Darwin
Marx
Wagner

Critique of a
Heritage

Jacques Barzun

Second Edition with a new Preface

THE UNIVERSITY OF CHICAGO PRESS
Chicago and London

The University of Chicago Press, Chicago 60637
The University of Chicago Press, Ltd., London

87 86 85 84 83 82 81   1 2 3 4 5

Library of Congress Cataloging in Publication Data

Barzun, Jacques, 1907–
    Darwin, Marx, Wagner: critique of a heritage.

    Reprint of the rev. 2d ed., 1958, with a new pref., published
by Doubleday, Garden City, N.Y.
    Includes index.
    1. Darwin, Charles Robert, 1809–1882.   2. Marx, Karl, 1818–
1883.   3. Wagner, Richard, 1813–1883.   I. Title.
CT119.B37   1981   920'.009'034   80-27274
ISBN: 0-226-03859-9 (pbk.)

CONTENTS

IV.   The Triumph of the Absolute

V.   The Reign of Relativity

Preface to the Phoenix Edition

The long life in print of this essay—forty years—testifies to a number of things: the fortitude of the reading public, the indomitable will to survive of the three figures dealt with, and no doubt a continuing intellectual need—that which prompted me in my youth to see in the combination of three influences the origin of our leading superstitions.

Much has happened in scholarship and public opinion during those forty years, but the understanding of the circumstances that gave Darwin, Marx, and Wagner their power over the modern mind has not greatly improved. Darwin has just been celebrated anew as the discoverer of evolution and the "painstaking scientist" who showed how it worked, thus "revolutionizing mankind's cosmic beliefs." That the facts are otherwise and his scientific contribution but a small part of his massive philosophizing makes no difference. All scientists are Darwinists ex officio.

Marx's principles and predictions have been shown wrong or false, and alert disciples have found it necessary to ransack his early writings for something to study and admire, but his fame as a great innovator persists, and innumerable scholars and publicists proudly call themselves Marxist and "apply his method."

Wagner's voluminous teachings about music and drama, art and society are no longer read or quoted, and the few who push their way through them term them obscure, inconsistent, and fallacious, but Wagner remains the exceptional artist who was also a great thinker and creator and who fittingly has a temple all to himself at Bayreuth. The religious cult of art still dominates the modern spirit.

Clearly, the power and influence of the trio differs from that of the great scientists, artists, and thinkers. It is rather that of kings and founders of religion, to whom all wisdom and authority is spontaneously ascribed and whose deeds are felt to have made, single-handed, the new era in which we live. It is a need of the people to invest its trust and worshipful emotions in figures imperfectly known. Gradually every good aim and great idea is attributed to the idol. It grows larger than life and impervious to criticism.

The choice of mortals to be canonized in this way owes something to chance, like every historical event, but it is not wholly arbitrary. It corresponds to widespread demands and powerful convictions. That is why the changes of forty years make so little difference. In our mental world, the faith in explanations from below is stronger than ever. We take as the genuine cause of things, as the ultimate reality, anything hidden and small and unsuspected that science or quackery "reveals." We accordingly rely more and more on automatic ways of controlling thought and behavior. A zoo director whose gorillas would not mate subjected them to long sessions of television. Many of our habits and enterprises follow the same logic.

For we believe in unchangeable "laws" of human action and social feeling, which should be discovered and observed for success, progress, sexual prowess, happiness, and other elusive goals. Every common desire and frustration is now a "problem," which means there is a "solution." The pattern has been set by science and technology, and the notion of permanent, unavoidable *difficulty* has perished. That is how it comes about that so many thousands "do research": let them look into the state of affairs, and it is bound to give up its secret—the hidden small cause—even to an ordinary intelligence, of which we have plenty.

These convictions, born in the time of Bacon and Galileo and grown strong by the mid-nineteenth century, prepared the ground for the work and the glory of our three men. What impressed their first adherents was the "painstaking." All three could (and did) boast of their heroic toil, their minute care, over small things, the one, in the observation of nature; the other, in the facts of history and economics; the third, in philosophy, history, esthetics, and the mosaic task of composition—not the making of mere operas but the creation of the first "total work of art." The impression given by these three efforts was: here is science, modern science, the triumph of method and system.

Darwin had a right to the label. Marx applied it to his work in defiance of common sense and made it stick: everybody accepts it, and he has an entry in the splendid *Dictionary of Scientific Biography.* By an oversight, no doubt, Wagner laid no claim to being a scientist, but he certainly was regarded as the equivalent for having solved by rigorous method the great artistic problem of his day.

All three, moreover, put forward a new system of the world. Had it been new, it would, of course, have met with general incomprehension; and had it been a system, it would have given no opportunities for the digging industry—the scholars and partisans who create the towering reputations while establishing their own. As things were, the three systems echoed what the active-minded already knew and felt, and the structures were perfect in their very imperfection.

But to gain universal sway, Darwinism, Marxism, and Wagnerism needed one thing more. Darwinian science implied a gloomy end to life and the solar system. Marx's class struggle and fated revolution meant bloody civil wars without end. The Wagnerian twilight of the gods came about because of greed and treachery and wound up in the destruction of the highest. General despair must follow these revelations. But tacked on irrationally to each vision of the future was a word of hope. Darwin concludes his evidence of the struggle for life by saying that from such war, famine, and death comes the best thing possible, the production of the higher animals. Marx similarly decrees an end to class struggle and promises the Utopia of absolute freedom without government. And Wagner is sure, like Darwin, that the production of something higher—art—justifies and repays for present anguish and coming agony.

These additions turned the grim harangues into Christ-like parables that have soothed and sustained millions of believers and helped to reassure skeptics as to their authors' good intentions. The thought of going to Darwin, Marx, or Wagner for consolation in a bad time is comic, yet it is true that their common outlook, gathering up as it does two centuries of speculation about man's fate, gives what our bewildered spirits apparently want: the satisfaction of feeling tough-minded—no "mysticism," no "romantic nonsense"—and at the same time the prospect of bliss to come once the exciting crisis is past; both moods validated, guaranteed sound and true, by scientific necessity.

The story of the men—many more than three—and of the troop of ideas that led us into these present beliefs is what the following pages try to relate intelligibly. The reader will probably want to begin at page 25 and see how the plot develops, postponing till after the end of the tale the intervening remarks which introduced the book to earlier generations by describing the state of mind of the time.

J.B.

January 1981

Preface to the Second Edition

Although the reader holds in his hands a sizable book, I should like him to regard it as an essay—as *one* essay, not three united by a common theme. The point of this suggestion is that here is something more than a comparison of great lives, something different from the stunt of finding common attributes in a trio of contemporaries. It is an attempt to treat an important cultural situation through the characters, works, and repute of figures that have attained the all-embracing power of symbols.

The situation so treated is of course unique but its type recurs. It shows how successive generations regard those just past—with hostility when close in time, with increasing fondness as great issues lose their power to threaten established ideas and become "truth" in their turn. It is the situation of the children toward the revered grandfathers. They are revered first as the founders of the new line, next as the obvious superiors of the fathers, and finally as the undisputed victors in the intellectual struggles of their own time. It is this last qualification which gives us convenient access to the culture of which they were a part, just as it ·is their eminence in ours which enables us to assess our relation to the still active past they represent.

An essay of this sort is clearly not pure biography, history, or criticism; it is a selection and fusion of all three, which is sometimes called cultural criticism. The chief justification for it lies in the degree to which it fits and serves the intellectual environment that brings it forth; it is thus *criticism*. And it must naturally correspond also to the ascertainable truth of the past and thus it qualifies as *history*. But it has a single purpose, which is to restore a balance that the writer thinks has been upset by prejudice, ignorance, or disturbing events.

When I was putting my essay through the press eighteen years ago, my publisher, sensing in the text this singleness of purpose, wished me to express it through the vivid fancy of a title more fashionable than the bald enumeration of proper names; whereupon a witty friend suggested *Three Pilgrims of Progress*. But no one word such as progress could denote the complex of interests and convictions which I saw as the properties, so to speak, that Darwin and Marx and Wagner had amassed for themselves, and on which we were still living, some off the capital, others more prudently on the income. I therefore contented myself with the subtitle *Critique of a Heritage*, trusting to the work itself to inventory what I called for short the legacy of 1859.

In 1940, before the significance of the Stalin-Hitler Pact had been fully taken in, and even for some years afterward, the intellectual class of this country was spellbound by the thought and character of Karl Marx. In written and spoken discourse he was omnipresent. A typical volume such as *Books That Changed Our Minds* proclaimed his influence. Others paid homage to his greatness as a thinker, even when they disavowed his political maxims or recoiled from his political consequences. The fact that congressional watchdogs took little notice then of Marxist "science" only shows how advanced the science was and how apposite to the needs of the Depressionist generation. It is this double quality, of being at a given time the appanage of the highest intellectual class and of serving all their needs at once, that characterizes the culturally symbolic figure. He may be as great as he seems, or only cast a huge shadow like Lucifer in starlight, he is all-important because to the advanced intelligence he has proved uniquely available.

To the same possessed minds, it was natural that the scientific method at large should seem the key of all our prisons, and in the preoccupation with social developments Darwin's assumed utility for large reference made him a second symbol of right reason. The memory of the time when he had been the all-explainer was still alive, and from him, like John Dewey in *Reconstruction in Philosophy*, every educated writer dated the modern universe of belief. In a series such as The Living Thoughts Library, Dr. Julian Huxley prefaced the extracts from Darwin with all the old unhistorical clichés, while in the novelized tracts of his brother Aldous Huxley the "facts" making for wit and disillusionment were traceable to the same fountainhead of science.

By 1940, it is true, some leading scientists had joined certain poets in the effort to make religious thought once more respectable. But among intellectuals this still was considered a personal matter. There was as yet none of that cachet and curiosity about theology which later produced the vogue of Kierkegaard and Berdyaev and the renown of Niebuhr and Tillich. The New Deal, after all, was an implicit denial of original sin, and the disciples of Freud had not yet gone softhearted and discovered that the theological virtues were also clinical. Science was still the most prestigious name of truth, and few dared harbor the thought that such an austere and successful goddess could work us harm.

In the arts, to be sure, the similar spell exercised by Wagner was less powerful than it had been, say, before the First World War. But the leading music and drama critics still belonged to the generation for whom Wagner was not simply a revelation but *the* revelation of art. To mention Berlioz or Verdi or even Mozart as artists of comparable depth, height, or width was then esthetic suicide. It argued not only a deficient sensibility but a feeble mind, for what made Wagner the greatest artist who had ever lived, the equal of ten Beethovens plus a hundred Shakespeares, was his encyclopedic grasp, his social, poetical, and philosophical doctrine—his system. Though few knew this ideology and fewer believed in it, many walked in awe of it, as of a magnate's reputed bank account.

Even more authoritative in our culture was the Wagnerian history of nineteenth-century art. According to its chronology, and despite the vigorous protest of the Wagnerite Shaw, poetic feeling and its expression had been lifted out of philistine crassness and infantilism about the year 1860. Independent evidence seemed to support this theory of sudden maturity and miraculous regeneration. The innocent American just discovering Baudelaire, Mallarmé, or Rimbaud in the 1930s and '40s found in them a mood and speech different from all he had known, and behold, Wagner was their leader and inspirer, the idol of the impressionists, realists, decadents, postimpressionists, and modernists down to Proust and Thomas Mann.

Surveying the three realms together—art, science, and social science—any reading and thinking American of the period I am harking back to would have had to be invincibly distrustful not to believe that he owed his true perceptions and refined sensibility to the triple revolution led by Darwin, Marx, and Wagner. The reasonable and the real, human life as against prehistory, dated from *The Origin of Species*, the first sketch of *Capital*, the full score of *Tristan*, all providentially brought to light in 1859.

Since the days of this clear conviction much has happened to spoil its *élan*. For one thing the momentum of the great flood of invective against the backward bourgeois came to a sudden stop on the shoals of acceptance and agreement. Darwin, Marx, Wagner became great men, great books, great bores. Their capacity to shock, to instruct, and to confer prestige through their vanguardism ended in due course. There comes a time for all systems when the ideas, and more especially the lingo, cease bubbling and taste flat.

And, as everybody knows, worse befell Marx and Wagner when political passion veered against them as agents of the totalitarian menace. The nonsense uttered about them in that phase is far from equaling the amount previously heard in their behalf, but it is no less offensive to the critical student of history. Nor does the esthetic religiosity of converted agnostics and repentant rationalists commend itself by the honesty of its facts and logic. The falling away from scientism as from socialism and Wagnerism has been as deplorable intellectually as the former infatuation.

Some years after the present essay, a large book undertook to demonstrate that Marx's ideas arose from his disagreeable character and German soul; later, another showed that Darwin was uncommonly neurotic and that the battle over evolution was fought and won by men, instead of angels as we had all thought; a third concluded that Wagner's overcompensation for inferiority produced the massive output in which one detects an absence of consecutive thought. These belated disclosures, expressed at scholarly length, were supposed to complete our disenchantment. Seeing what kinds of men these three were, we would know what place their ideas should hold in our minds. Yet lacking a sufficient historical grasp and nameable critical standards (as against opportunist carping), these studies and their echoes remained symptoms rather than dispellers of general confusion.

To say this is to say that possibly the present essay still retains some value for the student and general reader. There is need in any case for the kind of review and revision I first attempted nearly two decades ago. In spite of the noticeable increase in our knowledge of the nineteenth century, we still see it in jagged fragments. In literary and artistic circles the dogma of a total regeneration between 1860 and '70 is still strong. The caricature that usurps the name of romanticism persists and bolsters up the notion that only after the romantics could serious emotions and delicate art arise. Among students of society, the tacit assumption obtains that socialism, the economics of history, and a sane sociology had no existence before Marx. When he is not cited or alluded to, his distant heirs, Mannheim and Max Weber, do duty as his witnesses. As for the realm of physical science, all the signs suggest that the approaching centenary of the *Origin of Species* will afford publicists an excellent opportunity to trot out again the old catchword about "a revolution in man's thought" and will enable distinguished scientists to regain on the rostrum some of the brag and bounce they voluntarily gave up after Hiroshima.

Our imagination, in short, inhabits a stunted past, our thoughts fly under a low ceiling, bumping about like bats among familiar but incompletely known objects.

For the task defined by this situation I wish that my essay were better and fuller than it is. In the development of my own work it served as a preparatory sketch, the fourth and penultimate before I attempted to reconstruct the cultural image of an entire age in *Berlioz and the Romantic Century*. What *Darwin, Marx, Wagner* sought to establish first was the unity of the postrevolutionary era, 1789–1914. This could not be done without frequent glances at eighteenth-century enlightenment as well as at the elements of the new culture that was aborted by the First World War. But the internal coherence of the 125 years preceding that catastrophe became patent as soon as one worked free of the textbook convention which uses political dates to cut off the last third of the nineteenth century: the Civil War in the United States, the wars of unification in Germany and Italy, the emancipation of the serfs in Russia, the French Commune of 1870, the turn to empire and democracy after the Reform Bill of 1867 in England. All these are important, but they are not the great divides we think them; they are culminations, not points of departure; they bear a false meaning without their antecedents. And so it is with the cultural achievements attributed to our three symbolic figures. They are important, remarkable, awe-inspiring, but not as originators, not even as masterly synthesizers, rather as dogged eclectics whom a prepared public found representative of its own slowly acquired convictions. And they, too, are unintelligible apart from the creative minds that came before and prepared their triumph.

To the argument that it makes little difference what precise roles were played by various actors in a great movement, and that the busy modern reader cannot be bothered to go behind the scenes of popular successes, the answer is simple: it is on the whole better to call men and events by their right names; it is on the whole wiser not to make false diagrams of the way things happen. What, after all, are we so busy about? It is moreover interesting to go behind façades, and in the present instance it so happens that knowing the full story greatly enlarges the field of vision and choice.

Anyone who pretends to thinking for himself must obviously move beyond the narrow circle traced by the slogans of the schools, must re-examine not only his historical faith but also his historical facts, and must develop some principles of judgment adequate to the complexity of culture itself. This has practical consequences. Here is an example: at this moment the public and critics of New York are in some agitation over the unexpected success of Wagner's *Ring* at the Metropolitan Opera, after a period of marked anti-Wagnerism shared by the opera management. At once, an oppressed minority, silenced till now by the fear of being unfashionable, has burst forth in articles restating the extravagant claims about the master, at second hand, ignorantly. The claims are thus easily scouted in rejoinders that bear on details. To my knowledge none of the articles and letters so far has dealt with the true basis for a present revision of Wagner's fame, which must be the superb music his works contain. His new opponents mutter about Verdi and Moussorgski as if we should lose them again in the event of Wagner's renewed eminence. Nobody, it would seem, wants the whole repertory or a reasonable view of its makers.

Well, it is true in culture as in optics that if you hold a large object close to your nose, it will blot out the sun, moon, and stars. But that is the very reason why large objects should be viewed from a proper distance. We must work for perspective, under pain of never seeing more than one thing at a time, like infants with feeble grasp and unfocused eyes. Nothing but the fullest and clearest—which is not the same as the simplest—view of our cultural past and present should satisfy us. If the modern mind takes pride as it does in being discriminating, it is not enough that it should be hard to please in little things. The big ones are occasionally important too.

As I read over my sketch in the light of these obvious principles governing cultural criticism, I found myself wishing that I could improve my design and augment its detail. I am aware of regrettable omissions—Ruskin, Renouvier, Hardy, Meredith, among others, should have been more often cited or more fully treated. My neglect of the first two is to be accounted for like Dr. Johnson's confusion about the joints in a horse's leg—by pure ignorance. But Hardy and Meredith I knew adequately and with affection, so that I am without excuse save the lame one of inexperience in handling a crowded canvas.

I am quite sure it is too late to do anything about it. My present view of the performance is that of a stranger, and I should only spoil whatever is passable by patching and tinkering. A few glaring errors and a good many more repetitions and infelicities of phrase I have removed. But I have left the Introduction and the afterword essentially as they stood, period pieces which the present Preface will, I hope, sufficiently bring up to date. In short, I have contented myself with brushing and straightening and avoided anything like an overhaul.

In that lesser task I have been greatly helped by some letters from readers, and especially by the criticisms of my friend Professor Fritz Stern of Columbia University. He first endured this book as a student; later as a colleague he has enjoyed the moral man's revenge of improving it while putting me deeply in his debt. My gratitude also goes to my assistant, Virginia Xanthos, for making the new index.

J.B.

June 1, 1957

Preface to the First Edition (1941)

This book has not three subjects, but one. That one is simply the prevailing form of our thinking in an age of scientism and machinery. To speak of forms of thought is of course to speak of abstractions; the living observer of living men finds only concrete situations and individual opinions. But amid the multitude of these single facts he may discern a family likeness. It is the contour of this likeness that I have tried to draw in the following pages, by giving a critical account of mechanistic materialism in science, art, and social science, from the days of its great apostles down to ours.

Darwin, Marx, and Wagner certainly do not represent absolute beginnings, but neither are they arbitrary starting points. If we take up the history of certain ideas—the idea of struggle for life, of economic interpretation in history, of nationalism in art—we find ourselves discussing Darwin, Marx, and Wagner; but we also find ourselves embroiled in the present-day problems of democratic freedom, autarky, and cultural revolution.

Given this scope and this concern, the present book can, as I conceive, be used in a number of ways. The reader whose main interest lies in the three great figures, and who consequently wishes to plunge at once into narrative, should turn to page 25. He will find himself in mid-Victorian London, receiving the manuscript of Darwin's *Origin of Species*: the date, 1859; the place, John Murray's, publisher. Others, who would rather take hold of a guiding thread before going through the maze of particulars, should begin with the Introduction. It states the leading themes of the work and shows in what combinations they will be developed. As for those who would know from the start what my critique is aiming at in the present-day world and what my own "form of thought" may be, they should begin with Part IV and read to the end, then consult the Introduction and the middle chapters for substantiation of my position—or theirs.

Certain readers from each group might moreover like to know by what steps I was led to mark out the subject of this book. Some dozen years ago, while working on Montesquieu for C. J. H. Hayes's Seminar, I found in those back pages of *The Spirit of the Laws* that are so seldom read a full-fledged theory of the class struggle applying to eighteenth-century France. This theory, it soon appeared, was anything but a dead letter. It was a public controversy about the rights of the nobility and the bourgeoisie. Some said the nobles owed their privileges to their military conquest of the common people ten centuries before. Their opponents said no such conquest had ever taken place. Both sides, however, accepted the class theory of history as implying a fact of race: the nobility of modern times was presumed to descend in a pure strain from the conquering Franks, and so to deserve, by blood and might, the overlordship of the rest of the nation.

Montesquieu's seriousness and influence made me eager to trace this Race-Class dispute back to its origins and forward to its violent expression in the French Revolution. For it was at the outbreak of this revolution that a famous and decisive call to arms turned the ancient theory on its head: "Overthrow the nobles," it said, "and by right of a new conquest you commoners will become the power in the state." My account of this war of classes and ideas was published in dissertation form as *The French Race: Theories of its Origins and their Political Implications* (1932).

But the French Revolution did not settle the "class struggle" nor did it stop the race theorizing. Montesquieu's other theories—of conditioning by climate and of "scientific" history—had found multitudinous echoes in other minds, and by the beginning of the nineteenth century every discussion of social problems was permeated with would-be scientific notions of class, race, and soil. Nearly every one of these theories had some practical application as its corollary: political, social, or cultural; and meanwhile biological research, anthropology, and the science of language, had intensified, not abated, the use of "race-thinking." To carry forward my history of the French controversy therefore amounted to a general review of Western culture in the nineteenth century. After five years of research, I set down in 1937 a critical account of these ideas under the title of *Race: A Study in Modern Superstition.*

By that time, events were showing that my studies had nothing antiquarian about them. The daily newspaper told us what uses could be made in our own century of the protean idea of Race. Beneath the categories of Tribe, Class, Nation, or Species, and for deadly practical reasons, humanity and the individual had disappeared. No longer was race simply one among many issues, no longer had it to do solely with prejudice. Instead, it was the basic form of a struggle which many accepted as natural, progressive, inspiring. The appeal to race, class, or nation was in truth an epidemic attempt to supply a new motive power for social evolution. It expressed a desperate desire to breathe life into the two European idols of Progress and Fatalism.

Seeing the havoc which these clustered dogmas were wreaking in the rest of our culture, and seeing also the elements of new ways of thought making for a more livable scheme of things, I tried in *Of Human Freedom* (1939) to define what must replace the old idols and the new dogmas if democratic culture meant to survive.

The present volume builds on the previous ones. It seeks to bring together into one view the heritage of assumptions which we make about society, science, and culture.

Our ideas of class and race, of progress and determinism, reinforced as they are by our faith in science and evolution, may well seem to us inescapable. But that can be our view only so long as we ignore the criticism to which these ideas have been subjected in the last half-century; or so long as we misunderstand the new conceptions of nature and human nature which replace or refine on those of Darwin, Marx, and Wagner.

In the task of condensing and organizing the "chaos" which any century presents to the historian of ideas, I have naturally incurred many agreeable debts of gratitude. The generous help of friends and of colleagues, close or distant, has lightened my burden while increasing my responsibilities. Besides the authors cited in the text, I want to set down here my especially deep obligation to Lionel Trilling for his tireless readings of the manuscript; and to Professors Wendell Taylor, Robert Carey and Charles W. Cole, and James Gutmann for putting at my disposal their stores of knowledge in matters respectively scientific, economic, and artistic. Mr. Deming Hoyt has likewise put me in his debt for the inspired care with which he typed the several drafts. For the opinions expressed and the errors undetected, I am of course alone responsible.

J.B.

Introduction: *Why This Trinity?*

To name Darwin, Marx, and Wagner as the three great
prophets of our destinies is but to recognize a state of fact.
About the two former, there can be little doubt. Despite
quarrels and cavils, they rank in point of magnitude: Darwin as *the* scientist and Marx as *the* sociologist. And though
Wagner may in a sense be said to have been outgrown or
cast aside by our generation, there is another sense—popular
and profound—in which he figures side by side with the
other two as *the* artist. Open almost any book dealing with
the problems of our time and you will find these appraisals
more often than not taken for granted. You will find Darwin and Marx repeatedly coupled as the great pair whose
conceptions revolutionized the modern world; as the mighty
thinkers whose thoughts are now the moving beliefs of millions. And if any artist is felt to have exerted a comparable
effect as thinker or creator or both, it is Wagner who is
named and no other.

The most casual inquiry into the literature of the first
forty years of our century will confirm these assertions. The
references to Darwin, Wagner, and Marx are numerous and
often simultaneous. At times, indeed, there is a kind of

automatism about the use of these names, in pairs or in threes, as if each called up the others. In our universities and colleges where "great books" are read the *Origin of Species* and *Das Kapital* seldom fail to find a place, and in one academic institution they have been listed among the "Fifteen Decisive Books of the World." As for Wagner's position, the lists of gramophone recordings testify to his continued eminence in the popular mind.

But there is a still deeper sense in which Darwin, Marx, and Wagner have influenced our lives, and that is as the representatives of the dominant tradition we live by. Their thought embraces the three great relations that cause us the deepest concern—science and religion; science and society; society and art—and it is from them that on these subjects we have learned what we most familiarly know. To feel the extent of this debt one has but to imagine our speech and thought deprived of these words and phrases: struggle for existence, survival of the fittest, natural selection; economic interpretation, class struggle, exploitation of labor, dialectic materialism, scientific socialism; social significance (in art), national art, Nordic culture. And to these should be added the words borrowed from Wagner and which have now acquired the force of symbols: leitmotif, Beckmesser, music drama, Twilight of the Gods.[1]

OUR CENTURY BELONGS TO THEM

Not all these terms were invented by Darwin and Marx and Wagner, but the popular mind, when it thinks of giving credit, ascribes it to them. These terms, again, are not equally commonplace or current, but they have almost all acquired the widened significance of slogans: we all think we know what we mean when we use them, and when we do we are generally understood. It is a test of the universality

[1] These phrases and categories have lost potency since the end of the Second World War, which showed to what political consequences a literal faith in the trio might lead. [Note to the Second Edition.]

of a form of thought that a few catchwords not only serve as an adequate shorthand for it, but look as if they merely stated the obvious. It was no accident that Germany's West Front should have been named the Siegfried Line; that the totalitarian regimes should have taken the title of socialist; or that the powerful myth of race should be a mixture of biological, economic, and cultural dogmas. So far the twentieth century seemingly belongs to Darwin, Marx, and Wagner.

If there should be any doubt left on this score, it would be easy to invoke the authority of the great American who first perceived the fact. I refer to Henry Adams. Readers of the *Education* will remember that that painful process consisted in getting used to a Marxian, Darwinian, and Wagnerian world for which Adams's native environment had not prepared him. He got used to Wagner, he accepted Darwin,[2] and he feared Marx, but the burden of his misery was that the world which he saw as the fief of these three was an alien, cold, and chaotic world.

WHY A COLD WORLD?

The reason was that Darwin and Marx as scientists and Wagner as artist had seemingly made final the separation between man and his soul. Their labors had shown that feeling, beauty, and moral values were illusions for which the world of fact gave no warrant.[3] Man was no longer a cherished creature of the gods, first because there were no gods, and second, because cherishing was foreign to the nature of things. Art, as the embodiment of feeling, was a surcease from the pain of enduring reality, a narcotic, like

[2] Adams's prophecy that Darwin would mean nothing to the men of 1960 was based on the supposition that the biological work of the early 1900s would become generally known as refuting Darwin. Adams forgot the cultural lag or shortened it in thought.

[3] Wagner's reputation as a mystic does not contradict this fact. See below.

love; and *Tristan* fittingly united these two palliatives preparatory to death.

Things were the only reality—indestructible matter in motion. But even this matter in motion, on which all scientific progress depended, was constantly becoming less and less available for human uses. The log of wood on the fire was not destroyed as it burned, for the ashes, smoke, and heat given off were its exact equivalent; but you could not burn your log and have it too. This was a law—a law of physics and a law of evolution—and it caused Henry Adams enough anguish to make him trace our historical progress towards perdition in *Mont-Saint-Michel* and—the title is significant—in *The Degradation of the Democratic Dogma.*

SCIENTISM TRIUMPHANT

In such a world it was advisable to be tough-minded, "scientific," and so reap the only possible compensation—that of being able to undeceive one's fellows. Scientists could take delight in setting a date for the sun's extinction in accordance with the evolution of the planetary system. Scientific socialists could take pleasure in predicting the extinction of the bourgeoisie and all its values. Evolution was resistless, and though it could mean progress, it was strictly speaking progress without a purpose. Darwin's contemporaries deceived themselves into imagining a purpose, but Adams's lost that last illusion. Wagner made beautiful music out of the passing of the gods, but no one dared say with Emerson, "When half gods go, the gods arrive." For that was a romanticist's illusion—moonshine, so to speak, except that moonshine was a measurable vibration in the ether and consequently far more real than men's hopes and desires. As the Duke of Sermoneta—a distinguished scientist who was also a cultured man—put it in the nineties: "Neither the moral law nor the law of beauty can be found in nature, and without these, the world must be lacking in interest." The result of making matter the only reality was plain: a premium was put on fact, brute force, valueless existence, and bare survival.

Yet as I write,[4] the world is being told by some of its most conscientious scientists that the familiar unit of matter, the atom, is nearing the *in*tangible and that the sun *creates* energy. In the explanation of the latter phenomenon, we are told that at a certain point in the chain of events, "a miracle happens." In other well-informed quarters one hears that the old laws of conservation seem no longer to fit the data of matter and energy. Something has obviously happened to the world of fact since the complaints of Henry Adams and the delight of the sun extinguishers. In our mind and speech the world is still Darwinian, Marxian, Wagnerian, but beneath the thick crust are the fires of new thoughts which must modify or destroy the old.

THE NEW IDEALISM

Other signs of profound changes closer to daily life— Freudian psychology is one of them—compel us to reassess the late nineteenth-century legacy of mechanical change and moral fatalism. For the great danger is that under the pressure of new facts and new insights we shall swing back from materialism to an equally dangerous idealism, or even worse, to a know-nothing irrationalism.

Meanwhile it is obvious that the contempt for science preached by Hitler, the release of idealistic feelings which his crusade affords, and the racial mysticism which flavors the whole, are all explosive manifestations of a humanity starved on mechanical materialism and goaded to violence by its concrete results. But though irrationalism is exalted as a virtue, the new ideal is nonetheless scientifically armed and mechanized. The notion of race so dear to Wagner pretends to be not only cultural but also scientific. And national socialism, though it repudiates Marx, appeals to

[4] In 1940. [Note to the Second Edition.]

economic motives both at home and abroad. In a word, the totalitarian states are as much embroiled as we are in the cast-off thoughts of Marx, Darwin, and Wagner. What has made possible the new Germany, like the new Italy and the new Russia, is simply the revivifying of feeling, the re-creating of the sense of purpose at the very heart of a mechanical and scientific culture. And what has happened there can happen wherever the need for enthusiasm and action is given a goal. It is easy enough to manufacture slogans out of current superstitions—race, autarky, the cultural revolution—and make them seem genuine outlets from the impasse into which a narrow science of nature and human nature has led us.

THE PRAGMATIC ATTITUDE

Since belief directs action, it behooves us to take stock of the teachings characteristic of yesterday and today, for the very sake of reason, science, and art. We have thus two motives, one theoretical and one practical, for going back to the sources of our intellectual life. I am far from saying that the world events we are living through are the result of "mere ideas": that would be to espouse the very idealism I condemn. Ideas by themselves cause nothing. They are as inert as facts by themselves; or to put it another way, closer to the pragmatic view of history, facts and ideas do not occur separately from each other. Every significant fact occurs as an idea in some mind and certain combinations of ideas enable us to discover new facts or to alter old ones, in short, to change the given reality which we know only by purposeful handling. Events are thus the result of our wishes and our notions, our wills and our brains, acting in conflict or co-operation with the physical world. That is all that is meant when we hear that myths, not facts, move the world; which is far from saying that one myth (idea, dogma, hypothesis) is as good as another, or that its "working" is a thing that can be tested by anybody in five minutes.

THE LINKAGE AT THE SOURCE

I said above that Darwin, Marx, and Wagner were in some way responsible for the prevailing form of our thought and I listed a series of phrases which obviously belong to the three categories of science, social science, and art. Meantime I have spoken of their contributions as forming a single stream of influence which I have called mechanical materialism: the cold world in which man's feelings are illusory and his will powerless. This merging of three disciplines and subject matters under one head calls for explanation. The explanation is that none of our three men was content to stay within his specialty. Darwin made sallies into psychology and social science; Marx was a philosopher, historian, sociologist, and would-be scientist in economics; Wagner was an artist-philosopher who took the Cosmos for his province. Moreover, after allowing for superficial differences, we find so many links uniting Darwinism, Marxism, and Wagnerism that the three doctrines can be seen as the crystallization of a whole century's beliefs. Each of the systems may be likened to a few facets of that crystal: at the core they are indistinguishable. Though the three authors worked independently and were acclaimed by their own age at different times, they expressed with astonishing unity one common thought; they showed in their lives, and even in their characters, one common attitude; they imposed on their contemporaries one unified view of themselves. So much so, that it would be hard to find in the whole history of Western civilization a corresponding trio to share the mirroring of a single epoch with such perfect parallelism.

THE THREAD OF EVOLUTION

This means that the materials of our proposed stock-taking will be diverse: biography, criticism, history, philosophy—all converging on the same point, which is the dominance of materialism. Some of the biographical connections are of course well known. It is a commonplace that Marx felt his own work to be the exact parallel of Darwin's. He even wished to dedicate a portion of *Das Kapital* to the author of *The Origin of Species*.

Meanwhile Wagner's restlessly acquisitive mind was taking up, direct or secondhand, all the notions that the age had to offer. From vegetarianism to race theories and from Feuerbach's philosophy to Bakunin's anarchism, his ear was attuned to every doctrine. But his somewhat haphazard national, racial, artistic, and socialist views supported his main contention that he was building the artwork of the future—an evolutionary and totalitarian product surpassing Bach, Beethoven, and the Greeks. This explains why he has recently become the object of attacks as the father of German fascism. It is not merely that Hitler has annexed him for his cultural crusade, but that Wagner's pretensions as a thinker and dramatist, his friendships with Nietzsche and Gobineau, place him at the heart of the biological and sociological theorizing which sprang from the idea of Evolution.

THE WEB OF MATERIALISM

It remains to specify very briefly what ideas each of these three men stamped with his name and personality, but first I must say a word on the meaning to be attached in these pages to the phrase "scientific materialism." Materialism is a battered epithet which we too often use as a term of reproach. We tack on the adjective "crass" or "gross" and speak as if every materialist were a glutton. Or again we speak as if materialism meant believing in what is really there, whereas idealism means believing in the doubtful and invisible. In this last sense we are all, fifty times a day by turns, materialists and idealists; for we must believe not only in the presence of brick walls, but also in many things which cannot be seen or handled—say someone's grudge against us or someone's faith in patent medicines.

We must likewise believe in conditions that are material but hidden, as when we refer someone's bad temper to his bad digestion or his good behavior to his good environment.

But the systematic materialist or idealist goes beyond all this in an effort to reduce *all* observable phenomena to one or the other of these two "causes"—Matter and Idea. I need not speak here of the rival merits of each system. The important thing to grasp is that mid-nineteenth-century scientists chose to assume that matter was the source of everything in the universe, including life and consciousness. Everything else was either an illusion or else a subjective impression which could be "reduced" to material fact. We still use the word "subjective" to mean unreal, and "objective" to mean genuine, as if the subjective feelings inside us had no real existence or as if they were identical with the objective state of our bodies at the moment.

The idealist, on the contrary, perceiving that for objects to be as we know them there must exist a living mind endowed with certain powers, tries to reduce all phenomena to an act of perception, either human or divine. For him it is matter which is the illusion. And he can show without fear of contradiction that matter is nowhere to be found. There are only sensations, which admittedly depend on a perceiving mind. Both thinkers, the matter-ist and the idea-ist, consequently end up with two worlds each—a real world and a show world, because both insist on making only a single abstraction from the concreteness of daily experience.

THE FALSE DEMONSTRATION

Now materialism in science produced such magnificent results in practical life that to the men of the late nineteenth century these results seemed tantamount to a proof of the system. Thousands of miles of railway track, millions of yards of cloth, unlimited steam power, iron and steel machinery, devices for instant communication, and the multiplication of innumerable conveniences for the benefit of mankind—all struck the imaginations of men so forcibly as to make any questioning of the materialist assumption look like superstitious folly. At the same time, the age-old passion for uniformity drove the scientists to explain by material causes the inner life of man which alone gave value to the things. Vitalism was thus driven out of biology and man came once more to be considered a machine—a physico-chemical compound—as he had been in the middle of the eighteenth century. Lord Kelvin, speaking for many of his fellow scientists, asserted that nothing was scientific of which he could not construct a model. The model was a machine, and the machine was the model of all existences. Unfortunately, the new facts of electricity wrecked mechanism as a universal theory, and from that time forward materialism has had to beat a retreat until today we are expressly told that matter is a sort of fiction which can be resolved into electrical charges, and that the formulas of science can neither be imaged nor built into a mechanical model.

It is true that we are not bound to guide our daily life by the rules or assumptions that work in the laboratory, but the historical fact is that this is what Western man since the late nineteenth century has tried to do. Mechanism and materialism worked so beautifully—for a time—that even now we can sympathize with the enthusiasm of those who by its aid bequeathed to us the industrial world we live in. The misfortune was that when mechanism began to be questioned, for scientific reasons, the general public had become persuaded of its absolute truth; it could think in no other terms and it felt that all other views were simply "prescientific."

MECHANICAL EVOLUTION

Contrary to popular belief, Darwin's distinctive contribution to this movement is not the theory of evolution as a whole, but a theory which explains evolution by *natural selection from accidental variations*. The entire phrase and not merely the words Natural Selection is important, for the denial of purpose in the universe is carried in the second half of the formula—accidental variation. This denial of purpose is Darwin's distinctive contention. By an automatic or natural selection, variations favoring survival would be preserved. The sum total of the accidents of life acting upon the sum total of the accidents of variation thus provided a completely mechanical and material system by which to account for the changes in living forms.

In this way the notion of a Deity or Providence or Life Force having a tendency of its own, or even of a single individual having a purpose other than survival or reproduction, was ruled out. But since creatures obviously do possess consciousness and think they have purposes, these were looked upon as by-products of evolution, late in coming and negligible in effect. Exaggerating for the sake of brevity, one could interpret Darwinism as meaning that the whole of animal evolution had taken place among absolute robots, which reproduced their kind with slight, purposeless variations of form. Whence the common notion that man is the outcome of a long catch-as-catch-can beginning with an amoeba or one-celled animal, which has had advantageous faculties added to itself by a series of happy chances.

THE PROCESS OF HISTORY

The parallel to this natural evolution is the social evolution which Marx saw taking place in history. Here again the individual counts for nothing and has no original purposes of his own. It is the class that counts—a group determined by the forces of production operating at a given time and place. These forces are in turn reducible to physical factors—natural resources, modes of manufacture, means of communication, and so on, which form the social environment of a given class, just as a given area with its climate and food supply forms the natural environment of a species. In society also there is an illusion of conscious purpose on the part of individuals. They think they direct themselves and their fellows through beliefs, institutions, or leadership, but this is an illusion. The direction which the process of history takes is determined by material factors.

WHAT DIALECTIC MEANS

The process is in addition called dialectic because social changes follow a certain pattern. Material things in motion have a way of generating their opposites. Any action produces its opposite reaction or, in Marxian and Hegelian terms, *thesis* is matched and ultimately eclipsed by its *antithesis*, which is in turn eclipsed by a third form of activity, the *synthesis*. The dialectical process is thus like the dialogue of a continuous drama, and just as drama is the Greek word meaning conflict, so dialectical is the adjective corresponding to dialogue—the dialogue of action and reaction between conflicting social forces. It should be added that in society, action and reaction do not occur with the mechanical simplicity which we imagine when we think of an experiment in physics; and it is noteworthy that Marx and Engels's favorite example of the dialectical process was the germinating and growth of a plant from its seed—again the biological analogy—in which the germ is destroyed by its opposite, the plant; but is still in a sense part of it, in the same way that the new seed which the plant produces replaces its parent while continuing its form.

ARTISTIC MATERIALISM

After Darwinism and Marxism, a parallel consideration of Wagnerism necessarily has two parts. One part consists of the ideas that Wagner held at various times in his life— his nationalism and racialism, his theories of drama and revolution. The other part consists in the special theory and practice of his own art. About this last the question arises, how can art—particularly music—fit into the Marx-and-Darwin system? The answer is that Wagner too has a system, and as several critics have remarked, it is basically materialistic and mechanical. Not merely the subject matter of the dramas and the texture of the orchestration, but the implications of the Wagnerian leitmotif support this conclusion. The leitmotif, though it is the germ of a presumably free musical development, is also the sign, in Wagner, of a definite person, idea, or object; and this means that when the physical presence of these entities on the stage requires it, the musical development is bound to reintroduce the leitmotif. This not only encourages a mechanical manufacture of the so-called "unending melody" but it justifies calling Wagner's music "programmatic" in a stricter sense than usual, for the leitmotif is an identification tag in sounds.

Moreover, the Wagnerian work of art is meant to be an evolutionary, social, and nationalistic performance. It is part of a scheme which will make previous forms of art seem inadequate and which will usher in the regeneration of mankind through various means, of which the German nation is not the least. As a result, we have not only Wagner's music, but a movement—Wagnerism—a state of mind, a religion, which explains a number of occurrences unique in the history of music: the spread of Wagner's influence far beyond the confines of the musical world; the fanatical devotion of non-musicians to his name, and of Perfect Wagnerites to his cult; the appearance of systems upon systems to elucidate his works; and the production of an idolatrous technical literature which goes so far as to say that his music directly embodies scientific perceptions of the laws of nature, predicts the future history of Europe, and solves ethical problems with unerring precision.

In reporting these views, I am no doubt making it sufficiently clear that no one can interpret certain specified bars of music in Wagner or anybody else as "inherently" fascist or revolutionary or Christian or pagan. A musical system may be mechanical, like Wagner's, but the notes themselves are not on that account tinged with the political or metaphysical opinions of their creator. These opinions can only be discovered in works of literature, and it so happens that Wagner was no less prolix as a writer than as a composer. Hence the double role in which he will appear in these pages.

THE GHOST OF THE NINETEENTH CENTURY

In order to have shared so fully a common set of beliefs, we should expect Darwin, Marx, and Wagner to have occupied roughly similar positions in their century. This is indeed what we find. There is at the outset a remarkable conjunction in time in the appearance of their earliest characteristic work—all three in the same year 1859. We also find among them a singular unanimity of temper with regard to their immediate predecessors and contemporaries. All three stand, as they think, in isolation. They feel they are denying everything going on around them. With almost blind passion they ignore or misrepresent those closest to them—their colleagues, their rivals, and their own true teachers; and so strongly do they feel themselves to be missionaries and pioneers that they have managed in the teeth of historical evidence to persuade us of their essential originality.

Today, three quarters of a century after the event, it still seems a paradox to say that the ideas attributed to these three masters had been shuttling back and forth across Europe for more than a century. In spite of libraries full of scholarly and partisan studies, we still find educated opinion believing that Darwin invented biological evolution, that Marx was the first to analyze the contradictions of capitalism and explain history by economics, and that Wagner reformed opera singlehanded, making a profound experience out of a silly entertainment and changing art from a luxury to a socially useful institution.

One result of these beliefs is that we set Marx, Darwin, and Wagner over against a straw-man abstraction which we call The Nineteenth Century. Taken in the lump, as a foil for our three heroes, the nineteenth century is made to appear foolish, romantic, ignorant, complacent, Victorian, and superstitious. Darwin, Marx, and Wagner represent realism and scientific truth. Their achievements seem to come immediately after those of Copernicus, Newton, and Galileo.

THINKING IN PAIRS

So true is this that the ordinary educated man of today sees no third choice between the "scientific ideas" of the late nineteenth century and the "obscurantism and superstition of the Middle Ages." One can imagine him saying: "You are not a Darwinist?—You must be a Fundamentalist." "Not a believer in economic causation?—You must be a mystical Tory." "Not a materialist?—You must be an idealist." The implication is that if you are all of the latter things you must be on the side of ignorance, folly, and "reaction." And since these are justly dreaded evils, any critique of scientific materialism must be an attack on right reason.

The reply is simple: the evil world we live in is not a world which has been denied access to the science of Darwin and Marx and the theories and art of Wagner. Had their answers truly solved the riddle of the Sphinx, no obscurantism could subsist, for we are animated by—I will not say, the precise ideas of the three materialists—but surely by their deeper spirit, their faith in matter, their love of system, their abstract scientism, and their one-sided interpretation of Nature:

> Thus, from the war of nature, from famine and death, the most exalted object of which we are capable of conceiving, namely, the production of the higher animals, directly follows. There is grandeur in this view of life. . . .

This is not Mussolini speaking, but Darwin, and his voice re-echoes in our ears:

> War is not in contrast to peace, but simply another

form of expression of the uninterrupted battle of nations and men. It is an expression of the highest and best in manhood.

This is the comment of Dr. Robert Ley, head of the Nazi Labor Front, on the war of 1940.

I am not saying that Darwin would have accepted the results of his "philosophy of nature," nor am I seeking three individual scapegoats in the past to bear the burden of our present ills, but I do say that the ideas, the methods, the triumph of materialistic mechanism over the flexible and humane pragmatism of the Romantics has been a source of real woe in our day. Yet if the original conceptions of modern evolution and science and culture in the Romantic Era were broader and more humane, what happened to turn them from their first intention?

THE REALISTIC OBSESSION

The answer is wrapped up in our common use of the word "romantic" to describe the first half of the past century and of "realistic" to describe the second. We contrast the Utopian socialism of Fourier and Owen with the "scientific" socialism of Marx; the conscious or purposive evolution of Lamarck and Erasmus Darwin with the mechanical evolution of Charles Darwin and Alfred Russel Wallace; the romantic opera of Weber and Berlioz with the realistic music drama of Wagner.[5] And we infer that we have truth in the place of illusion.

But it is obviously one thing to say realistic and another to say reality, just as it is one thing to say romantic and another to say *un*reality. Realism is a slogan, not a certificate of success. Romanticism is an historical nickname, not a sure mark of imbecility. If our own generation is witnessing a violent outbreak of feeling, of irrationalism, of

[5] Realistic at least to the extent of having done away with arias, recitatives, and ballet music, and of having introduced "serious" issues of a philosophic cast into opera.

action for its own sake, of myths for destructive ends, it will give us small comfort and no help to call it Romanticism. Anyhow, we cannot have it both ways, saying first that Romanticism was a delicate flower that withered under the touch of "real" forces, and saying next that the upshot of these forces in our own day is a revival of Romanticism. The true diagnosis of the New Irrationalism is that it manifests live powers too long confined in a false mechanical world priding itself on its realism. Between this outburst of repressed human will and nineteenth-century Romanticism the only common ground is the recognition of the human will as a "real" force.

THE PRAGMATIC TEST

Beyond this the two movements are as diametrically opposed as the ends which they subserve. Romanticism was a constructive effort after a great revolution which had leveled off old institutions and old notions—including the mechanical materialism of the eighteenth century. Romanticism, as we all know, valued individual freedom, subjective feeling, human reason, social purpose, and above all, art. Granted that it failed to win the world, it was the right kind of failure; and the replacement of this productive Romanticism by the neo-materialism of the mid-century was in fact a regression we are now paying for in the form of private neuroses and public massacres.

The moral is not that we should go back and repeat Romanticism, which is in any case impossible, but that we should examine its merits with as much calm as we can muster, discover in it the true shape of the ideas which Darwin and Marx and Wagner absorbed—since they were born in the middle of the romantic era—and make a fresh start toward a working ideal for the Western mind. The elements lie ready all about us. The only danger is that we shall overlook them in favor of the old seesaw—from materialism to idealism, from disembodied rationalism to overbodied irrationalism—that has so far beguiled us.

THREE LIVES

This is only another way of saying that the study of Darwin, Marx, and Wagner will yield the first premises of what we seek. As it happens, their several biographies are interesting in themselves and can help focus the glancing lights into a beam. Wagner led what most people would call an exciting life and Marx an heroic one. Darwin, calm though his days were after his return from the cruise on the *Beagle*, awoke to find himself famous and lived to enjoy the adulation of the whole world. All three were conscious of their mission and communicated that awareness to the world in every act of their lives.

Three lives, that is to say also three legends, partly spontaneous, partly designed by overzealous followers to conceal real defects in the mortal men. For they have this likewise in common, that though they did not lack hero-worshipers, they can be called heroes only in a Pickwickian sense. Marx —apart from tenacity of purpose and domestic devotion— was a singularly disagreeable character, self-centered and insensitive to the point of cruelty. Wagner is too often despicable and, considering his luck, seems so with less excuse than most artists. Darwin, it is true, passes for a Galahad of fairness and pure intention, yet in the realm of ideas he treated his predecessors and contemporaries with something so like dishonesty as to raise a serious doubt. Of the entire trinity it can be said that they were ruthless to their opponents, and that despite the biographical evidence accumulated in fifty years there has been no joint retrial of their case.

THE PRAGMATIC TEST AGAIN

Faults of character mean much but they do not of course refute the ideas that they are linked with. We must beware of discrediting a doctrine because of what we know about its author. Otherwise we fall into the very error we are combating, the error of supposing that to know about a thing we need only know how it got there; to judge a man we need only inquire into his antecedents; to test an idea we need only discover its author's foibles and diseases. This is the "genetic fallacy," in many ways the worst product of evolutionism. For it denies the need and the possibility of judging things by what they are worth. According to it, the proof of the pudding is not in the eating, but in the cook's pedigree. True practicality bids us look the other way—not at origins but at results. If the village idiot says that the sun is shining, he may be speaking the truth and we may have to agree with him. Let us by all means be wary of accepting his testimony unchecked, but let us not pass once for all on his mental equipment and use him as a touchstone for truth, on the principle that if he asserts something it is false. Similarly, to gauge a great idea, a far-reaching theory, we must look to its fitness and its consequences. We must relate it to all that we know as having to do with the purpose in hand. There is no short cut through the biography of the man or the analysis of his soul, even though there may be through these a valuable insight into the way the finished product came to be.

This inclusiveness means that we must look not only at the works of Darwin, Marx, and Wagner, not only at their lives and personalities, but also at their imitators and detractors, their friends and enemies, their forerunners and followers. The gallery is neither obscure nor dull. Darwin brings into our ken Spencer, Huxley, Tyndall, Samuel Butler, Weismann, Haeckel, Bernard Shaw, and a choice group of Bishops and noble Lords. He makes us go back to Buffon, Goethe, Lamarck, Cuvier, and his own grandfather, Erasmus. Marx introduces us to Lassalle, Proudhon, Bakunin, Comte, Adam Smith, Shaw once more, and Lenin; while Wagner ranges freely over the notables of the century, beginning with Beethoven, Weber, Berlioz, George Eliot, Schopenhauer, and Liszt, and ending up with Gobineau, Nietzsche, Meyerbeer, von Bülow, and the ubiquitous Shaw, ultimately to reach H. S. Chamberlain, and through him the Kaiser and Adolf Hitler.

THE YEAR 1859

Our starting point, for tactical reasons, is the year 1859. It seems in retrospect a pivotal year. Not only did it see the appearance of Marx's *Critique of Political Economy* (January), the completion of Wagner's *Tristan* (August), and the publication of Darwin's *Origin of Species* (November), but it really opens the age with which we ourselves have living connections. Eighty years, in these hygienic days, can be the active life span of a man. Of course, much of what belongs to 1859 is dead and gone. It lies as far back as the crinolines just then coming into fashion; as Lord Macaulay whose sudden death cut short a great Victorian career; as the violent incident of John Brown at Harpers Ferry, which has already become American legend and poetry.

In that year, too, Europe was still trying to balance a protracted peace upon the four great powers—England, France, Austria, and Russia. It knew as yet no united Germany or Italy: a new era of conflict was beginning with a war over the unification of the peninsula. It was a Europe relatively unimproved, from our point of view—without electric light, telephone, automobiles, airplanes, or radios; without armored tanks, blackouts, TNT, or portable machine guns, though the germs of all this progress lay close to the surface. The Suez Canal was not yet built and Bismarck was still a mere ambassador, but the tide was turning.

As a hint of nearness consider that that same year 1859 saw the birth of some of our most distinguished contemporaries. I pick at random: John Dewey, Sir Arthur Conan Doyle, Bergson, A. E. Housman, Pierre Curie . . . the Kaiser. When the *Origin of Species* precipitated the fight on evolution, George Bernard Shaw was three years old, as was Viscount Haldane, of whom we shall have more to say. Justice Oliver Wendell Holmes and Thomas Hardy were youths old enough to discuss the "new" ideas. William

James, aged seventeen, was picking up what schooling he could in Geneva, a schooling which probably did not include Spencer, whom he would later destroy as a psychologist; while Samuel Butler, who was to make the fiercest attack on Darwin's theory, was sailing from England to New Zealand to raise sheep, not bothering his head with any other sort of biology.

When our story opens, Henry Adams, who survived the great war that he had predicted in evolutionary terms, was reaching his majority. The French biologist Paul Broca was founding in Paris a new society for scientific anthropology —the first of its kind, and the nursery from which so many of our modern ideas of race were to come. Across the Rhine, Fechner was finishing his great work on Psychophysics: the Man-Machine and the Race-Group were starting on a new chapter of their long career, in company with Natural Selection, the Class Struggle, and the Wagnerian warriors.

I

The Biological Revolution

There exists but one animal. The Creator used only one pattern for all organized beings. An animal is an entity taking its shape, or rather its different shapes, from the environment in which it develops. Zoological species are the result. . . .

I saw that in these regards society resembled Nature. . . . There have always existed and will always exist social species similar to zoological species.

BALZAC, *Foreword to the*
COMÉDIE HUMAINE, 1842

1. 1859: The Origin of Species

*November 24. A divine day. I walked out and Mrs.
Congreve joined me. Then music, Arabian Nights,
and Darwin.*

GEORGE ELIOT's *Diary for 1859*

In the spring of 1859, Charles Darwin completed his fiftieth year and, together with it, the manuscript of the
Origin of Species. This 500-page essay was only an abstract
of the great work that he had planned, but even so it had
been a hard pull to get it done—twenty years of observation
and note taking, a battle with incessant ill-health, and a
battle also with an inner demon of postponement amount-
ing to a neurosis. But at last all obstacles had been overcome—his friend Lyell, the geologist who had spurred him
on to write it, would see the book published, by subsidy
if necessary; though this need did not arise. On April 1,
acting on Lyell's recommendation, John Murray the publisher accepted the manuscript sight unseen.

Worn-out with the effort, Darwin could not even face
the objections to his style made by certain friends to whom
he had shown the work. He had slaved to make everything
clear; yet he was not quite sure of the character of his book:
"It ought to be popular," he wrote to Murray, "with a large
body of scientific and semi-scientific readers, as it bears on
agriculture . . . the history of our domestic productions,
and on whole fields of Zoology, Botany, and Geology." At

the same time he added: "My volume cannot be mere light reading, and some part must be dry and even rather abstruse. . . . The whole is one long argument."

Murray, who was an enthusiastic amateur geologist, tackled the long argument and found it unsatisfactory. He submitted it to his advisers, felt sure he ought not to print more than 500 copies, and gave it as his opinion that Darwin's theory was "as absurd as contemplating the fruitful union of a poker and a rabbit." Lyell was again called into consultation. Though he had not read the whole work he felt it advisable to print ahead of Alfred Russel Wallace, whose identical theory had reached Darwin in letter form eleven months before. The publisher now suggested to Darwin that he bring out only his observations on pigeons —"everybody is interested in pigeons"—together with a brief statement of his general principles. The book would then find reviewers in every journal in the kingdom and would soon be "on every library table"—that eternal goal and farthest reach of publishers' hopes.

But the mere thought of recasting his "abstract" was too much for Darwin. He balked and then collapsed. Only a complete rest at a water resort and the reading of an exciting new novel, Adam Bede, by an unknown novelist named George Eliot, restored his balance. Coming back in June, he found the proofs of the book as he had written it. It now struck him as full of obscure ideas and clumsy expressions—the common lot of authors after too many rereadings of their own sentences. Darwin bewailed and corrected and confided to his friends that a better man would have made a better book.

Nevertheless Darwin's first guess about his popularity was right. The small green volume priced at fifteen shillings which appeared on November 24, and which the author of Adam Bede was herself reading on that day, rapidly sold out a first edition of 1250 copies. A new edition of 3000 was called for—Darwin making very few changes in the text —and was ready early in the new year 1860. Two respectable American firms were already pirating the first edition, so that Darwin's friend at Harvard, Asa Gray, was unable to act in the interest of copyright. Gray banked on the need for a corrected edition to recoup the loss. But by this time Darwin was eager to pursue the major work of which the *Origin of Species* was the abstract, and he contented himself with adding to that lesser book a short "sketch of the progress of opinion on the change of species," which became the Historical Sketch now found at the head of most editions. We shall have occasion to return to its surprising contents a little later.

The essay itself, the "mere abstract," consisted of fourteen chapters setting forth a theory clearly summarized in the full title: *On the Origin of Species by Means of Natural Selection, or the Preservation of Favoured Races in the Struggle for Life.* The first five chapters contained the fundamentals of the theory and most of the applications which could be verified in the then state of science. Chapters Six to Nine anticipated certain objections. Chapter Ten dealt with the geological record—the successive kinds of organic beings preserved in fossil form. Eleven and Twelve discussed the geographical distribution of plants and animals over the earth's surface. Chapter Thirteen viewed the facts of classification, morphology, and embryology in the light of the theory, and the final chapter recapitulated the argument.

By "his theory," Darwin could only mean, of course, the idea that elimination by death, which he called Natural Selection, was the means by which species had come to be. He was not dealing with the origin of life, but with the origin of more or less fixed differences in those living forms that naturalists call *species.* Nor was Darwin arguing, except indirectly, for evolution, which was then variously termed "the development theory" or "descent with modification." He was proposing merely to explain the mechanism by which such modifications or development or evolution might occur. Least of all was he purposing to refute the Book of Genesis, dispossess the philosophers, or start a new natural religion. Most of the facts which he adduced were either common knowledge or available in the vast literature of natural history. The very idea of a Struggle for Life had come to him—as it had to Wallace—from reading Malthus's *Essay on Population* published sixty years before. The belief in gradual evolution was already established in geology and tentatively accepted in astronomy, and the Book of Genesis had been "contradicted" long before. It was the organizing of biological observations and evolutionary ideas around the central fact of natural selection which constituted Darwin's "long argument." Accordingly he had thought at one time of entitling his work simply "Natural Selection."[1]

If Darwin really wanted to rouse the British public, changing his title to *Origin of Species* was a stroke of genius. He had known he would not be loved by some of his colleagues for meddling with species, and had shrewdly hoped for a better hearing from "semi-scientific" and lay readers. But he had not expected the general furore which greeted his book. His instant fame was not due to the fact that "everybody is interested in pigeons." The real reasons were many, but the most immediate was the magic effect of the four great phrases of the title. *Origin* had an alluring ambiguity: it irresistibly suggested, as it still does to casual readers today, the beginning of all things. *Favoured Races, Struggle for Life, Natural Selection*—all repeated the same idea of strife with tangible rewards for the winners. So that if from the beginning all life had followed this "iron law" of struggle, then everything taught in the name of morality and religion was doubtful, at odds with the fundamental law of nature, and very likely an impediment to human progress. Purpose especially, the purpose of Providence or of man himself, had nothing to do with progress.

Contrary to common belief, not all the "good scientists" ranged themselves on one side with Darwin, nor all the

[1] *Proceedings of the Linnaean Society*, 1858, iii, 51; *Life and Letters of Darwin*, i, 480.

clergymen on the other against him. Kingsley, the novelist and preacher, was among the first to send Darwin a eulogistic letter. On the other hand, the influential scientist Sir John Herschel expressed his decisive contempt by saying that Darwin's idea was "the law of higgledy-piggledy." Whewell of Cambridge, the author of the great *History of the Inductive Sciences,* would not allow the *Origin of Species* in the library of his college. Edmund Gosse's father Philip, a biologist of note, was shattered by the book but remained unconvinced; and there were other men of recognized achievement in science—Sedgwick the geologist, Owen the anatomist, Harvey the botanist, Andrew Murray the entomologist—who firmly declined to accept the theory.

In America, the Harvard naturalist Agassiz, whose *Essay on Classification* had been republished earlier in the year, was unmoved by the argument of the *Origin.* His colleague Asa Gray pointed out in vain how many inferences and opinions he really shared with Darwin. The acceptance or rejection of the theory clearly depended on the amount of explaining which "natural selection" was made to do. Carlyle had seen this from the first and had taken sides against the theory: "That the weak and incompetent pass away, while the strong and adequate prevail and continue, appears true enough in animal and human history; but there are mysteries in human life and in the universe not explained by that discovery."[2] Gray bent all his efforts to showing that belief in Darwin was not incompatible with belief in God, and gave Darwinism in America a fair start. In France, where evolution had been discussed for over a hundred years, the *Origin of Species* might have been expected to find favor, but the general movement of ideas, always dependent on politics, was then at a low ebb. The Second Empire, to soothe Catholic susceptibilities, tried to enforce a literal orthodoxy, and publishers indignantly refused the book. But its appearance was only postponed. Mlle. Clémence Royer, a leading follower of the late

---

[2] Wilson, *Life of Carlyle,* v, 517.

Positivist philosopher Auguste Comte,[3] was shortly at work on a translation and defense of Darwin.

These warring opinions of 1859–1860 are still cited as being merely for or against Darwin. Those who pronounced against him at that time we feel a certain pleasure in blacklisting as bigots or fools. But in so doing we falsify history. It is partly Darwin's fault. Owing to his loose use of the words, it was never clear from the outset whether "my theory" meant Natural Selection or the gradual change of form in plants and animals which we now call Evolution. Hence we are apt to imagine that every objection to Darwin's thesis was an objection to evolution, whereas many of the objections were only to natural selection. Not every reader of the *Origin of Species* mistook the one for the other, though after almost a century of confusion it is hard to say exactly what single idea it was that "triumphed" with the *Origin of Species*. It was rather a cluster of ideas, a subject matter and not a theory. Indeed, to the theory of natural selection itself some of Darwin's supporters did not fully adhere. Lyell, despite his share in begetting the book, withheld assent to the inclusion of man in Darwin's scheme. Huxley, though Darwin's lifelong defender, maintained to the end a serious reservation. Darwin himself, with praiseworthy candor, offered in his own book objections which he was unable to answer; and he steadily diminished the scope of natural selection in every new edition of the work, until genuine Darwinians could say in 1900 what would have seemed "reactionary" to the evolutionists of 1860.

This early impatience with finer judgments is of course characteristic of a battle and it only proves that the *Origin of Species* was greater as an event than as a book. If the work is, as G. H. Parker says with a certain exaggeration, the most important publication of the nineteenth century, this is at least as much because of what it brought seething

[3] Born 1798, died 1857. For his evolutionary and scientific philosophy, see below.

out of the European mind as because of what it put into it. Darwin's genuine bewilderment at its reception and long after shows that the public ran ahead of him; so much so that he despaired of making himself understood.[4] Still there is a reason why we are repeatedly asked to wonder at the "revolution in thought" which emanated in 1859 from Darwin's "quiet Kentish home." This revolution was, in truth, hardly contemplated, much less engineered, by the Kentish scientist, but the Darwin legend is in itself significant, just as the "amazing coincidence" of Wallace and Darwin's hitting upon the same idea simultaneously is significant. The force of accumulated ideas always transcends the power of the man to whom they are ultimately ascribed.

But the question remains, why was it Darwin's book that set off the powder trains? Why *Darwinismus*, as the Germans promptly called the movement? Why not for instance *die Wallace'sche Theorie*? In England, Wallace was better known to the reading public than Darwin. He was a far clearer and terser writer, and a more consistent believer in natural selection—a hypothesis which he had as much right as Darwin to call "my theory," since he had arrived at it independently.

The answer lies in the special fitness of the man and the book to the times. In the first place, Darwin did publish his book before Wallace, and his was not a mere article written in two evenings. The *Origin of Species* came forth as a work of science—a large book which the author considered small—and it was crammed full of facts. Darwin told his public that he had been gathering them for more than twenty years with a consistent purpose in view. He said this in a diffident-confident tone calculated both to impress and to reassure. He had previously made himself known in his profession by writings on special subjects which had earned him esteem without enmities, and long before publishing the *Origin of Species* he had communi-

[4] "I must be a very bad explainer." *Life and Letters*, ii, 111.

cated his general principles to a few close friends—Lyell and Hooker and Gray in particular—and had familiarized them with his notions. He was not therefore going out altogether naked into the world, or sending his book, as many others have done, to almost certain death by neglect. He had also the merit of convincing the fiercest polemical writer of his generation—Huxley—and the good fortune that Huxley was given, almost by accident, Darwin's book to review for *The Times*.

Likewise to Darwin's advantage was the fact that he was not in any way a public figure. He had not taken sides on any of the great philosophical, religious, or political issues, nor dealt in popular articles and popular lectures. His was consequently a fresh voice, neither academic nor journalistic, a disinterested and pleasingly hesitant, even a confused voice. Huxley said that after thirty years of reading the *Origin of Species* he thought it "one of the hardest books to understand thoroughly that I know of. For exposition was not Darwin's *forte* and his English is sometimes wonderful."[5] By "wonderful" Huxley means of course "to be wondered at" for its often hopeless tangles. The friends who had read the MS. and objected to the sentence structure, and Darwin himself, who had complained of obscurities when he read his own proof, were both right. But that did not matter—on the contrary. Even the educated reader expects science to be abstruse, from whatever cause, and considering the mass of materials, the book was adroitly organized. The main argument was fully stated in the first four chapters, and for those whose attention could not stretch so far, there was a Recapitulation which could be read in half an hour. Indeed, it was one of those ideal books, like Marx's *Capital*, that need not be read to be talked about.

So much accounts for the popular response to the *Origin of Species*. It does not describe the way in which it was examined by Darwin's fellow scientists. If Huxley is right

5 Huxley, *Life and Letters*, ii, 190.

about the book's difficulty, their examination could only be superficially done in one or even more readings; and we know that it took the remaining forty years of the nineteenth century, with its profusion of scientific genius, to criticize and assess the value of natural selection as a hypothesis to explain the appearance of species. What happened at the time and on the spot was merely the "conversion" of a few well-prepared scientists and the establishing of the hypothesis as one worthy of prolonged discussion. This in turn required the drilling of certain words and bare notions into the public mind—a task which popularizers like Huxley, Spencer, Lewes, Asa Gray, Clémence Royer, John Fiske, Haeckel, and many others of lesser note, took into their charge. And for this purpose the increasingly powerful periodical press was ready to hand.

Earlier, as the example of Darwin's own grandfather shows, a new scientific theory would have reached but a very small circle of readers. Later, it would have been lost amid the clatter of front-page headlines. In the middle of Victoria's reign, however, press and public were in the right mood for the close and protracted discussion of ideas. The readers of that era did not thrive on the light fare which we find nourishing enough. They sustained themselves on fifty-page reviews of new books, exhaustive surveys of public questions, and party polemics whose weight could be measured on the open palm. Popular science of a high order was in demand, and it was still permissible, in dealing with science, to consider its philosophical bearing. Moreover, the leadership of the various sections of the press was remarkably unified in the hands of an elite.

Consider, for brevity's sake, all the personal relations wrapped up in the brief extract from George Eliot's diary which I have put at the head of this chapter. Why was the novelist reading the *Origin of Species* on the day of publication? Because an advance copy had been sent to her

husband, George Henry Lewes,[6] who was to review it for
Blackwood's. In *Blackwood's* he had already published two
popular series of Seaside Studies which Huxley had praised.
But Lewes was something besides a scientific reviewer. He
was an historian of philosophy and the first great biographer of Goethe. More than that, he had in the fifties edited
the first of the skirmishing weeklies, the *Leader,* born of
socialist and scientific convictions. It had had an important
following in Parliament, the clubs, the universities, and
among literary bohemians and self-taught workingmen. As
early as 1852 these readers had found in Lewes's journal
articles by one Herbert Spencer setting forth very precise
ideas of universal evolution based on the biological work of
Lamarck. They could follow Spencer also in the *Westminster Review,* and this is how George Eliot—herself a journalist—enters the scene, for she was until 1854 assistant editor
of that periodical. She was thus a close friend of Spencer's,
through whom she met Lewes.

At the *Westminster* were grouped the philosophical
radicals, once Benthamite, with J. S. Mill at their head,
and a host of younger men whose names were soon to become famous: John Morley, Alexander Bain, Frederic Harrison, W. S. Blunt, Richard Congreve—and it was with the
latter's wife that George Eliot took a walk on the "divine
day" of the *Origin's* publication.

But to mention Mill, Harrison, and Congreve is to name
another important element in the receptive atmosphere
that sustained Darwinism from the start. I mean the Positivists, or followers of Auguste Comte. We have seen that
in France it was a female Comtist who took up and fur-
thered Darwinism. In England Comte's ideas had gained
a hearing through Lewes, Mill, and Harriet Martineau, and
Congreve had become the leader of a small but active
group. Their allegiance to the new system meant "a belief

[6] I follow her usage and his, though they were not legally married. The "stuffy" Victorians did not on that account boycott
their writings.

in evolution, the generalizing of science, and the systema-
tizing of social forces."

These selfsame men who wrote for the public on such
high matters also met with the pure scientists in discussion
groups. There were the frequent "physiological feasts"
where Lewes, Piggott, Owen, and Redford argued the development theory, years before the *Origin of Species*.
There was the X-Club, which met the first Thursday of
every month—affording the hard-working Spencer his only
social pleasure—and from whose ranks came three presidents of the Royal Society and five presidents of the British
Association. There was finally the Metaphysical Society,
where "Archbishop Huxley" first coined the word "Agnostic," and where men of diverse callings and opinions
wrangled over every important intellectual issue. Add to
these intellectual societies the Workingmen's Colleges
which began to spring up about 1860, and at which the
Huxleys and the Tyndalls lectured; add to the intellectual
periodicals the new monthlies at a shilling, like *Macmillan's*
(1859), the *Cornhill* (1860), and the *Fortnightly* (1865),
and it becomes clear that a fertile soil awaited and helped
to spread the new popular heresies.

To be sure, these instruments of discussion and propaganda would have been nothing without the Victorians'
moral earnestness. We can laugh at it if we will, for its
ludicrous side has been made obvious. But its strength is
something we would do well to note and to compare with
other forms of force. A fresh insight into it was given us
when Bertrand Russell published a two-volume selection of
his parents' letters and diaries. The characteristic flavor appears in even the most casual passages, one of which happens to be in point. The year is 1866 and Kate Amberley,
Russell's mother, then aged twenty-four, writes down for
Sunday, June 17: ". . . Later came Mr. Herbert Spencer
(the philosopher) and Mr. Hill (an editor of the *Daily
News*) and Miss Garrett the woman doctor whom I had
heard lecture on Physiology at her own house. . . . We
dined at 6 (excellent dinner) delightful general talk, it was

most pleasant. The talk was on Comte, G. Evans and her new book *Felix Holt*,[7] on Nottingham, on Herbert Spencer's theory of the sun coming to an end and losing all it's [*sic*] force. . . ."

Truly delightful talk, as Lady Amberley says! It is such things as these that made a distinguished biologist of our time look back with longing to the Victorian age as the Era of Intellect.[8] For although the *Cornhill*'s circulation of 80,-000 or the *Leader*'s influence at the universities may seem slight when compared with the reach of our tabloids and radio, they are staggering when we take into account the nature and quality of the matter circulated. Occasionally, it is true, more modern distractions interrupted the Victorian public's devotion to marine biology and the *Origin of Species*; when, for instance, all England and America went mad in April 1860 over the first international boxing match, between Tom Sayers and J. C. Heenan, America's "Benicia Boy"; or when Napoleon the Third's need for dictatorial prestige led him into war with Austria over the unification of Italy.

But the interest in the origin of species and natural selection did not cease. There was indeed nothing incompatible between this interest and those other forms of struggle, individual or national. The very object of the Darwinian controversy was the idea of struggle. To advance natural selection as the means of evolution meant that purely physical forces, brute struggle among brutes, could account for the present forms and powers of living beings. Matter and Force, taken in any and every sense, explained our whole past history and presumably would shape our future. If there was for a time an ambiguity about the meaning of *Favoured Races* in Darwin's title ("race" stands there for the technical term "variety"), the public found in the text

[7] G. Evans is of course George Eliot (Marian Evans), and *Felix Holt the Radical* is a politico-social novel saturated with Comtism. (*Amberley Papers*, i, 513.)

[8] William Bateson in his lecture before the Eugenics Education Society, 1919; *William Bateson, Naturalist*, 1928, 380.

of later editions the alternative phrase "Survival of the Fittest," borrowed from Spencer and plain to the meanest intellect in an age of competition. Progress seemed assured, and ten thousand readers more bought Samuel Smiles's *Self-Help*, the best-seller of 1860.

There were, to be sure, some prophets of gloom. Darwin's old friend and teacher, Adam Sedgwick, who as a geologist believed in "development," that is to say in evolution, denounced natural selection as "a dish of rank materialism cleverly cooked and served up merely to make us independent of a Creator." Like Carlyle, Sedgwick feared that the denial of the "moral and metaphysical part of man" would ultimately brutalize and degrade mankind. Darwin's latest biographer, without admiring his subject the less, thinks Sedgwick saw into the heart of the matter and was right. In that case, it is no longer possible to view the storm around the *Origin of Species* merely as a battle over evolution—man's "descent from the monkeys" or the literal truth of Genesis—much less as the victory of unprejudiced inquirers into Nature's secrets over the forces of bigotry and darkness. It appears, rather, as a major incident, though neither the first nor the last, in the dispute between the believers in consciousness and the believers in mechanical action; the believers in purpose and the believers in pure chance. The so-called warfare between science and religion thus comes to be seen as the warfare between two philosophies and perhaps two faiths. Sedgwick's all-important distinction between evolution and natural selection is one indication that the issue is not local and limited but universal and permanent. Another proof of this is the fact that, our impression to the contrary notwithstanding, evolutionary theorizing did not begin with Charles Darwin.

2. The Evolution of Evolution

> There was an ape in the days that were earlier,
> Centuries passed and his hair became curlier,
> Centuries more and his thumb gave a twist,
> And he was a man and a Positivist.
> *Nineteenth-Century Ditty*

The word "evolution" does not occur in the first edition of the *Origin of Species* and Darwin did not use it until some years afterwards. But the idea it denotes had been put forward and discussed in Europe for at least a hundred years before 1859. These "sources" of evolutionary thought may be reduced to four: German philosophy, geological and astronomic evolution, biological evolution proper, and the new history—and the greatest of these is history.

Until the middle of the eighteenth century, history as we know it, the habit of dealing with all problems by recording their career in time, had hardly been invented. Historians were mere chroniclers who either neglected the whole European past since the fall of Rome, or else made it into a replica of their own age. The historical attitude becomes dominant first in the works of Montesquieu, Voltaire, and Gibbon, and it is significant that in all three historical-mindedness is allied to religious skepticism. Their earlier Italian contemporary, Vico, was in fact the first to conceive a distinctly evolutionary scheme of history, but he was then

and long thereafter neglected precisely because of his inno-
vating spirit. He called his work the *Scienza Nuova* or new
science, and it is clear that the success of the physical sciences had a good deal to do with rejuvenating the muse of
history. The popularizing of Newtonian ideas in France and
England bred the feeling that the modern period was superior to all others, that it depended on the achievements
of the period just past, and that there might be in history a
continuous improvement called progress. Seeking progress,
man would soon discover evolution.

The idea of progress created the need for "a science of
society" which would test the idea and show how conscious
change and natural fact co-operated. Accordingly Montesquieu tried to ascertain how states rose and fell, how climate conditioned human affairs, and how human laws
themselves, not arbitrarily made by man, must follow natural laws. A little later, before the Revolution, the French
economist, Turgot, showed that the old idea of historical
cycles must give way to that of historical continuity—
change within regularity; and the mathematician Condor-
cet, during the Revolution—in fact while awaiting execution
in prison—sketched a brilliant account of the intellectual
evolution of mankind.

Likewise in the eighteenth century, Leibniz opposed the
accepted world systems of Newton and Descartes. Theirs
was static and fixed.[1] His included the fact of change and
presupposed in all things an inherent perfecting principle.
It was a mere travesty of his idea that Voltaire ridiculed in
Candide by showing that the world was anything but perfect. Leibniz had not said this was the best of all conceivable worlds; he had said it was the best of all possible worlds.
At any given time the world was as perfect as it could possibly be, exactly as in the *Origin of Species*. Juggling with
these ideas, the second half of the eighteenth century devoted itself to the study of change and progress, and before

[1] Although Descartes' idea that from any given chaos a universe such as ours would result by the operation of existing mechanical laws is the archetype of all "mechanical" evolution.

the century was out, astronomy and geology had made considerable headway. On the one hand, Kant and Laplace conceived the famous Nebular Hypothesis to account for the development of the solar system; and on the other, Buffon, Lamarck, and Hutton substituted a uniformitarian theory of the earth's development for the former teachings of change by catastrophe. Shorn of details the new principle was that the present state of affairs on the earth or in the solar system could be explained by the continuous action through long ages of the same natural forces that we observe today.

This formula was a legacy of capital importance for the future. It is no exaggeration to say that the whole of nineteenth-century thought relied on the likelihood of imperceptible forces acting continuously. There was for the men of that century something inherently plausible about small doses. For example, Huxley and Spencer scouted the idea of a Creator making a live creature: that was incredible and superstitious; everything must be explained by the "more rational" system of small increments; but almost in the same breath they requested their hearer to grant them, for scientific purposes, the creation of life in a single small piece of matter. Only grant it and they would explain the rest. They also required an enormous length of time for the small increments and changes to add themselves up, and this the geologist and astronomer were ready to provide.

But the two great sciences of inert matter were not the only ones affected by the eighteenth-century notion of change. The same men who replaced a static earth and heaven by an evolving one also paid attention to living beings. The word "evolution" was first applied to life by Charles Bonnet, but he lacked the true idea and it was Buffon who first stated a complete theory of biological evolution.[2] Nature, said Buffon, does not make things in

2 The ancients, particularly Empedocles, Aristotle, and Lucretius, had more than mere glimmers of biological evolution; and in the Middle Ages a commentator on Genesis had spoken of a chain of being linking all animals together, but the continuity between

bunches. There are only individuals, and these individuals reveal a certain similarity of plan at the same time as they show a tendency to change. As director of the largest zoological garden in Europe and compiler of the encyclopedic Natural History that bears his name, Buffon had at his disposal a mass of facts, first and second hand, which exceeded in bulk and variety any other collection before his time. He had, moreover, a truly philosophic mind and a gift of style which, though it made him a classic in the French tongue, earned him the suspicious dislike of many of his colleagues.

This dislike was heightened by the fact just mentioned that he cast doubt on the reality of specific differences. In describing certain animals as common as the pig and the ass, Buffon permitted himself to speculate on the relations which might link them all together. When one examines their skeletons and the use of their limbs, he argued, one is tempted to arrange them in a series which would make them all derive from one another or from common ancestors. One would say all this, he added, if one were not told by revelation that they were all separately created. Buffon knew of course that the Sorbonne and the Court, exercising joint censorship in France, would not permit modern heresy.[3] He was a reserved and polite gentleman, fond of his place and of his friends, and he saw nothing but the inevitable obstruction of his work if he made himself a martyr. He therefore clothed his speculations in the form of paradoxes, as if he were only toying with ideas which he knew that Genesis set at naught. But in spite of this ironic attitude, he went so far as to hint of a means whereby species might change their form. He spoke of favoring and disfavoring circumstances in the environment, and enunciated the principle of the struggle for life which results from the discrepancy between animal fertility and a limited

these ideas and the modern movement remains doubtful. See H. F. Osborn, *From the Greeks to Darwin, passim,* and Hollard, *De l'homme,* 1853, 5.

[3] He had been compelled to retract his account of the origin of mountains in 1750.

supply of food. True, Buffon did not write any work exclusively propounding his theory of evolution, and even had he chosen to do so he would have lacked many kinds of proof needed for its acceptance. But he was the first to put into an authoritative work of natural history the idea of change of species, together with repeated suggestions of how modification might take place.

These opinions of Buffon's, published between 1750 and 1788, came at a time when other scientist-philosophers were also circling about the idea of change of species. The Scotch skeptic, David Hume, was speculating about the survival of the fittest and the unity of species long before he dared to publish the remarks embodying these views.[4] The Head of the Berlin Academy, Maupertuis, no doubt influenced by Leibniz, published a definitely "transformist" essay in 1751. Diderot, co-editor of the great *Encyclopedia*, in his "Thoughts for Interpreting Nature" (1754) and other papers, clearly set forth the doctrine of the survival of the fittest and the development of species through long ages. Bonnet, whom I have mentioned as the first user of the word "Evolution," drew up a scale of organized beings,[5] and concerned himself, like Buffon, with embryology: the mechanism of heredity was obviously the mysterious link between change from parent to offspring and change in species.

The next step was taken by Lamarck, a botanist and geologist, whose labors created the most elaborate and scientific system of evolution of his time.[6] As everyone knows,

---

[4] *Dialogues on Natural Religion*, written ca. 1750, published 1779.

[5] The classifier Linnaeus was no evolutionist, but he put man among the higher primates and in the last edition of his great work (1766) admitted the possibility of species "degenerating" through intercrossing and the action of climate.

[6] His *Natural History of Invertebrates*, 7 vols., 1815–22, and his *Fossil Shells of the Paris Region*, 1 vol., 1825, being works of description and classification, were universally acclaimed by the scientific world. This should be enough to dispose of the im-

Lamarck received nothing but jeers for his pains, the great anatomist Cuvier greeting every new volume of Lamarck's as a fresh sign of madness. It was these volumes, appearing between 1802 and 1809, that brought into common speech a number of now familiar images and ideas. The neck of the giraffe, for instance, is a Lamarckian example which it would be unprecedented to neglect.

According to Lamarck, the neck of the giraffe was not always long. It grew long owing to the effort of the creature to reach high foliage. The use of the organ stretched it just as the use of the muscle swells out the blacksmith's biceps. This lengthened neck was transmitted to the giraffe's off-spring until it reached its present size and became a perma-nent possession of the animal. The meaning of the La-marckian phrase "use-inheritance" is clear: use alters and heredity transmits "new characters," and species thereby evolve. Species are related, as in Buffon; environment changes their form, as in Buffon; but Lamarck asserts that new needs are the agency through which the environment acts upon the creature. And by the contrary process of dis-use, Lamarck explains the presence of rudimentary organs.

In reality, the climate theory by which Montesquieu had explained forms of government was being applied first by Buffon, then with greater refinement and precision by Lamarck, to explain forms of organic life. The new evolu-tionary geology had meanwhile shown that change in the environment was a fact. But so far change was not viewed as mechanical. Lamarck overstated his case when he said: "To perfect and diversify animals, Nature requires only matter, space and time"; for he also admitted the possi-bility of a perfecting tendency, and his theory really re-quired the presence of purpose in creatures to make them stretch their necks. It was this supposition of purpose that led to his being ridiculed. He was credited with the notion that if a giraffe wanted a long neck it would grow one. Baldly stated it sounds absurd. But, it might be asked, how

pression that Lamarck was an amateur with "crude" ideas of plant and animal life.

can any creature grow even into its usual mature form unless it exerts its will to live and to grow? In an age of simple and rigid ideas about willing, the question would have had no meaning. True, Cabanis, a physician, and Schopenhauer, the philosopher, who were contemporaries of Lamarck's, independently put the question to themselves and laid the foundations for the work of Nietzsche and Freud upon the Will. But Schopenhauer's influence did not properly begin until the 1850s, and Cabanis' theories were condemned as "abject materialism," which left Lamarck high and dry with an "absurd theory" of animals growing tails, horns, and necks "at will," and dropping them in the same fashion.

All the while there was a far more serious objection to Lamarck's scheme, and that was the doubtful possibility of inheriting acquired characteristics. Lamarck had boldly taken it for granted that the giraffe with a stretched neck would have offspring with necks longer than the usual size. It is true that we know but little even today about the giraffe's early days, but we can easily observe that the blacksmith's son—and daughter—are not born with appreciably larger biceps, for all their father's work at the anvil. Yet without inheritance, use and disuse are—of no use. So Lamarck died, blind, poor, and despised as a fool, without seeing his theory of animal evolution receive even the negative criticism that it deserved, much less the credit for deep knowledge and stubborn thought.

Fortunately, ideas make their way even into the minds that refuse them entrance, and so make easier the path of the same idea when it presents itself in a new guise. A few contemporaries of Lamarck's did take heed. The anatomist Geoffroy Saint-Hilaire was one. Bory de Saint-Vincent was another. Across the border, Goethe, who seems to have been familiar with the work of both Buffon and Lamarck, was led to establish through researches of his own a related theory of change which he called the Metamorphosis of Plants. Goethe was less happy when theorizing about the human skull, but when, after Lamarck's death, a new battle over the fixity of species arose in France, Goethe was on the side of the "Unfixed." His young friend, the Swiss botanist Soret, has described the scene for us:

> "Tell me," cried Goethe as I entered. "What do you think of the great event? The volcano has broken out, everything is in flames, and it's no longer something going on behind closed doors."
>
> "A dreadful affair," I replied (the revolution of 1830 had just broken out) . . . "the reigning family will be driven into exile."
>
> "We do not seem to understand each other, my dear fellow," rejoined Goethe. "I am not speaking of those people . . . I am speaking of the open break that has occurred in the Academy between Cuvier and Geoffroy St. Hilaire over a matter of the highest importance to science . . . you cannot imagine what I felt on hearing the news of the meeting of July 19."[7]

Geoffroy's debate with Cuvier bore no immediate fruits. Fortunately in England, another botanist, who happened to be the future Charles Darwin's grandfather, had arrived independently of Lamarck at the conclusion that species evolve, and had even gone farther than he in analyzing the process. More concerned than Lamarck with the problems of reproduction, Erasmus Darwin anticipated many nineteenth-century ideas, such as the unity of parent and offspring, the continuity of instinct as buried memory,[8] as well as the theory known in his grandson's work as sexual selection. In fact, the elder Darwin's awareness of struggle for survival, of the reproduction of the strongest animals, of the greater variations in animals under domestication, and even of what was later accepted for a time as protective coloration—all this set forth in plain English before 1800— is what enabled his future biographer to say, with the approval of Charles Darwin, that for every volume by the

[7] *Gespräche mit Eckermann* under date of Aug. 2, 1830.
[8] Hering in Germany and Samuel Butler in England rediscovered this idea, while Asa Gray and Joseph Leconte laid claim to it in the United States, each unaware of the others' work.

grandson there was a corresponding chapter by the grandfather.[9] The burden of his doctrine was that all animals originated in "a single living filament" and that evolution took place through the desire of creatures to survive, fit new environmental conditions, and diversify their structure. Desire and power, both in small amounts, kept pace with each other and the results were "selected" by favoring or unfavoring circumstances.

Though his person and character enjoyed universal respect, Dr. Darwin's generation was content to settle the questions he had raised by coining the verb "to Darwinise." It was a pity, too, that he should so often have used heroic couplets to convey his ideas and that his mind and interests should have been so wide-ranging. He predicted the use of steam cars and flying machines, wrote of the loves of the plants (ridiculed in a famous parody, "The Loves of the Triangles"), and could be eloquent even upon such a thing as the evolutionary significance of the opposable thumb:

> The hand, first gift of Heaven! to man belongs;
> Untipt with claws the circling fingers close,
> With rival points the bending thumbs oppose
>
> . . . .
> Whence the fine organs of the touch impart
> Ideal figure, source of every art. . . .[10]

Coleridge might class him, erroneously, with the materialists, but Shelley could penetrate the uncomely verse and absorb the best of the Doctor's philosophy, making it the substance of his own evolutionary thought in *Prometheus Unbound*. Clearly, the spirit of evolution hovered over the cradle of the new century. So far it was not tied to any underlying philosophy. It followed its subject matter: mechanical action in astronomy and geology; unconscious will and purpose, or use and disuse, in biology; climate and the conscious aims of men in the social progress revealed by history.

[9] Krause, *Life of Erasmus Darwin*, N. Y., 1880, 132.
[10] *Temple of Nature*, 1802, canto iii, ll. 122–28.

Side by side with proponents of evolutionism, however, the eighteenth century could boast a flourishing school of materialists. From La Mettrie, who in 1749 wrote a popular treatise called *Man a Machine*, to Frederick the Great, who made La Mettrie his physician and lifelong friend, the century numbered many distinguished men who would have quoted with approval Lamarck's incautious word about Matter, Time, and Space being sufficient for "Nature" to accomplish her ends.[11]

As speculation increased about what Nature was, the simple mechanical view became less and less plausible. Diderot, an early materialist, approached closer and closer to Vitalism. Rousseau's influence worked in the same direction: he not only inspired the fad for botany in place of Newtonian physics, he replaced mechanical explanations by vitalist in every realm of thought. And after the disastrous return to a more mechanical faith during the French Revolution, the Romantic movement was a reassertion of the living principle in all things. Evolution thereby became the general law of existence.

The so-called Biological Revolution[12] is simply this recognition that the laws of life, rather than those of mathematics and astronomy, should serve as a pattern for thought and a guide for action. This meant preferring the organic to the inorganic; the fluid and flexible and growing to the solid, rigid, and inert. For the Romanticists, the world was a scene of diversity, change, and contradiction, not a formal dance of fixed elements following a geometrical pattern, as the worshipers of Newton and Locke had imagined. Yet it was the Newtonian ways of thought which, by making men proud of scientific progress, had now

[11] Napoleon: "A man is only a more perfect being than a dog or a tree. . . . The plant is the first link in the chain of which man is the last. I know that this is all contrary to religion, but it is my opinion that we are all matter." *Table Talk and Opinions*, London, 1868, 51.

[12] The word "biology" itself was first proposed, independently, by Lamarck and Treviranus in the same year, 1802.

led to ideas of evolution denying the Newtonian rigidity and fixity. This is the sense in which the nineteenth century grows out of the eighteenth while repudiating it.

Combining the new views of evolving life with the older one of historical progress, the early nineteenth century produced a powerful hybrid, the Philosophy of History. A vast increase in historical research on the part of the Romantic School in Germany and France produced innumerable such philosophies, all constructed on evolutionary lines. Perhaps the most famous is Hegel's, though the ideas of Burke, Herder, and Fichte came before and exerted a great influence. Hegel showed how mankind had passed from the Oriental period of despotism, through the Classical period of slavery, to the Modern period, characterized by the idea of universal freedom, an idea of Germanic origin fittingly embodied in the state.[13] The influence of this work on Karl Marx and on many other nineteenth-century historians is well known: it made historical evolution a recognized subject matter; it accounted for the onward march of humanity according to a definite pattern, and it defined the function of the Great Man in that process. Its most practical conclusion was that institutions and states, like individuals, have to grow. They cannot be made out of hand by writing down constitutions. They live through "stages" and obey definite "laws." Though Hegel was little known in England before the middle of the century, Edmund Burke had earlier made the same point in attacking the French Revolution, and the spirit of his teaching survived in historians like Carlyle and jurists like Austin.

The Revolution had also taught French thinkers to question arbitrary political innovations and to insist on the need for social and economic reform as well. These reforms, they felt, should not spring ready-made from the brain of the reformer. They must be grounded in the historical past and evolve naturally. The philosophy of Saint-Simon, a

[13] Not such an absurd view as it now seems, if we remember that the enemy of freedom was Napoleon, the heir of the Roman ideal of Imperium.

French nobleman who fought under Washington, accordingly discovered another law of three stages describing the progress of humanity from Egyptian times to the present. The present was clearly the age of science and industry, requiring the leadership, not of kings or popular representatives, but of scientists and manufacturers—hence, the precise form of socialism that Saint-Simon urged on Europe.[14]

Coming one generation after Saint-Simon, his disciple Auguste Comte borrowed his method and made it, with many changes of his own, the most powerful doctrine of the century. There were at any one time but few professing *Comtists*, but the majority of thinking men either declared themselves *Positivists* or acted as such without knowing that they were.[15] What then is Positivism? It is three things—an evolutionary view of the past, an ordered scheme for the sciences, and a sociological creed. This last I shall leave to a later chapter; its goal suggests fascism and the passion of its adherents, Marxism. But the other two features belong here as showing the mood in which Darwinian evolution was received and the prophetic hopes which it fulfilled.

What chiefly struck independent thinkers like Mill and Spencer in Comte's system was his notion of the way human ideas had evolved from primitive times to the present. Comte discerned first a theological stage, then a metaphysical, and finally a positive or scientific stage. Each of Comte's three stages takes its name from the prevailing type of explanation given to natural phenomena. In the theological stage, a demon or a god is held to be the cause of an event: when Jove is angry he thunders. In the metaphysical stage a hidden power or entity accounts for the observed fact: thunderation, so to speak, is at work. In the positive or

14 See below.
15 "Hegel's dialectical evolutionism has been amended by that of Darwin or Spencer, and Auguste Comte's Positivism has influenced us all, even those amongst us who are not Positivists." J. Reville, speaking at International Congress of Arts and Science, St. Louis, 1904; Boston, 1906, ii, 644.

modern stage of thinking, science discovers the actual relations of matter and electricity and embodies them in
mathematical laws.

The three stages, however, do not follow each other
evenly and simultaneously in all human thought. Each
branch of learning must separately go through the three
stages. At the time he wrote, Comte felt that many of the
sciences—notably the biological—were still in the metaphysical stage. "Metaphysical" in this sense is a key word
for the understanding of Darwinism and its allies. Darwin's
Natural Selection was devised to protect evolution against
"metaphysical" perfecting tendencies, and no word in the
mouth of a late nineteenth-century scientist could carry so
much reproach and contempt as "metaphysical." To be
clear about the Positivist's use of it, one need only remember the joke in Molière which hinges on the reason why
opium puts people to sleep. The candidate is asked that
question by the medical faculty and the expected answer is
that opium puts people to sleep "because of its dormitive
power." Obviously, dormitive power is only another name
for the fact that opium induces sleep, and it is easy to
laugh with the satirist and with the Positivist at the in-
adequacy of the explanation; yet the problems of science,
as we shall see, are far from fully solved by ruling out hidden essences.

Comte went one step farther in his effort to create an
orthodoxy for science. He minutely set forth the relations
of the sciences to one another, making a "positive" hierarchy of their methods and contents. This is where his influence—like that of Feuerbach in Germany—made directly
for a revival of materialistic mechanism and paved the way
for Darwinism. Comte divided the sciences into static and
dynamic, depending on whether they dealt with structure
or function. Anatomy, for instance, is static because it sets
forth the number, form, and arrangement of organs; but
physiology is dynamic because it describes their actual
working. Yet the one rests on the other, and if one considers
the utmost range of scientific endeavor, it is possible to

start with the static parts of chemistry and physics, and rise, through physiology and biology, to sociology (Comte's own coinage for the science of society), finally reaching ethics at the top of the pyramid. Now Comte from time to time recognized that although ethics must take account of the sciences below it, right down to physics, yet the facts of ethics are not themselves reducible to mere chemical and physical formulas. But his passion for order and system betrayed him into that prevailing fallacy of reducing the complex to the simple absolutely.

It is the error which dogs the evolutionist, the error of believing that if you isolate the elements or label the beginnings of a process you have thereby grasped the process in its entirety. Because living things depend on certain chemico-physical things, therefore human beings *are* physico-chemical combinations and nothing more. This error is the so-called "genetic fallacy" and I shall refer to it under that name as occasion demands. It is a common error, and the very one, incidentally, that both sides fell into when disputing over the origin of species. When Bishop Wilberforce, for instance, asked Huxley at the famous meeting of The British Association in 1860 whether he, Huxley, was descended from an ape on his grandmother's or his grandfather's side, he was assuming that such an origin, quite apart from the visible facts of Huxley's appearance or personality, would be thought degrading and that Huxley would repudiate it. Huxley sensibly accepted it, though he later turned right-about-face and tried to prove that Wilberforce was only matter by referring to the fact that at one time the potential Bishop was a speck of jelly no bigger than the tip of Huxley's pencil case.

Both should have known that becoming or growing, if it means anything, must mean a change not reducible to the stage before, much less to the original stage of the process. Something exists at the end which was not there at the beginning. An oak may come from an acorn, but it is not identical with an acorn, nor even with an acorn plus all that the oak has absorbed of moisture and food in the process of growing upwards. This problem of Becoming was the staple of discussion for the whole half century of Romantic thought before Darwin and Spencer. To the Germans particularly—Hegel, Schopenhauer, Schelling, and Fichte—we owe the establishment of the basic evolutionary notion that Being is Becoming and that fixity is an abstraction or an illusion.[16] Unfortunately, this view was linked in biology with the principle of vitalism, or life force, which, though it inspired very fruitful researches into the nature of living cells, ultimately proved untenable. The difficulty is that if there is no superadded life force in living beings, seemingly nothing but matter is left.[17] Remove the mysterious, "metaphysical" soul or controlling power, and mere physical and chemical units remain behind. From these everything else must now be explained in "positive" terms. Hence the violent, almost angry reversion to eighteenth-century materialism which coincided with the Darwin-Wallace publication of Natural Selection.

The links between philosophy and science in this period are plain enough. Comtism, comprising under this head the group of doctrines based on science and history, and Hegelism, comprising those based on logic and philosophy, jointly suggested that human history was a part of natural history and that natural history was characterized by the process of change-according-to-law which we term growth. Evolution is thus in a very real sense the science of sciences, that is to say, it is a complete world outlook. The influence of this generality on the early nineteenth century was overwhelming, as can be seen in the steady approach to what we now call Darwinism. Between Lamarck and the *Origin of*

[16] Emerson and Thoreau made these ideas familiar to Americans, Theodore Parker was an evolutionist before Darwin, and the whole Transcendentalist Movement in this country was independently in tune with European speculation.

[17] Certain biologists today make use of "form" or *Gestalt* to dispose of the difficulty, saying for example with Holftreter that "Pattern rules particles." [Note to the Second Edition.]

Species, or, what amounts to the same interval, between Erasmus Darwin and his grandson, the purely biological idea of change of species was frequently reiterated. Lamarck's theory was hardly discredited, for it had never been credited. But as early as 1832, Lyell had made an abstract of it and printed it in the first edition of his *Principles of Geology*.[18] Lyell then disbelieved utterly in change of species, but he adduced Lamarck's thesis as a kind of parallel to his own theories of geological change, and he reprinted it in subsequent editions, after Darwin, "in justice to Lamarck."[19] Again, between 1810 and 1854 a score of other qualified scientists published their belief in the mutability of species.[20] In addition, at least three men during the same period applied the Buffonian-Malthusian idea of the survival of the fittest to the evolution of life[21]—Dr. Charles Wells, the famous investigator of dew, in 1813; Patrick Matthew, a writer on Naval Timber, in 1831, and Naudin, a French botanist, in 1852.

More important still, England had a foretaste of the furore that greeted the *Origin of Species* fifteen years before that book. An anonymous author, who turned out to be the publisher Robert Chambers, wrote a work called *The Vestiges of Creation* which was the sensation of the year 1844, and which sold ten editions in the following nine years. The work is not in any sense an advance on the Buffon-Lamarck-Erasmus Darwin theories with which the author showed his familiarity: it is rather an attractively written survey of

18 Vol. ii, ch. 1.
19 Ed. 1872, vol. ii, ch. 34, note.
20 See H. F. Osborn, *From the Greeks to Darwin*.
21 The *fact* of natural selection was generally recognized by innumerable nonscientific writers before Darwin. Schopenhauer, for example, wondered whether smallpox vaccination would not keep alive many weaklings whom nature would otherwise have pruned away. A century before, in the *Discourse on Inequality*, Rousseau had likewise noted the fact of natural selection. What constitutes a new departure in Buffon and his followers is to make this fact an agent of change; and what constitutes a still further novelty is Charles Darwin's making it the *sole* agent of change.

the entire field of evolutionary speculation, including the inorganic world of astronomy and geology as well as living things. Where the book failed, like its predecessors, was in its inability to point with assurance to the "mechanism" of evolution. Chambers did not agree with Lamarck's use-inheritance; he believed with Leibniz in an inherent perfecting principle—precisely the sort of explanation that Comte and Darwin would have denounced as "metaphysical." It was like saying that what makes the railway engine move is an "inner locomotive power."

Nonetheless the book had a tremendous influence in popularizing the idea of a general evolution. Disraeli, known at that time chiefly as an aspiring politician and a writer of smart society novels, could plausibly parody the argument as it was talked about by intellectuals: the hero after whom his novel *Tancred* is named is urged by the charming Lady Constance to read *Revelations of Chaos*. "You know," she gushes, "all is development—the principle is perpetually going on. First there was nothing; then there was something; then—I forget the next—I think there were shells; then fishes; then we came—let me see—did we come next? Never mind that; we came at last, and the next change will be something very superior to us, something with wings. . . ."[22] And Tancred, appalled at the possibility of her developing wings, changes his mind about marrying Lady Constance.

Though there was nothing aggressive about Chambers's theology—he made the Creator establish the laws of development just as Asa Gray did sixteen years later in behalf of Darwin—the conservatives in religion took alarm: "Prophetic of Infidel times," said the *North British Review*, "and indicating the unsoundness of our general education, *The Vestiges* has started into public favor with a fair chance of poisoning the fountains of science and sapping the foundations of religion." No plainer testimony could

[22] *Tancred*, John Lane ed., 148–49.

be given about the fears that Chambers had aroused or about his influence.[23]

It was to a more sophisticated public, though one prepared also by *The Vestiges,* that Herbert Spencer addressed his articles entitled "The Development Hypothesis," and "Progress—Its Law and Cause," between 1852 and 1857. Spencer had adopted Lamarckism entire, but it was no doubt the scope and generality of his evolutionary ideas that found an echo in the minds of his audience. It was he who coined the phrase "Survival of the Fittest" and he who carried out Comte's plan of a general "scientific" sociology. After gathering his first essays into a volume, Spencer was encouraged by his friends—including the scientists Huxley, Hooker, and Tyndall—to propose for public subscription the plan of a vast philosophic system based on evolution as a universal process. The prospectus was drawn up and sent out some months before the appearance of the *Origin of Species.*

Anyone, in fact, who would gauge the familiarity of the European mind with evolutionary ideas before Darwin need do no more than reread Tennyson's *In Memoriam.* There he will find not only the "Nature red in tooth and claw" of natural selection, but likewise man's kinship with the ape, the chain of beings, their development, and the consequences to religion and morals of the thoroughgoing naturalism of science. Now *In Memoriam,* after being mulled over by the poet for seventeen years, was published in 1850. The gropings of eighteenth-century philosophers and historians and the formulations of early nineteenth-century scientists and thinkers had borne fruit. Progress: its law and cause; the vestiges of creation; all is development; the principle is perpetually going on—these phrases signalized the coming age of evolution and the birth and transfiguration, at one stroke, of Darwinism.

[23] An evangelical preacher named Cumming sold 15,000 copies of an ignorant "refutation," *The Church Before the Flood.*

3. Darwin Answers the Sphinx

There is warrant for the belief that Evolution can
end only in the establishment of the greatest perfection and the most complete happiness.

SPENCER

A mind like that of Darwin can never sin wittingly
against either fact or law.

TYNDALL

The publication of the *Origin of Species* marks the
Hegira of Science from the idolatries of special creation to the purer faith of Evolution.

HUXLEY

It looks almost as if coming at the end of this triple tradition of history, philosophy, and science, Darwin had had
little to do. But the hallmark of accepted science, the active
support of a body of popularizers, and the downing of religious orthodoxy were all-important testimonials which no
theory of evolution had yet received in the full light of
public opinion. They must first be secured before the world
could take the new principle as axiomatic.

In achieving these results the importance of the idea of
natural selection cannot be overestimated. By putting it
forward as "his theory" for explaining the presumably
technical point of how species originate, Darwin addressed
himself to scientists and seemed to ignore lay opinion. He
made no frontal attack; his book was not about Evolution.

But by bringing together with the greatest care the geological, geographical, and embryological evidences of change of species, he turned natural selection as it were inside out, and showed that evolution was the real upshot of "my theory."

To scientists and laymen alike, the appeal of natural selection was manifold. It had the persuasiveness of "small doses"; it was entirely automatic, doing away with both the religious will of a creator and the Lamarckian will of his creatures; it substituted a "true cause"[1] for the "metaphysical" sort of explanation; lastly, natural selection was an exact parallel in nature to the kind of individual competition familiar to everyone in the social world of man. By joining the well-established notion of natural selection to the development theory which had been talked about for a hundred years, Darwin was felt to have solved the greatest problem of modern science. He had explained life, or almost. He had at any rate shown the primary animal basis of human progress and told "its law and cause."

This may not have been what Darwin consciously intended, and it is no measure of the worth of natural selection; for scientists now agree—and Darwin was among the first—that the struggle for existence was largely misunderstood as a process and very much overrated as a force. But Darwin may be said with a slight exaggeration to have found the right wrong idea for cementing together in the minds of his contemporaries the elements of doctrine which had repeatedly been proposed along separate lines of thought. Indeed, in the middle versions of the *Origin of Species* there was a dash of all the disputed hypotheses —a little Lamarckian use and disuse, a little Buffonian change by direct action of the environment, and a little

[1] It is significant of the evolutionists' neglect of philosophy that they generally use the phrase *vera causa* (true cause) as if it meant "the one real cause," whereas it is a technical term meaning "an additional cause, whose working is obscure, but which is truly a cause nevertheless."

curtsey before the Creator, who is mentioned by name. Natural selection nevertheless dominated the scene.

Darwin started with an analogy drawn from the breeding of domestic animals. Animals and plants under domestication are known to vary, that is to say, to produce offspring slightly different in shape or color or character from their progenitors. From these the breeder or grower selects those best suited to his purpose, preventing the rest from reproducing their kind. Luther Burbank, for example, owed his remarkable success in developing new varieties of plants to the skill with which he could pick out a dozen seedlings from a mass of several thousand. The bonfires of rejected ones testified to the degree of his selectiveness. Similarly Darwin starts with random variations—unexplained[2]—and the selection of certain of them by man for the breeding of specially useful varieties or "races." Natural selection is the same process occurring in the wild state. But how can selection be said to take place in the wild state? Simply by reason of the Buffon-Malthus observation that there are more animals and plants than can find means to survive. "Eat or be eaten" as Darwin's grandfather had put it. This struggle for existence must select certain individuals for death and others for survival—and survival means the opportunity of leaving offspring.

The only question left is what rationale of selection does nature apply? The obvious answer is that those individuals would be selected whose characteristics gave them special opportunities of escaping their enemies, catching their prey, and so forth. Any random variation—say longer legs —would enable its possessor to survive and produce "favored races." The small random variations would accumulate, and in course of time lead to partial or complete change of form. New species would arise bearing new and useful characteristics; for all changes, in order to be perpetuated, must be adaptive, that is to say, must be of help to the creature possessing them.

[2] This amounts to an "innate tendency" of a sort, since without Variation there could be no change.

Such is Darwin's "distinctive theory," and its correspondence with the argument of the classical economists to prove that unlimited competition brings out the best and cheapest product is complete. Even now, after a century of criticism, the persuasive exposition of either theory leaves the mind paralyzed with enchantment. It is so simple, so neat, so like a well-designed machine. Even better than a machine, in that it really provides for perpetual motion; the struggle for existence is constant, so is variation; improvement should therefore be endless. After its beauty had once been grasped it was difficult not to fall down and adore the theory. In this country John Fiske, among others, could not tire of repeating how natural selection would seize unerringly upon every really useful variation in plant and animal forms. It would preserve whatever was truly beneficial to the development of the race. Nature acted like that miraculous agent in economic science, The Market, which will theoretically not allow a slightly better or cheaper can opener to fail of enthusiastic reception. But Fiske was a devout man and he therefore combined with his worship of natural selection a verbose theism which he purveyed to his compatriots in lectures and writings that sold by the tens of thousands.

Even apart from these considerations, natural selection was what many believers in development had long looked for. It made entirely unnecessary the Lamarckian assumption that acquired characteristics are transmitted by way of generation. And since the science of genetics was still unborn and nobody knew how offspring came to possess the same traits as their parents, a theory which worked without any assumptions about heredity was all the stronger on that account. Natural selection was as simple as the shotmaker's slide, which allows only the perfectly round shot to reach the bottom. Only, with living beings you can count on the "fittest" giving birth to similarly fit progeny. "How very stupid not to have thought of it!" as Huxley somewhat tactlessly exclaimed.

It came so pat that it soon was overworked. From explaining the origin of species, natural selection became the explanation of all adaptations, beginning with one-celled animals and ending with man's latest ideas. Spencer quietly dropped the use of Lamarck's name and made selection explain all the facts in his special province—psychology, sociology, and ethics. Walter Bagehot, in a very popular work, *Physics and Politics*, explained how a natural selection was at work among human societies, favoring desirable innovations, so that political forms grew into perfection through conflicts and yet gradually. Trench, a bishop of the church and an authority on the English tongue, who in 1859 had declared the cause of linguistic change a mystery, showed with assurance, after 1859, that language grew and old words died in virtue of the great principle of the survival of the fittest. It was a cheerful thought that no good thing was ever lost and that no lost thing was any longer any good.

It is but fair to say that Darwin himself soon began to have doubts about the universal efficacy of natural selection. Just before the publication of the *Origin of Species* his faith in it was so strong that he believed a slight adaptive variation in a single trait would turn the scale in favor of survival. But as early as 1862 he had begun to waver, and by 1865 he talked increasingly of the direct action of the environment and of use and disuse as factors of change. Successive editions of the *Origin of Species* tried to coordinate these doubts and shifts of opinion.

Darwin's difficulty had several aspects. For one thing, the presence of vestigial organs could hardly be accounted for by natural selection. It could not be a critical need of the creature to lose useful organs—the toes in the flipper of the whale or the eyes of the mole. The more these vestiges suggested evolution, the less they supported natural selection. Darwin fell back on the Lamarckian factor of disuse. Then there were differences between related species such as the varying number of hairs on the head of certain insects, or the tuft on the breast of the wild turkey, which fulfilled no visible purpose. Yet natural selection required life-and-death utility before it could come into play, so Darwin had to suppose direct environmental influence à la Buffon or selection through sexual preference.[3]

In other words Darwin was slowly coming back to some of the positions of the early nineteenth-century evolutionists, including his own grandfather's ideas. And in the last revised edition of the *Descent of Man*, he had to express again his indecision about the factors causing evolution. But needless to say, the public, including many scientists, paid not the slightest attention to *these* variations in the mind of their oracle. Darwin was and remained the man who had made evolution thinkable by proposing a cast-iron cause. Darwin's co-discoverer, Wallace, never departed from his faith in his own theory, and the apostolic succession continued to the time of Weismann, whose application of selection to the reproductive cells of the body earned him and his followers the title of neo-Darwinians. And to this day in many an excellent textbook one finds, after a careful list of the undisputed objections to natural selection, that it is "the only theory of any consequence" that will account for the facts.[4]

It should have been possible, even before Darwin came around to it, to criticize the whole imagery of natural selection and the survival of the fittest.[5] But if we except Samuel Butler and one or two other unheeded critics, everybody preferred "Nature red in tooth and claw," and either regretted or rejoiced that it was the only means of making improvements in species. Some obviously feared that if natural selection were discarded evolution would be endangered. They thought the two theories inseparable and foresaw a rebirth of superstition. But dropping natural selec-

[3] A now discarded theory which Weismann once described in words which it would be a pity to abridge: "It arises from the rivalry of one sex, usually the male, for the possession of the other, usually the female." *Darwin and Modern Science*, 42.

[4] See for example J. W. Folsom's *Entomology*, 3rd ed., 1922, 198–211.

[5] See below, pp. 107 ff.

tion leaves the evidence for evolution untouched.[6] It was
not even a question of dropping natural selection, for natural selection is an observed fact. It was a question of seeing
—as Darwin came to see—that selection occurs *after* the
useful change has come into being: therefore natural selection can cause nothing but the elimination of the unfit, not
the production of the fit. To use once again the analogy
of the shotmaker's slide, the perfectly round shot have to
be made before they can be selected, and it is nonsense to
say that it is their trial on the slide that makes them
round.

The nonsense, however, captivated a generation of
thinkers whose greatest desire was to get rid of vitalism,
will, purpose, or design as explanations of life, and to substitute for them an automatic material cause. They saw
adaptation and utility, but they wished to explain them
both by unintentional necessity. This is what Thomson and
Geddes meant—orthodox evolutionists though they were—
when in celebrating the fiftieth anniversary of the *Origin
of Species* they said: "The substitution of Darwin for
Paley[7] as the chief interpreter of the order of nature is cur-
rently regarded as the displacement of an anthropomorphic
view by a purely scientific one: a little reflection, however,
will show that what has actually happened has been merely
the replacement of the anthropomorphism of the eighteenth century by that of the nineteenth. For the place va-
cated by Paley's theological and metaphysical explanation
has simply been occupied by that suggested to Darwin and
Wallace by Malthus in terms of the prevalent severity of
industrial competition; and those phenomena of the struggle for existence which the light of contemporary economic

[6] Huxley, *Nature*, Nov. 1, 1894.

[7] The author of the classic *Natural Religion* (1802) which
argues the existence of the Deity from the evidences of design in
nature. "It is difficult now to realize the impetus which the works
of Paley gave to the study of Natural History." Professor E. B.
Poulton, "The Value of Colour in the Struggle for Life," *Darwin
and Modern Science*, 272.

theory has enabled us to discern have thus come to be temporarily exalted into a complete explanation of organic process."[8]

Malthus had witnessed the growth of population under the new factory system, the gathering of poverty-stricken masses in industrial slums, and the relative shrinking of the home-grown food supply as a result of urbanization— in short he had first observed and then put into formidable prose the subject of Goldsmith's *Deserted Village*, and he had concluded that if it were not for a beneficent Providence everybody would starve. For population increased in geometric progression, food production in arithmetical— 2.4.8.16.32 . . . against 2.4.6.8.10. . . . The beneficent Providence consisted in the natural checks to the growth of population: war, famine, and disease. It followed that any interference with these checks through almsgiving, hospital care, or peace societies, was cruelty to the rest; while starvation, pestilence, and bloodshed were merciful gifts from on high.

By substituting Natural Selection for Providence, the new science could solve a host of riddles arising in practical life, though by the same exchange the new science had to become a religion. This necessity is what makes the Darwinian event of lasting importance in cultural history. We do less than justice to the men of the nineteenth century who first did battle for evolution if we think that it was altogether for secret or unconscious economic motives that they clung to Darwinism. A man like Huxley may have been tempted by his pugnacity and evangelical passion to overstate his conclusions, but he was neither stupid nor dishonest. He had the highest kind of courage, and a Calvinistic desire to be chosen for the right reason, which for him was the possession of truth. "Science and her methods," he declared, "gave me a resting place independent of authority and tradition."[9] His rejection of everything untested by

[8] *Ibid.*, 15.
[9] Clodd, *Thomas Henry Huxley*, N. Y., 1902, 15.

him was radical, revolutionary, heedless of consequence. And it left him and his world naked before moral adversity. Europe became more and more like the vaunted jungle of the evolutionary books, and Huxley died heavyhearted with forebodings of the kind of future he had helped to prepare. We are face to face with the typical contradiction of nineteenth-century enlightenment. How did it come about?

Before the *Origin of Species* Huxley was familiar with evolutionary ideas but unconvinced. Darwin's book converted him "by means of natural selection," so that in 1863 he could say "it is Darwinism or nothing." Yet from the very first he had held against the completeness of the theory the fact that it lacked experimental proof. Until from a common stock varieties could be produced which were infertile when crossed together (for only then would one have seen species originate) Huxley was not satisfied with the Darwinian theory. He saw no reason to change between 1860 and 1887 when he reverted to the problem. No amount of human selection had yet produced distinct species, and the theory consequently presented an "insecurity of logical foundation."[10] Nevertheless, Huxley maintained to the very end an "unshaken belief in the theory propounded by Mr. Darwin thirty-four years ago." He characterized it as "the only hypothesis at present put before us which has a sound scientific foundation."[11]

Are we to conclude that a sound scientific foundation is one which is also insecure in its logical basis? To the skeptical, Huxley kept affirming that evolution is "no speculation but a generalization of certain facts which may be observed by anyone who will take the necessary trouble."[12] Yet it was the fact of observation that Huxley himself was seeking and waiting for. Until it was produced, evolution should have remained, at least for one who loved fine distinctions, speculation and not theory.

[10] *Ibid.*, 102.
[11] *Ibid.*
[12] Huxley, *Collected Essays*, v, 41-2.

Having ruled out vulgar motives, how can we explain this inconsistency in the most tireless and most intelligent of the Darwinists? Why was evolution more precious than scientific suspense of judgment? Why do scientists to this day speak with considerable warmth of "the fact of evolution," as if it were in the same category as the fact of combustion, which "may be observed by anyone who will take the necessary trouble"? One answer is that Darwinism acted as a test case for freedom of scientific inquiry, by which is to be understood not unlimited intellectual freedom but freedom for scientists. It gave over to them everything in heaven and earth without restriction. They had their way in clerical as well as in civil courts, in education as well as in the popular mind. The spread of evolution was truly world-wide. The *Origin of Species* was translated into the language of "newly awakened" Japan and that of hardly emancipated Hindustan. The scientists won on vaccination and vivisection, Bible teaching and table rapping. By won, I mean that opposition to their views on all these things put one in a minority even in the opinion of the ignorant. Materialism, conscious or implicit, superseded all other beliefs.

Nor is it hard to understand why it did, for it satisfied the first requirement of any religion by subsuming all phenomena under one cause. Darwin's merit was to have tackled all the facts which made other religions and philosophies bulge uncomfortably and to have given them spacious accommodations under a few simple laws. The most fundamental of these laws he received of course from the Newtonian tradition of matter and force; but by his application of them to living things there was no realm left outside as an exception. The scientific quest and the religious wish, both striving for unity, were thus fulfilled at one stroke. That is why Huxley called Darwin the Newton of biology,[13] why he called the evolutionary debate a New Reformation, and why he liked to date events in the history

[13] Wallace seems to have been the first to use the phrase.

of human thought as pre-Darwinian and post-Darwinian—under the old dispensation or the new.

This profound emotional and intellectual victory once gained, it would have taken a superman or a coward to retreat from it for so trifling a cause as lack of final proof. The scientific principle being sound, demonstrative proof would be sure to follow in due course. Besides, retreat to what? The cosmogony of Genesis was swamped under an avalanche of contrary geological facts. The notion of inherent perfecting tendencies smacked of metaphysical thought. Creation by divine fiat was of course still believed in by many, but they were those who had never budged. No one of any intellectual standing went back to Personal Creation. On the contrary, intelligent clerics and their flocks adapted Evolution to Revelation in exactly the same way that their grandfathers had adapted Gravitation to it. Darwin was indeed the successor to Paley. In the United States especially, the most fervent evolutionists were deists: Asa Gray, Joseph Leconte, Theodore Parker, John Fiske, young William James—none of these in welcoming evolution denied a supreme being. They only made ampler room for natural laws and included biology under the sway of Newton. Others who claimed for themselves the freedom of agnosticism or atheism were in fact just as deeply committed to dogma—the infallibility of the new church—as any prince of the old.

Lest it be thought that I am exaggerating the religious aspects of Darwinism I must again refer to Huxley, whose remark about the "Hegira of Science from the idolatries of special creation" and "the purer faith of Evolution" was made, not in the enthusiasm of 1859, but after fifteen years' reflection.[14] Huxley could truthfully call himself an agnostic and a religious man at the same time, for he was completely devout about the new faith. For it he was "prepared to go to the stake," and he was so full of hope, as

[14] *Academy*, Jan. 2, 1875.

he confessed in criticism of Spencer, that he "did not care very much to speak of anything as 'unknowable.' "

What gave Huxley such confidence was the sense of unity which I have already mentioned; but it was also the vastness of that unified scheme. It was the same feeling that thrilled Tyndall when he tried to beguile the unbelievers in mechanism by saying that "at the present moment, all our philosophy, all our poetry, all our science, all our art —Plato, Shakespeare, Newton, and Raphael—are potential in the fires of the sun."[15] The very word "potential," with its happy suggestion of latent geniuses—or genii—in the fiery clouds, added to the grandeur of the fact. A new beauty was being given man to enjoy—scientific eloquence, of which Huxley and Tyndall were in English the two great creators. Huxley's sermons, compounded of defiant assertion, elaborate caution, terse blows, genuine humor, and pompous polysyllabification, created a style that has remained characteristic of a certain type of science; just as Darwin's gentler vanity concerning his patience and thoroughness can still seduce us into the belief that only scientists are patient and thorough.

Freedom, authority, unity, vastness of outlook, and esthetic pleasure combined into the final satisfaction belonging to the religious emotion: I mean the mysteries of the new teleology—the answer to the riddle "how what was purposive in the universe could be brought about without the intervention of a directing power."[16] I quote Weismann's words celebrating the fiftieth anniversary of the *Origin of Species*, because they carry the authority and the retrospective wisdom of one who remained faithful to natural selection. What we scientists find by research, says Weismann, is matter and force—nothing else; but what we see in the life around us is clearly purposive, adapted—and in very fine fashion—to the uses of life. Since the conditions of life cannot be determined by the animal itself, the

[15] *Fragments of Science*, ii, 131. Compare the poet's "nightingale music sleeping in the egg."
[16] *Darwin and Modern Science*, 21.

adaptations must be called forth by the conditions. Yet if you make Chance your creator, you are likely to get nothing but monstrosities as your creatures; you cannot make an alarm clock by whirling bits of scrap iron in a closed box. But natural selection, without smuggling any intelligence into the box, produces perfect adaptation, for what is poorly adapted perishes. No wonder that Weismann transferred to his principle the former attributes of the Deity and spoke of natural selection as possessing omnipotence.[17]

The theory of evolution would not have made its way so quickly, Weismann goes on to say, if Darwin had not discovered a principle capable of solving this problem in a simple manner. He is probably right. The Roman philosopher-poet Lucretius, in the first century B.C., had wrestled with the same difficulty in his effort to supersede the old gods and explain creation by the chance collision of atoms. But he had failed where Darwin, Oedipus-like, had answered the Sphinx. After him natural selection was indeed the new providence, the new book of Genesis, with "each form appearing precisely at the right moment in the history of the earth—the trichina at the same time as the pig."[18] One is tempted to ask about the mustard, though Weismann was not a botanist. Like Huxley, his status is that of a believer; for when we ask him whether the small random variations in nature are important enough to decide between the life and death of the creature, he replies with great candor: "Even one who, like myself, has been for many years a convinced adherent of the theory of selection, can only reply: '*We assume so, but cannot prove it in any case.*' It is not upon demonstrative evidence that we rely when we champion the doctrine of selection as a scientific truth; we base our arguments on quite other grounds."[19]

[17] The All-Sufficiency [All-Macht] of Natural Selection, reply to Herbert Spencer, London, 1893.
[18] Darwin and Modern Science, 21.
[19] Op. cit., 25.

By the time that Weismann was making this concession —seemingly so damaging to the omnipotence of natural selection—others were recording their dissatisfaction with it in a more brutal way. "No one," said William Bateson, "can survey the work of recent years without perceiving that evolutionary orthodoxy developed too fast and that a great deal has got to come down."[20] Clearly, both believers and unbelievers in Natural Selection agreed that Darwinism had succeeded as an orthodoxy, as a rallying point for innumerable scientific, philosophical, and social movements. Darwin had been the oracle, and the *Origin of Species* the "fixed point with which Evolution moved the world."

[20] *Op. cit.*, 101.

4. *The Newton of Biology*

If Mr. Sullivan is right about Newton, as there is every reason to believe, the oft-repeated comparison between Newton and Darwin signifies something more than high praise.
Though many of the external reasons of its triumph remain
to be set forth, Darwinism, as we just saw, conquered in the
guise of an "infallible world outlook." But it would not do
to suppose that all the reasons were external. The personality of Darwin and the character of his writings had a great
deal to do with the availability of his doctrine; so that apart
from the biographical interest which always attaches to
those whose names signify a world system, we must now
interrupt our account of the uses of Darwinism in order to
examine Darwin himself.

The first notable fact about Darwin as a man is the near
unanimity of opinion concerning him. With the single
exception of Samuel Butler, every writer has praised his
modesty, sincerity, and industry. Butler has consequently
suffered for his rashness—if rashness it be to have an independent opinion, with reasons in support, on so important
a subject. This question need not concern us here. We may
take it as proved by the testimony of those who actually
came in daily and lifelong contact with Darwin that he was

as described—a modest, industrious, and wholehearted man.

Probably owing to a lack of understanding between the young Darwin and his father, Charles found his vocation somewhat late. There was never anything of the promising lad about him. Like many another who is destined for fame he did not distinguish himself in school—the renowned Shrewsbury School made famous by Dr. Butler, the namesake and grandfather of Darwin's critic—and as a youth Darwin continued to show no particular talents. No career, from preaching to physicking, seemed to attract him. At Cambridge he only liked going out into the country with his dog and shooting in desultory fashion. At the University of Edinburgh Medical School he was a poor scholar, too easily disgusted at the dissecting bench. But he made a friend of Dr. Grant, who was an ardent Lamarckian. Finally, in spite of the shape of his nose,[1] he secured the place of naturalist on *H.M.S. Beagle.* It is in connection with this appointment that we hear for the first time a prophecy of fame. It comes, poetically enough, from Sedgwick, in a letter written to Darwin's former headmaster, Dr. Samuel Butler: "I suppose my friend Dr. Darwin is a member. His son is doing admirable work in South America, and has already sent home a collection above all price. It was the best thing in the world for him that he went out on the voyage of discovery. There was some risk of his turning out an idle man, but his character will now be fixed, and if God spares his life he will have a great name among the naturalists of Europe."[2]

When Darwin returned from the trip around the world, he edited the *Journal and Remarks* on the ship's voyage— his first important appearance before the public—which has remained the best introduction to his mind and work.[3] He appears there as an acute observer, a meticulous narrator of

[1] Captain Fitzroy, who had the power to appoint, was a convinced phrenologist and physiognomist, and he had grave doubts about Darwin's nose.

[2] *Collected Works of Samuel Butler,* xi, 144.

[3] In the popular revision of 1845.

detail, and a mildly speculative mind. I say mildly, for it is when the question of genius is raised that opinions about Darwin begin to differ.

Some, and they are in the majority, assert without hesitation that he was one of the greatest thinkers of the nineteenth century, if not the greatest. They place him in the long line of British scientific genius that begins with Bacon, Newton, and Locke. Others, while recognizing in him the gift of immense industry, deny his greatness as a thinker. This division of opinion was already apparent on his death, though it was obscured by the fact that the critics of Darwin's philosophizing powers were themselves philosophers of an opposite school. We strike here the usual biographical snag: professional opinion is biased and lay opinion lacks professional authority. Still it may not be unfair to quote the impression made upon the Duke of Argyll by the reading of Darwin's *Life and Letters*: "I have a great respect for Darwin's mind. He was the greatest observer that ever lived. . . . The *Life* raises him as a *man*. I do not think it raises him as a *philosopher*. On the contrary, I could not review it without pointing out the extraordinary defectiveness of his philosophical faculties."[4]

The best confirmation of this view comes of course from Darwin himself. He says: "I have no great quickness of apprehension or wit. . . . My power to follow a long and purely abstract train of thought is very limited; and therefore I could never have succeeded with metaphysics or mathematics. My memory is extensive, yet hazy. . . . Therefore my success as a man of science, whatever this may have amounted to, has been determined, as far as I can judge, by complex and diversified mental qualities and conditions. Of these, the most important have been—the love of science—unbounded patience and long reflecting over any subject—industry in observing and collecting facts—and a fair share of invention as well as common sense."[5]

[4] G. Paston, *At John Murray's*, 1932, 269–70.
[5] Darwin, *Life and Letters*, i, 82, 85–6.

Whatever the fair share of invention came to—and it does not seem to have been his luckiest trait—Darwin was pre-eminently an observer and recorder of facts. He came to ideas and he came by ideas very slowly, as he himself repeatedly tells us: "The great leading idea is quite new to me, viz., that during late ages, the mind will have been modified more than the body; yet I had got so far as to see with you that the struggle between the races of man depended entirely upon intellectual and moral qualities."[6] Darwin frequently found Wallace and Spencer and Huxley indispensable sources of ideas: "Bates was quite right: you are the man to turn to in a difficulty," he writes to Wallace. "Spencer's prodigality of original thought" astonishes him, and he admits "I always feel as if my books came half out of Lyell's brain."[7]

We might interpret this as modesty and caution if Darwin had been able to do without suggestions from others or if he had not naïvely prided himself on his own inventions. Darwin's temper and habits, quite apart from the written testimony of his works, show that facts impinged on his mind far more deeply and significantly than abstractions. He could map the distribution of plants and animals over large areas of the world's surface—an immense labor—with far greater ease than he could suggest or explain a hypothesis to cover the facts when found.[8] He was slow and not sure. Hence even though he considered himself and was considered an innovator and an iconoclast, he really worked most of the time with others' assumptions and ideas. "He owed far more to the past," as H. F. Osborn says, "than is generally believed or than he himself was conscious of, especially as to the full and true conception of the evolutionary idea, which had already been reached, to

[6] *Ibid.*, iii, 89.
[7] *Ibid.*, iv, 235, 117.
[8] "A naturalist's life would be a happy one if he had only to observe and never to write." (June 1, 1867) *Life and Letters*, ii, 248.

the nature of its evidence, and, to some extent, to the line of its factors."[9]

We saw in a previous chapter what this tradition was which Darwin inherited. His originality in the sense of his power to hit afresh upon an old hypothesis is of course not capable of assessment. In any case it is of minor interest for the history of ideas. A man might unaided rediscover Euclidian geometry tomorrow and still not receive much thanks for his pains. But the fact that Darwin was a great assembler of facts and a poor joiner of ideas was of great importance in making his *general* views prevail. For at certain moments in history (think of political elections) it will not do to be too clear. Straightforward assertion and distinct theory are a handicap. It is better to throw a haze of seeming explanation about a difficult problem, particularly if one can do it unaware.

Darwin thus often benefited from his arguments in a circle, just as Natural Selection benefited from Darwin's confused words about the origin of random variations in animals. He unintentionally gave the impression that the cause of these variations was—Variation.[10] He denies that they can be "caused by chance," yet admits that he has previously spoken of them as if they were. The same habit of mind—one might almost say habit of words—repeatedly leads him into tautology, as when the origin of conscience and the moral sense in man is explained by "well-developed social instincts" which "lead an animal to take pleasure in the society of its fellows."[11] When Darwin begs a question it is not at first obvious because the begging generally covers pages of circumlocutory matter.

Huxley, a far keener thinker, put down these tail-chasing explanations to Darwin's lack of command over language.

[9] *From the Greeks to Darwin*, 229.

[10] "Variation will cause the slight alterations. . . ." *Origin*, ed. 1876, 146. This is pure "metaphysical" explanation, the dormitive power of opium.

[11] *Decent of Man*, Chs. IV and V, especially pp. 108–20, ed. 1882.

Some critics—in the very office of Darwin's publishers—put the same objection more bluntly. "Though much which Darwin tells us is as notorious as the multiplication table, he often also expresses himself very darkly, and it would take a long time to find out what he means."[12] A decided admirer, like the American physician George M. Gould, put forward a clinical theory of Darwin's haziness. It is that Darwin's eyesight was excessively astigmatic.[13] This would explain also Darwin's early neglect of study and his lifelong ailing, with nausea, inability to read, use the microscope, or work more than a couple of hours at a time.[14] But since similar troubles attended the careers of Spencer and Huxley, who are clear writers, the clinical view seems inadequate.

A worse fault than obscurity, in view of the wide faith accorded by the nineteenth century and ours to scientific works, is Darwin's hedging and self-contradiction; for it enabled any unscrupulous reader to choose his text from the *Origin of Species* or the *Descent of Man* with almost the same ease of accommodation to his purpose as if he had chosen from the Bible. But the Bible is a whole library, written by different men at different times, whereas Darwin's books are supposedly consistent from beginning to end. On the subject of war, for example, Darwin can be used equally well to prove its utility to the race or the reverse, and this without any indication that war may have contradictory virtues.

When at the turn of the century, geneticists like Bateson or later T. H. Morgan, wished to assess Darwin's works in the light of new facts, they were compelled to make what has been called a "lawyer-like" re-examination of his

[12] Whitwell Elwin, editor of the *Quarterly Review; At John Murray's*, 232.

[13] *Biographic Clinics*, i, 103. See also "The Ill-Health of Darwin" by W. W. Johnston, *The American Anthropologist*, iii, I, Jan.–March, 1901.

[14] His letters are one long complaint of ill-health, which water cures, rest, and the help of innumerable friends did not alleviate. Some of his friends thought him a hypochondriac.

words. Lawyer-like can be meant as a slur on the critic, but the blame should rest on the original author whose works contain more than a few casual or strictly verbal inconsistencies. We can note and forgive Darwin's regret at "the bad term Natural Selection."[15] But what are we to think of the scientific writer who says: "I have called this principle . . . by the term natural selection. But the expression often used by Mr. Herbert Spencer, of the Survival of the Fittest, is more accurate, and is sometimes equally convenient."[16] Or, in the same vein, the extraordinary hodgepodge made in the *Descent of Man* with the Sermon on the Mount and the Benthamite greatest-happiness principle? Darwin hedges by saying that the seeking of pleasure and the avoidance of pain is a "nearly safe standard of right and wrong." Why nearly? Does it mean not quite ever safe or not always safe? In one of his many revisions, he changes "I do not know of any . . ." to "I know of hardly any. . . ."[17] What shade of difference would he indicate, what does he know or not know? It is idle to argue that things in nature cannot ever be rigidly pinned down. True, nothing is ever absolutely white or black but rather more-black-than-white. But precisely because of this fact of experience abstract statements can and must be made exact if they are not to mislead. Modifiers and exceptions, which will inevitably occur, must be stated in equally clear fashion. As Darwin's text stands we do not know whether he believed in Bentham as the founder of ethics or in the author of the Sermon on the Mount. We do not know whether he thinks the term Natural Selection less proper or more proper than the term Survival of the Fittest. If less proper, how can it possibly be that the more proper term should be "*sometimes* equally convenient"?

We must do Darwin the justice of believing that his devotion to fact, to the great mass of his facts, and his sound instinct about the mutability of all things, betrayed

[15] See below, page 115.
[16] *Origin*, 49.
[17] *Origin*, 2nd ed., 227; 6th ed., 224.

him into these endless shufflings with words. He carried over into his utterance the sense of flux and indecisiveness which he felt in observing nature. Species changed, varieties were flexible, things were in endless motion. Yet we must not forget that the main issue was of a different order and of clear-cut significance to man and civilization. Darwin's function was not merely to gather facts and group them correctly; he pretended to organize them under general laws. It was on that higher level that his admitted faults[18] became magnified. His hesitancies were bound to give rise to an inextricable puzzle about his conclusions, certainly about his "distinctive theory." This theory, as we know, was natural selection. But it is clear that "the *Origin of Species* without use and disuse would be a materially different book." Gray himself in defending the *Origin* in America took it as an extension of Lamarck.[19] "A certain vacillation on this point," as Bateson gently calls it, hardly begins to describe the fact.[20] Osborn concludes that "starting with some leaning toward the theories of modification of Buffon and Lamarck, he reached an almost exclusive belief in his own theory, and then gradually inclined to adopt Buffon's, and then Lamarck's theories as well, until in his maturest writings he embraced a threefold causation in the origin of species."[21] But, says Osborn after recording another minor shift of Darwin's, "these decided changes of opinion were, in part, a tacit acceptance of work done elsewhere, rather than the direct outcome of Darwin's own observations."[22]

The word "tacit" here should be underscored and kept in mind, for it might suggest disingenuousness on Darwin's part. It is an accepted rule that where doctrine is concerned, particularly doctrine that the public is likely to

[18] ". . . facts compel me to conclude that my brain was never formed for much thinking." *Life and Letters*, i, 506.
[19] Gray, *Darwiniana*, ed. 1876, 52.
[20] Bateson, op. cit., 220.
[21] Osborn, op. cit., 230.
[22] *Ibid.*, 243.

follow as authoritative, the authority who expounds has no right to shift his ground without clear announcement of the fact. A Catholic theologian who became converted to Buddhism, a Soviet theorist who turned Quaker, would be in duty bound to notify their readers of the change. A scientific writer who makes his appeal to the lay public as Darwin confessed that he did is no less obligated. Yet how did Darwin signify his change of mind and take leave of the whole question of cause? In a way which seems to me conclusive proof not of his dishonesty but of his shy inability to speak out loud and clear. Change of species, he says, "has been effected chiefly through the natural selection of numerous, successive, slight, favorable variations; aided in an important manner by the inherited effects of use and disuse of parts, and in an unimportant manner—that is, in relation to adaptive structures, whether past or present—by the direct action of external conditions, and by variations which seem in our ignorance to arise spontaneously. It appears that I formerly underrated the frequency and value of these latter forms of variation, as leading to permanent modifications of structure independently of natural selection."[23]

The only fitting comment upon this is Swinburne's remark about a passage from one of the Elizabethan dramatists: "Which he who can parse let him scan, and he who can scan, let him construe."[24] Darwin was therefore being candid and accurate when he said, "I must be a very poor explainer." It would do violence to these same two qualities of candor and accurate observation to suppose him better than his own estimate, or for that matter, better than Hux-

[23] *Origin*, ed. 1876, 421.
[24] I think it may be construed as follows:
   a. change of species is effected mainly by the accumulation of spontaneous variations,
   b. aided by the inherited effects of use and disuse (important), and of direct action (unimportant),
   c. as well as by spontaneous variations (unimportant);
   d. I formerly underrated these last variations,
   e. I still think them unimportant (statement c.).

ley's. Yet there are passages in all his books, particularly the *Beagle* journal, which satisfy all the canons of descriptive prose. When he describes a natural scene or tells a story of animal behavior or gives an account of his own procedure, he is clear, direct, and unpretentious. Hence many handbooks of writing quote excerpts from Darwin as models of scientific prose. They are samples rather than models, for they could be matched by equally good ones in hundreds of other writers. They do not in any case justify the extravagant opinion occasionally heard that the *Origin of Species* is a masterpiece of English literature—an opinion which can come only from revelation by faith and not from the experience of reading the work.[25]

Darwin's best modern biographer, Mr. Geoffrey West, ends his account of Darwin's life by a balanced chapter of criticism in which Darwin is called a Fragmentary Man. The description applies equally well to Newton but Newton's fragmentariness is very different from Darwin's. Neither was perhaps a profound philosopher, but Newton's achievement was ultimately based on the power of sustained thought. He characteristically refused to correct small errors in a late edition of the *Principia* because they did not come from faulty reasoning but were factual errors which the reader could correct for himself. Newton, moreover, had a clear idea of science and scientific method, which necessarily includes a sense of their limitations. In fact, far from loving science, like Darwin, he treated it in a rather lordly way and put the greater part of his energy into historical writing and theological speculation. Lastly, though he mixed a doubtful philosophy with the physical laws he enunciated, the very nature of his researches left the formulas as independent of his philosophy as their accuracy was independent of his prose style.

On this basis Darwin's performance reads like the reverse of Newton's. His formulas were inseparable from his

[25] Cf. *British Authors of the 19th Century*, art. Darwin.

philosophy or its verbal expression; and this philosophy he imbibed, whether he knew it or not, from the economic, social, and metaphysical speculations of his time. It did not arise spontaneously from his facts. Malthus and Spencer, combined with Lamarck and Positivism, provided him with the needful assumptions and attitudes, both seemingly so simple and so common in their kind as to pass for matters of fact. What brought him rapid victory and prolonged sway over his age was thus the ability of the age to recognize itself in him; but where these assumptions and their consequences clashed, there we inevitably find in Darwin contradictions and uncertainties which reveal the fragmentariness of his thought, the derivation of his metaphors, and indeed the secret of his power.

When the coming of age—as it was called—of the *Origin of Species* was celebrated in England two years before Darwin's death, a book written for the occasion by Grant Allen spoke in excited words of the atmosphere of evolution which the young Darwin must have breathed at the house of his grandfather Erasmus. To those who remembered the opening paragraph of the *Origin* or had read the Historical Sketch prefixed to the third and following editions, this biographical guess must have come as a surprise. We now know that Darwin had read his grandfather's *Zoonomia* before going to Edinburgh, that he had met there an enthusiastic disciple of Lamarck and that he had subsequently read—on the *Beagle*—Lyell's *Principles of Geology* which devotes a chapter to Lamarck's theory. On board ship he had also read Humboldt's *Personal Narrative,* which comments farsightedly on the distribution of plants in South America. Later he had come across Malthus and read him to good effect. But from all indications given by Darwin himself[26] one would be justified in inferring his

[26] "When on board *H.M.S. Beagle*, as naturalist, I was much struck with certain facts. . . . On my return home it occurred to me, in 1837, that something might perhaps be made out on this question by patiently accumulating, etc. . . . After five years'

almost complete mental isolation, both from his predecessors and from his contemporaries. He conveyed the impression of a self-made thinker so strongly to his readers that
Grant Allen had to protest, in his eulogy, against the
universal identification of evolution with Darwinism.[27]

When we turn to the Historical Sketch itself our legitimate surprise at this self-sufficiency deepens into amaze-
ment. Professing to sketch the progress of the idea of
change of species, it is surely the most extraordinary piece
of writing bearing the word "historical" at its head. It dis-
misses Buffon; it misrepresents Lamarck, and it buries
Erasmus Darwin in the middle of a footnote stating that
"it is curious how largely my grandfather, Dr. Erasmus Darwin, anticipated the views and erroneous grounds of opinion of Lamarck. . . ."

With Robert Chambers's *Vestiges of Creation* it deals
at some length, not only because the book had been in
everybody's mind during the previous fifteen years, but because in the first two editions of his own book Darwin had
managed to misconceive Chambers's principal argument
and to call down on himself a peremptory summons to
correct the misstatement. The correction was made, though
without acknowledgment of the previous error. Lesser
writers like Matthew and Naudin, not mentioned in the
first 6000 copies of the *Origin*, are listed in the sketch,
but without entering into the importance of their views.
Forty years later the ever-generous Wallace hinted an
apology for the fragmentariness of these acknowledgments:
"In the later editions of that work Darwin has given an
historical sketch of the progress of opinion on the subject.
I shall therefore now only notice a few great writers whom
he has not referred to."[28] These are of course Buffon,
Goethe, Lyell, and Lamarck, for whose belated recognition
Wallace gives thanks to Samuel Butler. Darwin's major

---

work I allowed myself to speculate upon the subject. . . ." See
also letter to Haeckel, Oct. 8, 1864.

[27] Allen, *Charles Darwin*, N. Y., 1885, 177.

[28] *The Progress of the Century*, N. Y., 1901, 16–17.

trespasses against his fellow men were thus atoned for by the co-propounder of natural selection.

The greatest injustice was of course to Lamarck. According to Osborn, "the disdainful allusions to him by Charles Darwin . . . long placed him in the light of a purely extravagant speculative thinker."[29] These disdainful allusions are all the more reprehensible that they were misrepresentations, not excusable through ignorance, and made by an unavowed part-disciple. It is clear that Darwin would not have treated a pigeon or gasteropod in this cavalier fashion, and that coming from any other man than an "intellectual, modest, simple-minded lover of truth" the whole performance would have been damned as shamefully fraudulent.

Two arguments may be advanced in extenuation, only one of which has, in my opinion, any validity. First it may be said that Darwin's profession was not that of historian and that errors in this part of his work do not count. But this reasoning will not do. No one compelled Darwin to prefix a sketch of opinion to his work and no one requires now that he should have listed every one of the half-hundred evolutionists found by Osborn in the half-century before Darwin. At the same time, it required no historical training to avoid giving the impression throughout the first two printings of the *Origin* that the author had come upon his leading ideas entirely by himself.

The second argument is an extension of the one I offered in the previous section: Darwin was not at home with ideas. He very seldom grasped another's point of view in anything like its true contours. What more likely than that he also absorbed ideas without a clear line of demarcation between them and his own?[30] He certainly knew when he disa-

---

[29] *Op. cit.,* 156.

[30] Against this view, though perhaps not weighty, is Darwin's account of his skill at cribbing when a boy under old Dr. Butler: "I used at school to be a great hand at cribbing old verses, and I remember with fearful distinctness Dr. Butler's prolonged *hum* as he stared at me. . . . Now if I publish L's remarks as my own,

greed with a man, as he thought he disagreed with Lamarck, but this does not mean that he rightly judged of
the difference between the points of view. He got it stubbornly into his head that Lamarck stood for an inherent
perfecting tendency and nothing could shake it out. Huxley
may have got the same impression from Darwin for he
began by deriding Lamarck as *buccinator tantum*—much
cry and little wool—but he corrected his error before his
death and spoke as highly of him as did Wallace or any
other Darwinian who has actually looked at Lamarck's
work.[31] When Darwin himself in propounding his theory
of Pangenesis came belatedly to Buffon under Huxley's
urgings, he exclaimed: "Whole pages are laughably like
mine."[32] Had he said this about Lamarck the modern
reader might well think such a laugh in such a place a
singularly insensitive form of apology. Even about Buffon
it is a trifle crass when we know how Darwin adopted his
views and remember what is said of him in the Historical
Sketch: "As his opinions fluctuated greatly . . . and as
he does not enter on the causes or means . . . I need not
here enter on details."

What strengthens the likelihood of Darwin's ultimate
innocence is that he showed the same indifference to the
notables in his own family. Concerning his father he poses
one of his extraordinary verbal riddles: "He was fond of
theorising, and was incomparably the most acute observer
whom I ever knew. . . . Nor did he possess, as I think, a
scientific mind."[33] As for his grandfather, whatever may

I shall always fancy that the public is humming at me." "L" is
not Lamarck but Litchfield, Darwin's son-in-law and a founder
of Workingmen's Colleges. *A Century of Family Letters*, ii, 208.

[31] Professor Julian Huxley, in his recent Introduction to extracts from Darwin, continues the tradition of linking Lamarck
with Chambers as authors of "crude theories." Lamarck may have
been wrong, like Darwin, but his theory cannot be called crude.
Ptolemaic astronomy was wrong, but not crude, and it is pure prejudice to suppose that earlier=cruder, or error=crudity.

[32] *Life and Letters*, ii, 228–29.

[33] Darwin, Introduction to Krause's *Erasmus Darwin*, 84–5.

have been the atmosphere of evolutionary discussion at his house when Charles was a boy, the mature Darwin never really made amends for the unconscious egotism of saying that the older man had come "curiously close" to "erroneous views" which he himself reaffirmed.

All this is complicated by the very real possibility that Darwin was never sure before or after the *Origin* came out what his distinctive theory was. The Historical Sketch, we may note, did not purport to give the progress of the idea of natural selection—it hardly touched on it—it was to show the progress of the idea of change of species. This was in fact the Great Ambiguity on which Darwin's reputation rested. Unintentional, the ambiguity must have gradually cleared in Darwin's own mind, for Samuel Butler counted at least forty-five instances in which the word "my" before "theory" was deleted between 1869 and the final edition of the *Origin*. All these *my's* had been placed where they could only mean that evolution and not merely natural selection was "my theory"—an impression which in spite of a vast literature has hardly been dispelled to this day. As Darwin seemed to know when he refrained from changing Natural Selection to Natural Preservation, tampering with his own text was bound to make "confusion worse confounded." So if we accept the common verdict voiced by John Morley that Darwin was "an intellectual, modest, simple-minded lover of truth," it must be with the proviso that we qualify "intellectual," retain "modest," and attach in the light of Darwin's psychological limitations a very special meaning to "simple-minded lover of truth."

The phrase "Newton of Biology" now appears as a very loose description indeed. Darwin was not a thinker and he did not originate the ideas that he used. He vacillated, added, retracted, and confused his own traces. As soon as he crossed the dividing line between the realm of events and the realm of theory he became "metaphysical" in the bad sense. His power of drawing out the implications of his theories was at no time very remarkable, but when it came to the moral order it disappeared altogether, as that penetrating Evolutionist, Nietzsche, observed with some disdain.

Yet everything that can be said in praise or blame of Darwin deepens one's conviction that he was in every respect the man of the hour. Judged by the standard of survival he was evidently the fittest to teach the world evolution; and it is only as historians and critics, freed from the need to follow the crowd, though under the sway of other practical needs, that we dare analyze the book and the thinker and expose his shortcomings.

As a man, "our gentle Darwin," as Henry Adams affectionately called him, is the nearest description in a single phrase. He was simple, modest, gentle, and stubborn too. He loved quiet and hence compromise, was suspicious of vehemence or of energy applied to ends that he could not encompass.[34] He was an invalid for a great part of his life and needed a "bulldog" like Huxley to defend him. He was a man to call out the faithful attachment that dogs can give, and Huxley was not alone in admiring the "dumb ox-like sagacity" of his master. His friends urged, encouraged, warned, and shielded him, as they thought, in the struggle for scientific existence, though one is inclined to believe Darwin fully capable of taking care of himself in his own way. The Newton and John Bull of biology might even be a fitting epitaph for the most famous of the Darwins, if it did not invite misconstruction. Whatever other description might be preferred, the Fragmentary Man that Darwin was does not belong with the great thinkers of man-

[34] Marxists are especially annoyed at the timid letter in which Darwin declined the honor of a dedication offered by Marx; but with some inconsequence these critics choose to call Darwin a "Philistine" and "a mighty thinker" as well. (The Labour Monthly, 1931, 702–05.) See also Darwin's letter to H. A. Gaskell on birth control, where he fears the profligacy of unmarried women and the diminished colonizing power of the English if people learn how to limit their numbers. Life and Letters, iv, 49–50.

kind. He belongs rather with those others—men of action and feeling and unconscious power—whom Hegel termed world-historical characters because the world after them is not as it was before.

5. The Uses of Darwinism

> The souls of men have become void; into the void
> have entered in triumph the seven devils of Secu-
> larity.
>
> JOHN MORLEY, 1874

> Darwinism has superseded liberalism and socialism,
> which are anti-scientific and Christian doctrines.
>
> VACHER DE LAPOUGE, 1899

> History must revolve about the positive and biolog-
> ical notion of Race.
>
> LAUMONIER, 1885

"Newton banished God from nature, Darwin banished him
from life, Freud drove him from the last fastness, the Soul.
It was all latent in Newton, in Descartes, in Galileo; mechanism would conquer all, once it had conquered nature,
for man's body was sprung from nature and his mind from
his body." So speaks a contemporary critic.[1] It may not be
quite accurate to say that for Newton personally, God was
banished; and I shall try to indicate later that for Freud
the human soul is not a mechanism, even though one side
of psychoanalysis appears to continue materialistic science.
Be this as it may, the tendency of science since Galileo
has certainly been to push mechanism into every corner of
the universe and so get rid of Mind, although it is an his-

[1] Gerald Heard, quoted in West, *Darwin*, 325.

torical error to believe that the battle joined in the fifties and sixties of the last century ended in a final rout.

The facts somewhat resemble those concerning Free Trade: it used to be thought that nineteenth-century England had abandoned Protectionism; but when the record was examined, it was found that the movement started later and ended earlier than was commonly believed. It really triumphed for only two decades. The same is true of mechanism, though at a later date. The fifties and sixties saw its heyday among the thinking part of the world. Already in the seventies there were strong counter currents, which won recognition in the eighties and nineties, and which show that there was nothing inevitable about the pursuit of science leading to materialism. Popular materialism, however, was untouched by these new ideas and kept spreading. The new medicine and surgery in the sixties, free public education in the seventies, the widespread mechanization of life, and the rise of Marxian socialism in the eighties, all strengthened its hold.

The three men who rose with this popular materialism and did the most to persuade the English-speaking world of its final truth were Spencer, Tyndall, and Huxley, and it is not unfair to quote as a sample of their effectiveness a schoolboy's notion of science around the year 1880. The question posed was, "Why do water pipes burst in cold weather?" to which came the answer: "People who have not studied acoustics think that Thor bursts the pipes, but we know that it is nothing of the kind, for Professor Tyndall has burst the mythologies and has taught us that it is the natural behavior of water (and bismuth) without which all fish would die and the earth be held in an iron grip."[2]

This is not precisely what Spencer, Huxley, and Tyndall taught. But this confused science implies a clear philosophy. As philosophers, it is true, all three men repel in so

[2] Communicated by Professor Lodge, Science and Art Department, South Kensington; H. B. Wheatley, *Literary Blunders*, 186–87.

many words the doctrine of materialism. How then did their teachings come to such a bad end in a frozen pipe? Huxley gives us the clue when he says that he teaches a doctrine which is "not materialism though using the language of materialism,"[3] the object of this duplicity being, of course, to burst the old mythologies. Tyndall, working primarily in physics and geology, pushed Shakespeare and Newton back into the sun, but at the same time assured his Belfast audience that science cannot bridge the gap between matter and consciousness. Spencer, with his Unknowable as a sustaining element, circled the cosmos of Matter and Force, and deduced everything else from them, but confessed that our knowledge of phenomena could not be so deduced.

If all three, though engineers at heart,[4] admit that it is impossible to deduce consciousness from matter, an impartial observer would say that the gentlemen were in a dilemma and should choose. But Darwinism, so useful in the fight against theology, would not let them do it. They thought, at least, that it would not. In order to establish once for all the idea that species had not been separately created; that man was descended from an apelike form; that social life was affected by physical forces, and that the supernatural was inconsistent with science, they felt obliged to say that every phenomenon was reducible to the motions of material particles. This is materialism.

It is also mechanistic, or machinelike, because if one starts with matter, action can only occur through one bit of matter pushing another bit. Action at a distance is inconceivable. Matter must fill all that we call space, for since light travels through it, and is composed of waves, the waves must be *in* something—hence the luminiferous ether.

[3] J. M. Robertson, himself a materialist, says no doctrine can well be more materialistic than Huxley's. *Modern Humanists*, 235 n.

[4] Spencer and Tyndall started life as engineers. Huxley would have done the same had his means permitted.

Applying the same assumption, physics had discovered the mechanical equivalent of heat and the Law of Conservation of matter and energy: Physiology had got rid of the Vitalists' life force: there was nothing left but the mechanical impact of particles. The nervous system and the human brain were material, hence life and thought must rise from matter. As the French philosophers had said a century before, the brain secretes thought as the liver secretes bile.[5] Huxley entertained the theory that we were all automata, with consciousness as an "epi-phenomenon";[6] he even thought for a moment that he had found the link between Matter and Life.[7] Nor were the orthodox more free of the superstition. Hardly a single defender of established religion had metaphysics enough in him to ask what this Matter was which Huxley and Tyndall called a "cause." They accepted it ready-made from the Maker as much as the others did, and only insisted that a Maker there must be. Yet they so conceived Him that they lay open to their opponents' challenge to produce a definite proof of miraculous intervention. All this because of the conventional metaphors about a Great Architect, a "Supreme Being whose thoughts are the laws of Nature"—as if God were a super-Stephenson who made the world in the same way as the mechanic makes locomotives.

We may conclude from this that the God of the nineteenth century was materialistic, too, not because he was imagined as a fatherly idol with a Tennysonian beard, but because he was made into the image of the man that the century really worshiped—the scientific engineer. This generality, of course, does not include the handful of religious minds like Cardinal Newman, R. H. Hutton, and Samuel Butler, the reluctant agnostics like Carlyle, Burckhardt, and Matthew Arnold, or the large mass of literal believers in a childhood deity. I am speaking of the vast

[5] "Ohne Phosphor, kein Gedanke: without phosphorus, no thinking," had written Moleschott five years before Darwin.
[6] Fortnightly, Nov. 1874.
[7] Bathybius Haeckeli.

body of average "enlightened" opinion who give its distinctive character to an age—the Gladstones, Fouillées, Haeckels, Fiskes—and kindred leaders of public thought.

That some of them accepted Darwinism while others did not indicates at the most the conservatism of the human mind about details, for the historical criticism of the Bible from Strauss to Renan, taken together with the previous readjustment of Scripture to Newtonian laws, had certainly not left the Bible an undisputed authority on matters of fact. Not many persons in 1859 still believed in a central earth and a tentlike sky. Most of them had swallowed Copernicus. It should not then have hurt so much to swallow the Darwinian story of animal and human creation. As a matter of fact, many clergymen became excellent scientists and historical critics, and in the end most religious bodies gave in and absorbed the historical and scientific criticism of myths, religions, and dogmas.

To the results of this comparative method we commonly ascribe the decay of faith and the rise of a "coarse materialism." But this overlooks an important difference. Materialism, coarse or fine, does not come from scientific or historical method as such: it comes from the philosophy concealed in the use of the method or suggested by proponents of the method. And it is there that Darwinism can justly be accused of destroying faith and morality—not Darwin and his book, but the entire movement from which he sprang and to which he supplied impetus and a name. The genetic fallacy dating back to Comte is at the root of the trouble—the fallacy of reducing all experiences to one condition of their origin and so killing meanings by explanations. With its mechanical and historical bias, evolution reduced everything to something else. From fear of being anthropomorphic, it deanthropomorphized man. With its suspicion that feeling was an epiphenomenon, it made "refined music" into "a factor of survival." Nothing was what it seemed. As one scientific historian later complained: "The Devil may be the Persian Ahriman and the Logos a Greek idea, but their *meaning* changed with the new use to which they were put."[8] Yet as everybody was looking only for material or historical antecedents, it is no wonder that the seekers found nothing else; nor that they came at last to see that something had been left out of the reckoning.

While some of the best minds were whirling round and round in this vicious circle, it was not noticed that the words Matter and Force, particularly when applied to human beings, might find in daily life some dangerously simple applications. No one can continue preaching the sole reality of these "bare facts" without encountering someone who will take him literally. And when the idea of force is embodied in the notions of Struggle and Survival of the Fittest, it should be expected that men will use these revelations of science as justifications for their own acts. Darwin did not invent the Machiavellian image that the world is the playground of the lion and the fox, but thousands discovered that he had transformed political science. Their own tendencies to act like lions and foxes thereby became irresistible "laws of nature" and "factors of progress," while moral arguments against them were dubbed "pre-scientific." The only text they would heed was "Go to the ant, thou sluggard," because ants waged wars.

War became the symbol, the image, the inducement, the reason, and the language of all human doings on the planet. No one who has not waded through some sizable part of the literature of the period 1870–1914 has any conception of the extent to which it is one long call for blood, nor of the variety of parties, classes, nations, and races whose blood was separately and contradictorily clamored for by the enlightened citizens of the ancient civilization of Europe.

Unlike the Napoleons, Nelsons, and Wellingtons of an earlier day, who knew war at first hand and described it

[8] Harnack, *The Relation between Ecclesiastical and General History*. International Congress of Arts and Science, 1906, ii, 628.

for what it was, in simple, unpleasant words, the militarists of the second half of the century poeticized war and luxuriated in the prospect of it. With relative impunity for themselves, they took it for granted that all struggles *in* life must be struggles *for* life, and the death of the loser its "natural" goal. One spoke of the "beneficent private war which makes one man strive to climb on the shoulders of another and remain there through the law of the survival of the fittest."[9] Another, asking himself why an English village of colonists was indisputably superior to a native village of Australians, answered that the English can "beat the natives in war, take from them what they like and kill any of them they choose."[10] A third, smarting under the defeat of his country in the Franco-Prussian War of 1870, declared that "war is in a way one of the conditions of progress, the cut of the whip which prevents a country from going to sleep."[11]

If the vanquished said it, what else could the victors say? Through the mouth of the conquering Marshal von Moltke, a sensitive and cultivated man, they announced that "perpetual peace is a dream and not even a beautiful dream. War is an element of the order of the world established by God." The next generation, which might have reflected on the merits of peace as the older Bismarck did, were kept feral by the writings of Treitschke, Haeckel, Ratzenhofer, Gumplowicz, Ammon, and other "Social Darwinists." One of them, General Bernhardi, incurred odium for his *Germany and the Next War*, but he had his counterparts elsewhere. Across the Rhine, Arthur Boucher prophesied a *Victorious France in the Coming War*; the word *Struggle-for-lifer* was added to the chaste French vocabulary; Clémence Royer arranged nations on an or-

[9] Sir Henry Maine in *Popular Government* (1884), quoted in Nasmyth, *Social Progress and the Darwinian Theory*, 31.
[10] Bagehot, *Physics and Politics*, N. Y., 1873, 207. These words require interpretation to be properly understood. [Note to the Second Edition.]
[11] Renan, *La Réforme Intellectuelle et Morale*, 1871, 111.

ganic scale of superiority, and the scientist Topinard sent articles to a Chicago journal advocating a social free-for-all, *without* education, which might interfere with natural competition.[12]

In the United States, in addition to a good many sociologists preaching struggle like Lester Ward, William Sumner, and Benjamin Kidd, there was the Strenuous-Lifer, Theodore Roosevelt, whose sympathy with the German Kaiser was based on something like the same attitude towards the goal of human life. And in the smaller countries still striving for nationhood, the echoes of these scientific dogmas made up in virulence what they lost in volume. Everywhere this ideal fitted a time when strife seemed the quickest way out of the commercial and territorial tangles of half a century. It certainly comforted the holders of power, and one can understand why a Darwinian work in Germany should have been advertised as particularly interesting to the *besitzenden Klassen*.[13] But it was equally comforting to the *dis*possessed, for it promised them individually a Darwinian dog's chance of climbing on other men's shoulders and staying there by natural and social law. *Darwinismus* offered mankind as great a Utopia as later *Marxismus*.

Since in every European country between 1870 and 1914 there was a war party demanding armaments, an individualist party demanding ruthless competition, an imperialist party demanding a free hand over backward peoples, a socialist party demanding the conquest of power, and a racialist party demanding internal purges against aliens— all of them, when appeals to greed and glory failed, or even before, invoked Spencer and Darwin, which was to say, science incarnate. That Moltke appealed to God may be regarded either as an old-fashioned habit or as a shorthand term for what the others really meant. Race was of course

12 *The Monist*, 1895 ff.; also *Association Française pour . . . la Science*, 1897, ii, 660.

13 On the cover of Lombroso's *Political Crime*, German ed., Hamburg, 1891.

as convenient and as short a word for expressing the same
feelings of inner doubt and hatred. Race was biological; it
was sociological; it was Darwinian. No doubt the "favoured races" mentioned on the title page of the *Origin of
Species* referred to pigeons, but the extension of the term
to man was easy to make; indeed it seemed to receive Darwin's own approval on many a page of the *Descent of Man*,
where the struggle of races was a part of evolutionary advance. As for determining what these races were, ever since
1859 when an eminent French anatomist, Paul Broca,
founded the Société d'Anthropologie, there had sprung up
all over Europe groups of industrious researchers, meeting
annually, and broadcasting the results of their new science.

True, the materialistic test of race was elusive. Competent men might find that there were three or thirty or a
hundred distinct races. There also appeared to be a nationalistic bias in the choice of traits distinguishing the superior from the inferior stocks. Combining with complete
ignorance of genetics a Chinese reverence for the bones of
the dead as indices of class and race, and a very superficial
knowledge of modern European history, these men soon
made racialism a source of international animus, class re-
crimination, and private *parti-pris*. Not content to measure skulls and outlaw the longheads (dolichocephalics) or
the roundheads (brachycephalics); not content to examine
pigmentation and damn the yellow men for their racial
backwardness (at least until the "awakening" of Japan),
they discovered as well that individualists were one race
and socialists another; that the poor and rich, the burgher
and the peasant, the nobles and the former serfs, all were
races whose descendants, intermingled in the modern nation, were fighting a Darwinian struggle, a struggle which
Broca had the honor of calling Social Selection.

Sometimes the fittest was determined ahead of the struggle by the scientist himself; in which case one saw the
absurd spectacle of a clamor for the "preservation of the
fittest" by legislation against the *more powerful* mass of
the inferior race. Thus the blond Nordic was held to be

dwindling in numbers and he must be saved at all costs, like a rare specimen at the zoo. Another way of saving him was by eugenics, and attractive schemes were proposed, of biological segregation, sterilization, purification, and repro-duction, guaranteed to yield within twenty-five years a su-perior race of men who would "sweep back the present races" into the waste places of the earth.

To identify this hypothetical progeny with Nietzsche's Superman apparently taxed neither the public's intelli-gence nor its credulity. Count de Gobineau, who had writ-ten an *Essay on the Inequality of Races* in 1854, was like-wise made into a forerunner of these ideas, even though his book sought to explain the decline of civilizations and denied the possibility of turning back the current of his-tory by breeding a few blonds. He protested and at last virtually abandoned the idea of race; but to no avail. Rich-ard Wagner and other pan-Germanists took him up, despite the fact that he thought Germany non-Aryan; just as other readers made him a lesser Darwinian prophet, though he had said on considering the state of the world: "We are not descended from the apes, but we are rapidly getting there."

With the popularization of all these terms by pseudo-scientists and real journalists, the races born to rule and those born to serve could be picked out by any citizen, with the assurance of a cattle breeder among his stock. The only hybrid tolerated was the latest product of racialism, a new science called by its inventor *Anthroposociology*. First publicized in 1889, it won adherents and practition-ers at such a rate that in 1893 thirty works were published on the subject in Paris alone. It was highly plausible, as can be seen from its success then and now, for twentieth-century racialism has added but little to its stock of clichés.

In general, race thinking was compatible with every other form of classification: socialists like Ludwig Wolt-mann were racialists and Marx himself held strong racial-ist opinions. Believers in the class struggle often saw little difference between race and class, just as religious fanatics saw little difference between race and creed. As in Montesquieu's day, climate was also a good dividing line: the North and South of Italy were races, with the industrial North naturally superior. Anglo-Saxons and Latins were two races, since Protestantism and Industry could be aligned against Catholicism and centralized government. The Anglo-Saxons—which of course included the United States—must form a Teutonic Union to share all colonies and rule the world. Poets sang of it, Cecil Rhodes made his will in favor of it, the German Kaiser praised the idea as much as Mr. Joseph Chamberlain, while both helped build rival navies. By the side of this Nordic bloc—tall, blond, and blue-eyed to the last man—the Latin Union looked feeble, and possibly the Slavs would have to be asked in as first cousins, unless South America, with its "pure" Latin stock and faith in Auguste Comte, would join in.

That the alliances for the next war cut across these racial lines was no obstacle to the triumph of racial science. Diplomacy looked trivial by the side of "biological realities." Politics, art, religion, language, science, everything had a natural, therefore a racial, basis. Nations were races, and professions too; there were races of poets and races of sailors, races of democrats and races of pessimists, races of struggle-for-lifers and races of suicides. Apparently the only race not entered on the books was the race of true Christians.

Aside from the stored-up animus in these fancies, race thinking was made possible by the ambiguous relation between the individual and the group which had been preached since 1859. The Darwinists had shown that the individual did not matter—only the race. But the Darwinists had also shown that races were mutable, not fixed categories. There must therefore be struggle between individuals to decide which race was to survive. Carried over into society this was very confusing: should a man give up his life for the common good? Certainly not. His duty was to survive at all costs, that is to say on other men's shoulders, as Sir Henry Maine pointed out with the authority of legal lore. But in the *Descent of Man,* published immediately after the Franco-Prussian War of 1870—the first war, be it said in passing, to be interpreted Darwinistically on all sides—Darwin constantly wobbled between keeping man under the regime of natural selection and putting him under the modified regime of co-operation, reason, and love. He points out that among men wars operate a reverse selection—killing off the fit and leaving the unfit. But he believes that a short war is beneficial, because it brings out the social qualities of cohesion, selflessness, and mutual aid, without killing off too many good men. How short a short war is, he does not say.

Nor should one have expected that he would. Bringing all of life under one law was superhuman work. The materials themselves seemed to resist, forcing the social interpreters to contradict their own idea of evolutionary continuity. According to Darwin, man had probably sprung from a weak and gentle species, already living in society, and more akin to the chimpanzee than to the gorilla. But growing reason—not instinct—had led to wars, and wars had further developed reason. "The struggle between the races of man depends entirely upon intelligence and moral qualities . . . selfish and contentious people will not cohere, and without coherence nothing can be done." Yet, he added, continued war leads to the destruction of great civilizations—witness Greece. In the light of this account what was European man to do? Spencer, though usually clearer than his colleague, was here no better guide. Readers of the *Social Statics* had learned how "the stern discipline of nature which eliminates the unfit" results in "the maintenance of a constitution completely adapted to the surrounding conditions." And similarly with social organisms, "inconceivable as have been [its] horrors, . . . without war, the world would still have been inhabited only by men of feeble types, sheltering in caves and living on wild food." But suddenly, it seemed, this happy evolution must stop: "From war has been gained all it had to give."

Blown about on these conflicting winds of doctrine, modern man could only lose his head. Individual variations are useful, but they must not oppose cohesion;[14] selfish people will not cohere, but life is a free-for-all; war is the source of moral qualities as well as of civilized housing and cooking, but it operates a reverse selection that might destroy civilization. A modern, industrialized, democratic nation must therefore be a compact herd—of rugged individualists.

As in all human crises, however, heroism was abundantly displayed. Men sternly set their faces against the weakening influences of compassionate feelings. Doubts were stifled, fears ridiculed, complaints turned to good account, and only a detached observer with an historian's eye could make light of the contradictions: "These men, O Plato! are perpetually bewailing the shortness of human life, and saying unkind things about Death; protesting against that cosmic sadness which they are continually hugging to their hearts, and complaining of the shortness of those pleasures which they seem to enjoy like a stomach-ache."[15] Until nearly the end of the century, the prevailing attitude was that of hope against hope. Winwood Reade, a young explorer praised by Darwin, and a nephew of Charles Reade, the novelist, embodied it in *The Martyrdom of Man*—an aggressively hopeful cry wrung from disillusionment. Though its freethinking encountered the abuse of believers, it soon became the gospel of those who trusted, with a new Messianic faith akin to Marx's, that from violence and death and the sacrifice of Man, better men and a better life would evolve.[16]

[14] Darwin's cousin, Francis Galton, arrived at the important conclusion that "the fact of a man leaving his compatriots or so irritating them that they compel him to go is fair evidence that either he or they or both feel that his character is alien to theirs." *Inquiries into Human Faculty*, 1883, 200.

[15] H. D. Traill, "Hellenism in South Kensington," *Fortnightly*, July 1883.

[16] Sherlock Holmes, that is to say, Arthur Conan Doyle, sang the praises of Reade's book, just as he echoed the racial anthro-

Looking back on that troubled period one can only pity the blindness and bewail the misdirected faith. Like all other things, it had its *raison d'être*. Bitter though the creed of Darwinism was, it gave, as we have seen, some genuine satisfactions, noble or ignoble, to many kinds of people, however dearly purchased: first, it extended the hypothesis of matter and motion into the last realm of scientific inquiry, namely Life; second, it offered a universal rule for tracing the history of all things, namely Evolution; third, it provided an absolute test of value—survival —which could be applied as readily in nature as in society; fourth, it seemed to vindicate and perfect the speculations of a host of previous thinkers, from Buffon and Lamarck to Comte and Erasmus Darwin, taking in on the way the German philosophers, the French naturalists, and the romantic poets of all countries; fifth, it was well adapted to the economic, and later the political, purposes of important groups in each nation; sixth, it explained by phrases whose meaning lay within the intelligence of all how, without taking thought, adaptation and improvement occurred; seventh, it replaced various philosophies and theologies couched in poetic terms by a scientifically worded account of origins, which rested on the "more rational" and "credible" notion of small doses adding up through the ages; eighth, it surrendered to a new, active, and intelligent class —the scientists—the difficult problems of morality, feeling, and spirit. The age-old conflicts of philosophy and life were solved—at least for a time—by denying their real existence and substituting automata for men; ninth and last, the Darwinian orthodoxy provided a rallying point for all factions and parties that desired a better world along the lines of their own infallible prophecies. It did not matter how much they fought among themselves on other counts. Fighting was the order of the day.

---

pology and other features of Darwinism, e.g. *The Hound of the Baskervilles.*

6. Voices of Dissent

> Forty years ago, our friends always explained things
> and had the cosmos down to a point, *teste* Darwin
> and Charles Lyell. Now they say they don't believe
> there is any explanation, or that you can choose
> between half a dozen, all correct. The Germans are
> all balled up. Every generalisation that we settled
> forty years ago is abandoned. The one most com-
> pletely thrown over is our gentle Darwin's Survival,
> which has no longer a leg to stand on.
>
> HENRY ADAMS, 1003

The century was within six years of its close when T. H.
Huxley delivered at Oxford his Romanes Lecture on Evolution and Ethics. It was, on the testimony of his hearers, a
very moving occasion. The arena was substantially the same
as had witnessed his great duel thirty-five years before with
Wilberforce and Owen. But in those days the uttering of
animal evolution without reservations about man's soul had
been greeted with abuse. Indeed it had seemed a poor joke.
When the American Dr. Draper had tried to illustrate
the facts, "Let this point A be the man, and let that point
B be the mawnkey," the undergraduate contingent had
sent up a cry of "Mawnkey! Mawnkey!" Now the situation
was reversed. A whole generation had passed. They had
been born evolutionists, and to them Huxley had the up-
hill task of expounding the lesson that evolutionary ways
were not after all the best basis of ethics—nature was not to

be taken as a direct model. There was a cosmic process which Darwinism had lighted up; but it was a dangerous guide to human action. The ethical process must supplement it, for man in society was no longer a natural animal. Capital and labor, nation and nation, race and race, must live otherwise than as the ants. Co-operation and love, the Sermon on the Mount, were the more successful, the more "scientific" ways of life.[1] He might have added that even in the cosmic sphere not every creature is as warlike as the ant. The so-called wild beasts are not; neither are the apes. The albatrosses of the South Seas who occupy unmolested their own waters do not fight among themselves. Yet they form different species and must have evolved without benefit of struggle in the narrow sense. With this example, Huxley's sermon might even have recalled to the memory of the listeners the parable of the Ancient Mariner.

But the listeners were not in a mood to accept a partial retreat even from Huxley. The younger men had grown tired of his voice, so long raised in battle and now striving to roar like any nightingale. In the words of a prominent writer, lecturer, and M. P., Huxley had always been an "essentially negative mind . . . more concerned to evade compromising names than to clear them up . . . a crossing-sweeper of philosophy."[2]

Those are harsh words. Huxley, like almost every other scientific philosopher of the period, had been inwardly divided. Had the public followed him attentively, they would have heard him assail the Bible but insist on its use in the schools; scorn the believers, but declare no man should be unreligious; remind himself of a Hebrew prophet, but worship the calm austerity of the scientist. He peppered the journals with a gunfire of new definitions—of science, education, faith, truth. He asked workingmen to lend him their ear, assuring them that they only needed common

[1] Even in making this point, Huxley is not consistent. His speech was taken by some as a "senile recantation."

[2] J. M. Robertson, *Modern Humanists*, pp. 243, 236 n.

sense to understand science. Then he would denounce the "spurious metaphysics of vulgar common sense."[3] All this because his philosophic culture was inadequate to his needs. True, he studied Descartes, wrote a book on Hume, and rediscovered Berkeley. This made him end by preaching the sole reality of sensations, which are "immaterial entities in the strictest sense of the term."[4] But this dissent from his earlier dogmas, however sincere, came too late and with a kind of ill grace. He was trying to lay the ghost he had raised, but lacked the formula. He was enacting another parable from the Romantic period, that of the Sorcerer's Apprentice.

Huxley's motive was undoubtedly a growing disgust with life, a disgust shared by others. While he wished for a colliding comet to shatter the world to atoms, Henry Adams prophesied wars on a gigantic scale, with a possible escape through a violent return to superstition. In the press of Europe, the *fin de siècle* was greeted with cries of "decadence," the signs of which were read on every hand: a decreasing birth rate in France; the wretched size and health of Boer War recruits in England; increasing homosexuality in Germany and neuroses at the Salpêtrière; corruption in politics and perversion in the literature and art of every country. The only visible faith in this mass of dispirited mortals was the faith in drifting—a progress measured by pig-iron production and fated from the beginning of animal life upon earth.

When Spencer, also with second thoughts, began to assail English militarism and to predict the degeneracy of the nation through the rise of a new serfdom, he was scouted as a pacifist, a dotard, and a dissenter. The London *Times* celebrated his death with an article against him. English opinion was so violent that protests came from the continent. Forty years before, on the appearance of the *Origin of Species*, a Manchester journalist had shown that according to the author's scheme "might is right and there-

[3] *Essays*, vi, 318.
[4] *Ibid.*, vi, 302.

fore Napoleon is right and every cheating tradesman is also right." Darwin had not understood. But in the late seventies he had grown alarmed. "I am beginning to despair of ever making the majority understand my notions." This from the man who had "conquered the opinion of the world." No. The gladiatorial conception of the struggle for existence was there to stay, and as Geoffrey West rightly says, harking back to old Sedgwick and his complaint about neglecting the moral and metaphysical part of man: "He leapt . . . right to the heart of the matter in a prophetic passage whose insight should be the more apparent now, when the increasing brutalisation and degradation of humanity are no more to be denied than detached from conceptions of evolution and natural selection. . . ."[5]

The work of undeceiving the world about Darwinism and scientific materialism had to be begun by other hands. It had to come from the persistent efforts of those who throughout the Darwinian hegemony had said *non credo*. The influences that joined in this undertaking were naturally diverse. Some were philosophic, some religious, some superstitious. First in line was the scientific criticism directed at the theory of Natural Selection and leading to the Mutation Theory of De Vries and the new genetics of Gregor Mendel. They will be briefly dealt with in the next chapter.

Next came the philosophic criticism of materialism and scientific method which Huxley, Tyndall, and Spencer responded to but could hardly grasp. Its most enduring monument was Friedrich Lange's *History of Materialism*[6]—a sympathetic but uncompromising critique of both materialism and idealism by a man trained in both science and philosophy.

[5] *Darwin*, 252.
[6] This refers to the much enlarged second edition of 1873–75. The only English translation of it is a disgrace to everyone responsible for its appearance: it should be retranslated and reissued in readable shape.

In the same or the following decade came forth publications by younger men, little noticed at the time but significant in retrospect. In England, a group of nine, led by A. S. Pringle-Pattison and including the brothers J. S. and R. B. (later Viscount) Haldane, published *Essays in Philosophical Criticism*. In 1877 Samuel Butler began his onslaught with *Life and Habit*. In France Poincaré and Bergson, in America Stallo and William James, began the revolt against mechanism. Their work first received wide notice at the turn of the century, when the public became aware of the Haldane brothers' antimaterialistic biology, Bergson's Creative Evolution, and James's Pragmatism. These ideas coincided with the revision of mechanism in physics and the disenchantment about mechanistic psychology.

In addition to a scientific house cleaning there occurred in the same final quarter of the century a remarkable religious revival. Beginning with the Vatican Council of 1870, which promulgated the infallibility of the Pope in matters of faith and morals, and reasserted the unshakable opposition of the Church to the new doctrines of liberalism, socialism, Darwinism, and secularism, the religious faith of Europe overflowed into the most diverse paths. The Social Gospel was everywhere an occasion for religious ferment. Better men went into the ministry; new religions sprang up. No sooner, it seemed, had mid-century materialists destroyed the last remnant of belief in the hereafter than appeared Spiritualism, psychical research, Theosophy, Christian Science, Yogi, and innumerable shades of New Thought. The coincidence in the dates is remarkable. Spiritism had been growing stronger ever since D. W. Home (Browning's "Mr. Sludge the Medium") had made his appearance in the late fifties,[7] but most of the other

[7] The symptomatic importance of Spiritism—really a disguised materialism—can be seen from the fact that a number of eminent scientists from Sir William Crookes to the late Sir Oliver Lodge came to give it varying degrees of credence. The list includes such notables as A. R. Wallace, G. T. Fechner, Charles Richet, Camille Flammarion, Cesare Lombroso, and, even nearer to our own

new creeds burst forth between 1875, when Madame Blavatsky established her first Theosophic Society in New York, and 1882, when the Society for Psychical Research was founded in the two Cambridges, under the auspices of distinguished scientists and philosophers. The significantly named "Christ Scientist" had been promulgated by Mrs. Mary Baker Eddy of Boston in 1879.

To these intellectual religions we must add the power of the Salvation Army. Huxley's denunciations of it for fanaticism and regimentation hindered it no more than did the disdain of professional men, who seemed to think that spirit séances and Theosophical jargon were worthier expressions of their feelings. It was not until George Bernard Shaw made the point in *Major Barbara* that the so-called elite began to appreciate what General Booth's movement had done for the uneducated, pauperized, and drink-sodden masses which social Darwinism had complacently allowed to find their place under the heels of fitter men. Then it was seen that neither the fatalism of biological evolution nor the fatalism of "scientific" socialism could withstand a vigorous assault by people who believed in the power of the human will and had the wits to combine religion, social work, army discipline, and rousing tunes.

For those who remained outside organized religions and organized science, there were available in this same period a number of disembodied faiths which it will be sufficient merely to name, since they continue to act as substitute religions: social work, militant atheism, scientific socialism, pacifism, and art. The importance of art as a religious outlet in this period must not be discounted, even when esthetic pleasure is divorced from Anglican and Roman Catholicism. Merged or fused in a love of nature, art and religion can occupy a common ground and not be merely an arbitrary joining of separate emotions; so that given sensitiveness and a secular training, a late nineteenth-century European could direct his impulse to worship toward works

---

day, Sir Arthur Conan Doyle, F. C. S. Schiller, W. McDougall, and Alexis Carrel.

of art and their makers. Of these outlets for devotion the most important in numbers as well as degree of idolatry was the cult of Wagnerism.[8]

> Samuel Butler, the most brilliant and by far the most interesting of Darwin's opponents . . . whose works are at length emerging from oblivion.
>
> BATESON, 1909

England meanwhile had produced one man of genius whose opposition to Darwinism began shortly after the appearance of the *Origin of Species* and continued unabated on all planes of thought—biological, social, metaphysical, and religious—until his death in 1902. This was Samuel Butler, the grandson of Darwin's old headmaster at Shrewsbury. When the *Origin of Species* appeared, Butler was on his way to New Zealand to earn a competence raising sheep. He read the book there in the solitude of his ranch and at once became a convert to the idea of evolution. The hypothesis even spurred him to write for a local journal a sketch called *Darwin Among the Machines*, the leading idea of which—that of machinery evolving by itself and ultimately conquering man—has since acquired the taste of an unpleasant truth. This idea of course also contained the germ of the satire *Erewhon*, which Butler published after he returned to England, in 1872.

Further reflection and several rereadings of the *Origin of Species* made Butler dissatisfied with the Darwinian theory of Natural Selection. Perhaps his own fancy about the machines gave him the clue to the weakness of Darwinism—what he ultimately came to call "the Deadlock in Darwinism." The deadlock was simply that machines, having no purposes of their own, could not evolve; and since animals and plants were treated by Darwin as if they were machines, Darwinian evolution was impossible. Natural

[8] See below.

Selection might conceivably aid us to understand which forms survived, but it could never tell us how these forms had come to be. Natural Selection was an undoubted *fact*; it could never be a theory or a cause. As Butler put it, "To me it seems that the 'Origin of Variations,' whatever it is, is the only true 'Origin of Species.'"

In examining Darwin's text, Butler found that small random variations were taken for granted or occasionally ascribed to a metaphysical agent called Variation, so as to provide Natural Selection with something to work on. But Butler also found Darwin relying now and again upon use and disuse, and he traced the origin of this hypothesis to Lamarck, whose name and work Darwin openly discredited. This led Butler to Buffon, Goethe, and Erasmus Darwin, making him the first careful historian of the evolutionary movement. After comparing Darwin's theory in all its vacillating forms with the theories of the earlier trio, Butler came to the conclusion that the grandfather, and not the grandson, had met most nearly the difficulties involved in any evolutionary hypothesis. The grandson had of course marshaled many more facts indicative of evolution than the grandfather; he had, as Butler proclaimed, taught people about evolution; but he had not made out a convincing case for the way in which species changed. He had at most emphasized in Natural Selection a fact previously noted by zoologists that "those who can survive do survive." The secret of the Origin of Species still lay hidden in the Origin of Variation.

Had Butler contented himself with offering these criticisms, he might conceivably have gained a hearing for them. But once aroused he was not given to stopping short. Assuming that in the presence of established facts his thoughts upon them might be of use, Butler offered in *Life and Habit* a suggestion to replace—or rather supplement—Darwin's Natural Selection. Starting from the truism that the organism is a living thing and not a machine, Butler asserted that its characteristic feature is that it has an "interest": it wants to do certain things and not to do others.

In other words, the physical action of living beings is the expression of a mental action. Mental here refers not to Intellect, but to consciousness, however low and limited. This was going dead against Huxley's Automaton Theory, not yet discredited. It followed that for Butler, effort, endeavor, purpose, have something to do with biological evolution. From this, by a shorthand expression it could be said that living forms evolve because they want to: desires lead to efforts; successful efforts result in new powers; and new powers create new desires. As Butler saw it, the process was limited by the environment and the narrow powers of the creature, but the reality of it corresponded to what could be observed in the phenomena of growth, habit, and learning. Best of all, the hypothesis got rid of the inexplicable mechanism by which the evolution and the life of living things was made to result from chance push-pulls from outside.

Besides reinstating purposes into a world that had become a vast roulette table, Butler's notion made society something else than a Coliseum where human beasts strive with one another in moral darkness. Mind, feelings, ethics, art—all these things once again became real, instead of being the dreams of automata, accompanying the physico-chemical changes called digestion, respiration, reproduction, and death. It was still possible and instructive to look at these functions in their physico-chemical aspects, but to do so did not exhaust the meanings inherent in them.[9] Lastly, Butler's theory made the problem of religion one that could not be shirked or relegated to a superstitious past. Men live by some sort of faith, life is indeed a form of faith, and the repeating of scientific formulas is not its only ritual.[10] Though Butler often used scriptural lan-

[9] Asa Gray had said: "We advise nobody to accept Darwin's or any other theory as true. The time has not come for that, and perhaps never will. . . . The theory is just now very useful to science." *Darwiniana*, 175–76.

[10] Compare Whitehead's "Life is an offensive against the repetitive mechanism of the universe." *Adventures of Ideas*, 1934, 102.

guage, there was nothing orthodox about his religion. It was nevertheless a consistent set of beliefs, far from the atheism which a misguided modern critic has ascribed to him, though seemingly unintelligible to both the churchmen and the scientists of his own day.

What puzzled them was that Butler seemed to be striking out on a new line instead of choosing, like everybody else, between theology and materialistic science. For one thing, he wholly disclaimed for his theory any scientific warrant or even any originality. The hint of it, he said, lay in Lamarck, and it had been fully exploited by Erasmus Darwin. What Butler was doing was to give it another hearing at a time when a completely mechanical view of life was sweeping the field. Butler thought both theology and Darwinism inadequate, mechanical evolution even more so than supernatural creation, for creation was at least a fact of daily experience whereas mechanism was an abstraction born of scientific needs.

Unfortunately Butler's initial modesty was misplaced. Far from receiving thanks or intelligent criticism, he was assailed by both sides in truly professional manner as "lacking authority." Here was a man who had never worked in a laboratory or been ordained, who had made fun of churches in *Erewhon*, and who had the effrontery to criticize, speculate, and dogmatize. It was an infringement of monopoly. It seemed to the gentle Darwin "clever and unscrupulous." It was of no use for Butler to reply that he took the very facts which the scientists supplied him with, that no one had detected him in a factual error, that his theory had never been criticized. Official science had no time to listen—only time to invoke the Principle of Authority and write insulting reviews.

Oddly enough, Spencer, who was no more a practising scientist than Butler and who was in truth a far more deductive, a priori, unscientific mind, was gravely attended to by the official Darwinians. He was on their side. Even when after twenty-five years of exclusive enthusiasm for Natural Selection Spencer made it share the throne with his earlier love, Lamarckism, no one thought it particularly "impudent" or "unscientific."[11]

Again, G. H. Lewes, who held and promulgated a theory of life identical with Butler's, was respected and quoted, though only on matters of detail, by the professionals. The reason for this discrimination seems to have been that Spencer and Lewes both paid homage to Darwin and set up no other idols—particularly earlier evolutionists—in his stead. Butler was too direct in his questionings of a famous man twenty-five years his senior, and it is doubtful whether even with the aid of scientific degrees and a less readable style he would have made any impression on orthodoxy. As it was, all parties grew more obstinate, Butler more and more peppery and irreverent, the churchmen more and more "pleasant-like and frothing at the mouth," and the Darwinians more and more contemptuously silent.

The result was lifelong neglect for Butler and the postponement until our century of the pleasure and honor of rediscovery. Bateson's recognition of Butler's importance in 1909, Shaw's successful campaign to give him his due place in English thought, and the numerous biographies of him which have appeared to date, do not begin to exhaust the points of interest in his mind and personality. The many anticipations of William James and Freud, for instance, that can be found in *Life and Habit* will delight and surprise the attentive reader. And it is increasingly apparent that, without knowing it, Butler was in line with the most fruitful speculations of his age. Unconscious Memory, for example, was a suggestion very much akin to the renascent interest in genetics. Butler perceived that if he made creature-purpose the moving factor in evolution, he had to explain how these purposes accumulated. He concluded that instinct, which was inherited, was a sort of memory buried in the germ plasm; and, anticipating Weismann, he argued that life was in fact continuous and not chopped up into the fragments we call individuals.

[11] "The Factors of Organic Evolution," *Nineteenth Century*, Apr. and May, 1886.

Shortly before publishing these views, Butler found that a German professor named Hering had given expression to similar ideas at a scientific congress not long before. Butler thereupon fathered his own theory on the shoulders of the accredited degree-holder, not suspecting that Asa Gray and Joseph Leconte in the United States had also attributed instincts to inherited memory. But once again Butler had no response. He none the less persisted, republishing his historical account of evolution and finally summarizing all his arguments under the crystal-clear title of "Luck or Cunning?"

Butler's criticism of Darwin is summed up in his objection that Darwin had banished mind from the universe. This does not mean, of course, that Butler's suggestions have been proved true, and G. H. Parker is right in saying that such ideas would require much hard work to verify. But neither does it mean that Butler's objections were grounded on a mere preference for the banished "Mind" as against the ever-present "Matter." Many materialists still think that a sense of personal deprivation is the sole ground of any such objection. The truth is that the objection is directed at the "inevitable tendency of analysis to disregard whatever elements it provisionally sets aside."[12] Mind was but the traditional name for those experiences that were not mere movements of particles. It was the name for those things which Huxley and Tyndall declared themselves unable to measure, account for, or lead up to by means of laboratory analysis. Let them set mind aside as much as they wished for certain purposes of investigation, still mind must not be forgotten like an inconvenient umbrella in the cloakroom. It must reappear somewhere in the final inventory. If it came to a choice of making mind all matter or matter all mind, Butler chose the latter as more consonant with the facts.

Lewes agreed with him, perhaps without knowing it, oc-

[12] Lewes, *Physical Basis of Mind*, Boston, 1877, 76.

cupied as he was in striking out new paths in biology. "Materialism," says Lewes, "in attempting to deduce the mental from the physical puts into the conclusion what the very terms have excluded from the premises."[13] His hypothesis, which would have satisfied equally Samuel Butler in 1887 and John Scott Haldane forty years later,[14] is that "the physical process is only the objective aspect of a mental process."[15] Nor was Lewes a new convert to this conclusion. As early as 1853, in his book on Auguste Comte, he had defined God as Life[16] and echoed the Roman poet's "Life is everywhere and nowhere Death."

Both in Butler and in Lewes this conviction came from a familiarity with more than one realm of thought. Just as Butler rediscovered Hegel's law of contradiction without reading Hegel, and carried forward Schopenhauer's notion of the will without reading Schopenhauer, so Lewes, who as a philosopher had read both, could anticipate the doctrine of Emergent Evolution[17] and stand out in amiable dispute against his century. As a competent and well-connected scientist, Lewes could draw confirmation for his theories from many quarters. Paget on the tissues, German cell physiology and neurology, French work on medicine —all seemed to converge on the point that, though Supernaturalism was a metaphysical mistake and a stumbling-block for science, materialism was untenable too, and for the same reasons. Life was not just atoms in a bag.

Unfortunately, Lewes died prematurely in 1878, and his work never won the place which it deserved. But its merit can be tested, like Butler's, by the fact that the younger generation was falling in with its tendency. It was in 1875–1876 that the young William James, saturated with Ger-

[13] *Ibid.*, viii.
[14] *The Sciences and Philosophy*, Gifford Lectures, 1927–28.
[15] Lewes, *op. cit.*, viii.
[16] *Comte's Philosophy of the Sciences*, 54.
[17] He coined this phrase, later used by Lloyd Morgan, S. Alexander, G. H. Parker, and others, and adopted by H. S. Jennings of Johns Hopkins to describe his non-materialistic biology.

man science, began to wean himself away from Spencerism and psychophysics, that Lange brought out the second edition of his polemical *History of Materialism*, and that biologists in many parts of the globe began to make those attacks on Natural Selection which led to Darwin's "tacit" recognition of their weight.

7. After Darwin: What Is Science?

> The temperature of our atmosphere decides that no liquid carbon shall be found on the face of the earth; but we do not suppose that the form of the diamond has been gradually achieved by a process of Selection.
>
> WILLIAM BATESON, 1909

Though in 1909 scientists united in celebrating the fiftieth anniversary of the *Origin of Species,* the comments I have already cited from the pages of Bateson and Weismann make it clear that by then the Darwinian orthodoxy showed an open rift. Darwin had admitted long before his death: "I suppose natural selection was a bad term; but to change it now, I think, would make confusion worse confounded, nor can I think of a better. 'Natural preservation' would not imply a preservation of particular varieties and would seem a truism, and would not bring man and nature's selections under one point of view."[1]

The chief trouble with Natural Selection was not only that it was a bad term, but that it seemed incapable of taking enough hold on small creature-variation to get started. Weismann himself admitted this and furnished an example of what his opponents meant: the limpets that live among the breakers on a rocky shore have acquired thick shells—clearly an adaptation. But what degree of

[1] *Life and Letters,* ii, 111.

thickness was sufficient to decide "that of two variants of
limpet one should survive and the other should be elimi-
nated? We can say nothing more than that we infer from
the present state of the shell that it must have varied in
regard to differences in shell thickness and that these differences must have had selection value—no proof, therefore, but an assumption which we must show to be convincing."

"Must" in this sense is a hard word for a scientist to use
and when he is as honest as Weismann it wrings a con-
fession: "We are reasoning in a circle, not giving proofs,
and no one who does not wish to believe in the selection
value of the initial stages can be forced to do so."[2] Behind
this difficulty lay the nineteenth-century idea of small
doses. The selection of minute random variations resembled the Cheshire Cat in Lewis Carroll: specific characters
would appear or disappear gradually, either producing a
discernible cat or leaving only a vestigial grin. Yet the
Lamarckian assumption was little better. There was some,
though very little, evidence that acquired characteristics
could be inherited. Brown-Sequard's experiments had
shown that artificial mutilations might be inherited, but
only, it seemed, under conditions of disease. The outlook
was not hopeful. It was then that the work of Mendel,
Bateson, and De Vries came to the fore and gave research
a new impetus while changing its direction.

De Vries was a Dutch botanist who in 1901 asserted that
there were two kinds of variation—the random variations
previously observed by Darwin, and what he himself called
"mutations," or sizable divergences from the parent form.
Bateson had paved the way for this distinction with his
large work on discontinuous variations (1894), and the
theory which covered their combined evidence was that
such selection as nature might exert operated on large and
complete changes of form. The small random changes did

[2] *Darwin and Modern Science*, 25, 27.

not accumulate through long ages and were in fact irrelevant to evolution.

On top of this hypothesis came the rediscovery of Gregor Mendel, a Moravian abbot, who thirty-five years before De Vries had completed[3] some beautifully simple and clear experiments on the proportions in which the characters of the common or garden pea are inherited upon crossing.[4] "Mendelian factor" is now a common phrase, and the schoolboy babbles of recessive genes, but in 1900 Mendel was a new star in the scientific firmament. His neglect had been partly due to the fact that his work ran counter to the prevailing views of Variation, for even in 1900 it courted disbelief as unlikely on the face of it. The time was ripe, however, and disbelief was conquered. Publications on the new facts grew plentiful and voluble. Weismann was stimulated to further research in behalf of Natural Selection, whose field of application he now transferred to the reproductive cells of the body: selection occurred before the individual was born; it was "germinal selection" and the survival of the adult was of importance only as permitting procreation. Natural Selection was a mere retaining device which kept useful germinal variations from being swamped out of existence. The new biology, it seemed, was working away from an individualistic, competitive state of nature and into a microscopic world where invisible determinants did the work of evolution prenatally.

Darwin (and breeders before him) had of course recognized the existence of mutations or "sports," but he had held them to be exceptions of no significance to evolution; his idea suiting a time when the means of study and the interest in genetics were lacking. Besides, the plain analogy

[3] And published. The statement that Darwin left the *Origin of Species* in its final shape "twenty-eight years before the publication of Mendel's work" (Irene Manton, *Key to the Origin*, Oxford University Press, 1935, xiv) is inaccurate and tendentious.

[4] The efforts to produce uniformly improved cereals—notably in Germany, Scotland, and Minnesota—go back to the early nineties. "Single-ear sowing" for pure types was thus rediscovered.

between biological and slow geological evolution was convincing. Now, for reasons that may owe something to the human desire for novelty, evolution by jumps suddenly appeared much more probable. It was the time of quantum theory, of discontinuous change. "Do the new lights on heredity and variation," asked Bateson, "make the process of Evolution easier to understand? On the whole they do. . . . An Evolution by definite steps is more, rather than less easy to imagine than one proceeding by the accumulation of indefinite and insensible steps."[5]

When such a change of direction occurs in a science the immediate result is confusion. Some grasp a part, some all, of the new deductions and corollaries. There is a strong desire to patch old and new together, and another, less strong, to make a clean sweep and start afresh. There is also a healthy interest in the history of the science, which is studied in the hope of making things clear by presenting rival theories in their cultural setting and in the order of their appearance. Mendel was thus placed with due honor in his proper rank, Samuel Butler received a few posthumous apologies, biographies of Lamarck took on a eulogistic tone, and a great many men of science whose views had been too lightly dismissed, like Moritz Wagner, Nägeli, Wollaston, St. George Mivart, and Naudin, were given as nearly as possible their due.

The best historians of evolution, like Plate of Berlin, Kellogg of Leland Stanford, Osborn of Columbia, naturally maintained a judicial attitude. But many others expressed themselves in intemperate language. Darwinism was described as "on its deathbed," or else "as good as new." Living Darwinians were attacked as having softening of the brain, anti-Darwinians of earlier days were extolled, both groups of scientists speaking with singular malevolence and skill at imputing motives. Everyone naturally prefers moderation in others, but in retrospect it can be said that there

[5] *Darwin and Modern Science*, 99.

is a certain virtue in indignation, even in science. Science and human feelings are not separable, for science is not only man-made but man-used. When the Darwinians fought for a hearing, very little moderation was shown on either side, and the triumph of Darwinism was commensurate with the noise it made. Once in power the victors could afford to manhandle past and present dissenters or, applying a double standard, make all the exceptions in their own favor: allowing Lyell's reservations about man because he accepted Natural Selection; letting Wallace, for the same reason, believe in the separate origin of man's soul; overlooking Lewes's anti-Mechanism; allowing Spencer his ancient and revised Lamarckism because he joined Natural Selection to it, while Butler was boycotted; numbering all the American Darwinists as friends, even though theists, and yet keeping silence about Agassiz because he would not depart from original creation; overlooking Darwin's unlucky theory of Pangenesis, his confused expressions, and his occasional errors of fact as well as Huxley's "bathybius" blunder; and yet holding against Richard Owen the unfortunate business of the formation of the skull—none of this was felt to be "intemperate." But at times in the moral world contrary motion must go beyond its goal in order to reach it: to undo the Darwinian verdicts required an effort which was bound to generate in heat the equivalent of mechanical work done.

Other, less personal judgments had to be undone, too. The notion of species had to be re-examined for perhaps the millionth time. De Vries's work brought the "systematists," as they were called, back into favor, and with them their belief in the reality of species. A new regularity in species was thus reintroduced together with a new irregularity in descent. Species seemed to be much less easily changed than the early Darwinians had thought.

Around the numerous versions of Natural Selection—individual, germinal, cellular,[6] and so on—a confused mêlée

[6] A new adaption by Félix LeDantec of one of Lewes's hypotheses.

continued. Enough has already been said to show that the objections to considering selection an omnipotent cause were copious and acute. Yet in the inchoate condition of genetics, no one had anything conclusively better to offer, and lest evolution itself suffer from the riddling of Natural Selection, many scientists still made it their mainstay, though marking those limitations of which they themselves felt the force.

But just because the new discoveries made it evident that biology had spots of great regularity, the rest of the field seemed stricken with chaos. Paleontologists especially deplored the "mass of facts." They, the pathologists, and some botanists[7] markedly preferred Lamarckism. For Lamarck's theory offered a guiding thread through the labyrinth: creature-purpose responding to environmental needs. The contrary law of higgledy-piggledy hardly seemed competent to regularize what was complex but regular to start with. Whatever the merits of the case for Lamarck, Erasmus Darwin, and Samuel Butler, as against Charles Darwin and his cohorts, little doubt could be left in the minds of thoughtful scientists that the orderliness in the facts of Heredity and Variation could not depend on pure Natural Selection, whose essence it is to make chance produce adaptations, and whose operation can only begin after variations —however originated—have put in an appearance.[8] Mechanism was doomed unless a new mechanism was discovered in the germ plasm.

This new mechanism has not been forthcoming. In 1907, reviewing the proposed answers to the riddle of the Sphinx and asking himself which was the true one, Vernon Kellogg could not say that he knew. "Nor in the present state of

[7] "Acquired characters are inherited or I know nothing of plant life." Luther Burbank, Popular Science Monthly, lxix, 1906, 363.

[8] "Darwinian Natural Selection as the final arbiter of control is saved and clear of objections. But Darwinism as the all-sufficient or even causo-mechanical factor in species forming and hence as the sufficient explanation of descent, is discredited and cast down." Kellogg, Darwinism Today, 1907, 374.

knowledge does anyone know, nor will know until, as Brooks says of another problem, we find out. We are ignorant; terribly, immensely ignorant. And our work is to learn. To observe, to experiment, to tabulate, to induce, to deduce."[9]

Today, after thirty years of experiment, tabulation, induction, and deduction, which have brought many particulars to light, a worker in the same field must also write: "The nature of the genic changes which produce mutation is not known."[10] The geneticist continues to follow Weismann's idea of embryonic selection among variations in the genes—caused no one knows how. The Lamarckian idea is once again in the discard, but the establishing of theory remains extraordinarily difficult. The nineteenth-century temptation to think of the gene as a single mechanical agent is not dead. "It is hoped," says the author just quoted, "the reader will realize that the gene is not a self-enclosed, static performer of creations, but on the contrary is a concept . . ." composed of two subsidiary ones: "first the material particle on the chromosome, so to say the gene matter, and second, the interaction of that gene with given substances under various internal and external environments to produce an end result."[11] These unequal yoke-fellows, taken with the great complexity of the observed facts, make the research into evolution particularly treacherous. "The real experimental difficulties lie in the fact that geneticists, physiologists, or biologists in general have not yet made a concerted effort to clarify all the concepts involved in the theory of evolution. In fact, no science of evolution as such has yet been organized, and the applications of genetics to it are merely fortuitous." And he concludes, "The problem of the fitness of organisms should be omitted entirely from any evolutionary study . . . [a] vague anthropomorphic concept . . . which we cannot define or

[9] Op. cit., 387.
[10] Mark Graubard, Biology and Human Behavior, 1936, 250.
[11] Ibid., 254, 246. See also L. J. Henderson, The Fitness of the Environment, 1913.

make use of fruitfully. . . . It is more profitable to consider the situation as it really exists in nature."[12]

Whether or not it is possible to see "the situation as it really exists in nature," the general public of our century has never departed from the Darwinian faith that the scientist is the man to do it. On this latter-day public the new theories of mutation and genetics have had little effect. The interest, for example, in the Spencer-Weismann debate of 1893 had none of the violence and universality which had greeted the original onslaught of 1859. For one thing, the new sciences came out of the laboratory and required special training and equipment to appreciate. For another, the public holds to a touching belief in the absolute unanimity of science. Encouraged in dogmatic habits by the words of popularizers, it accepts what "science says" or trusts that "we now know . . ." as if some agency existed for creating agreement among the workers of a particular age or ascertaining their consensus. Lastly, the conviction that knowledge comes out of the observation of matter tended to dwarf the role of intelligence and idea.

In the ranks of science, to be sure, the new discoveries revolutionized more than the methods of study. They radically changed the notions of living organisms, and in so doing they did draw attention to the fact that our ideas affect our results as much as things affect our ideas. What Hegel much earlier had called the "duplicity of nature" was here illustrated. Make some assumptions about heredity and gradual change, speak of Natural Selection and Survival of the Fittest, gathering many facts in support of your hypothesis—and the whole universe will seem to respond by "proving" or "verifying" it. But let someone question an initial assumption or stick stubbornly to some discrepant fact,[13] and sooner or later the whole edifice is turned topsy-turvy. Natural Selection becomes a factor of stability and

[12] Op. cit., 289.
[13] E.g., the revival, around 1900, of the objection to Darwin based on the "shortness of geological time."

not of change; heredity becomes the source and not the mere channel of evolution. The cause is no longer a cause, but a mere condition; the question of the Origin of Species is reopened and the formerly accepted "means" becomes, perhaps, the very one that is clearly impossible.

This essentially philosophical revolution, I say, did not reach the great public. Its mind had only just grasped the fine distinction that evolution does not mean direct descent from the monkeys, but merely descent from "a common anthropoid ancestor," and it had taken the exact mechanism of survival so to heart that it was useless to insist on "a certain vagueness" in nature, which might allow some unfit beings to live while fit ones died. The ever-closer contacts with machinery, as the world passed from a period of factories and locomotives into one of domestic and individual machines—bicycles, automobiles, electric lights, and telephones—seemed to verify for good the great push-pull principle which works so well in common life.

Since, moreover, there were still hinterlands of theology to colonize, writers on scientific subjects continued to preach the plausible doctrine that science is merely organized common sense; from which it followed that any questioning of definitions, any tendency to distinguish between the matter we see, hear, feel, touch, smell, and the hypothetical matter of the physicist's atom, should be viewed with suspicious contempt. Matter being whatever is "out there," it is also the "cause" of what we feel, hear, touch, and so on. This belief was right, indispensable, "natural." The Positivism of Comte and Huxley, thoroughly absorbed, but without their later doubts, meant just that. To trust it was scientific; to doubt it, "metaphysical." As one Darwinist admirably put it, those who do not believe in matter must be perpetually weeded out of existence through the operation of natural selection.

Unfortunately, faith in science and the exclusive worship of facts had gone even further. It had destroyed the rival faith in the intangible. I quoted in the introductory chapter the wistful remark of the Duke of Sermoneta about "the moral law and the law of beauty" being absent from the universe. It is typical of the regrets so abundantly expressed by sensitive men at the turn of the century. The Duke was apparently so convinced of the primacy of material things that it never occurred to him to suppose that the moral law and the law of beauty *were* in the universe by reason of his wondering about them. Carried away by admiration for Spencer, who knew how fast the sun was shrinking, the Duke felt he had no warrant for admiring the sunset. It would have seemed to him "subjective" and not "objective" behavior and *therefore* illicit. Similarly, the moral law was a cultural accident. It had "grown out" of war, or anxiety about the spring crops, and *therefore* was not valid. Genesis, that is, scientific genesis, explained all things. Repinings were vain, for Nature herself was red in tooth and claw, and man should not be anthropomorphic.

And yet, as we have just been told on scientific authority,[14] no formula was ever more anthropomorphic than that of the Survival of the Fittest, no poetic metaphor more secretly flattering to pride than Natural Selection; which may be why mankind sacrificed its other feelings—albeit with groans—to make it the Supreme Law. For after measuring the skulls of apes and finding them as well provided with an occipital lobe as man, it was clear that there was as much to be proud of in the kinship as in denying it: man had evolved, the ape had not. Between them lay an impassable gulf, said Huxley. And man owed everything to steady victory in age-long struggle. Summed up in his superior brain, these victories had made White European man the Lord of creation . . . and of other races.[15]

The poetry of it was irresistible. It seeped down among the masses through public instruction after 1870, with its clear-cut images neatly fitting a world of obvious struggling. Darwin had tried, once or twice, to show his metaphors for what they were, but few read him. They read his ex-

[14] Pages 121–22 above.
[15] Clodd, *Huxley*, 127, 25–6.

pounders instead who dramatized the "story of evolution"[16] by stressing the business of chase, capture, and death. It was always a tiger and a gazelle, and the gazelle with slightly longer legs. . . . It would have been confusing to say "A plant on the edge of the desert is said to struggle for existence against the drought, though more properly it should be said to be dependent on the moisture."[17] And explaining that "the drought" does not exist and is merely a name for the absence of moisture would have sounded metaphysical. In truth, once the word "selection" was used, no other course was possible than that of personifying Nature and making *her* "watch and seize unerringly" those of her children who deserved survival. The idea of merely resisting the universe, sitting tight and enduring, was not sufficiently anthropomorphic. Competition with other species or individuals, victory earned because of inward merit or determination to win—these were intelligible principles. And by a peculiar twist of fate, it amounted to teaching the public a doctrine closer to Butler than to Darwin. To accept the absolute value of survival, the common mind wanted it to represent a "genuine" value. It would have been horrified to learn that "fittest" only means "those who survive," and that the sickly coddled child of wealth who lives and procreates is fitter than the robust laborer who dies of overwork and bad food.

The same injection of a selecting *mind* into natural affairs led to picturing animals as constantly at each other's throats. Enlightened opinion condemned as "sentimental" the view that Nature was harmonious; calling it "cruel" instead, and not seeing that to speak of cruelty in reference to the millions of seeds or eggs that perish is a piece of far worse sentimentality. For there is balance and interdependency among living things, whereas ascribing conscious agency to Nature can make it be anything one wants: Na-

[16] E.g., *Histomap of Evolution, From Flaming Planet to Modern Man*—"Ten Thousand Million Years of Evolution on a Single Page: One Dollar." (John B. Sparks, 1932 ff.)

[17] *Origin of Species*, 6th ed., ch. iii, par. 4.

ture is kind in that it solicitously feeds the frog with gnats; it is cruel in that it allows innocent gnats to be eaten by frogs. Still, as an excuse for human cruelty the ascription was endlessly useful, and it was only a few years ago that fox-hunting was defended in England as "Nature's way."[18] This is what came of confusing matter with things, mechanism with values, metaphors with laws of nature, and capital letters with personal powers.

But the gloom of some and the easy self-satisfaction of others were rendered negligible by the growing sense of esthetic delight in science. Its powers of prophecy, the virtue and modesty behind its "quiet and patient" work, the awe which its great practitioners inspired—"cold as ice, mighty as the Peak of Teneriffe"—left no real room for cavil. Yes, human pride could rejoice in the Darwinism that had at first threatened to abase it. Indeed, at each step in the progress of science, the first impression has been that man was degraded by its results. In the seventeenth century it was the removal of the earth from the center of the universe by Copernicus and Galileo. In the eighteenth century, the contemplation of distant worlds, which made our solar system seem insignificant, and the first hint that man was but an animal. In the nineteenth century, it was evolution, reducing man to aboriginal slime. Each time the idea seemed bound to crush man's self-conceit. Each time he rose above it and turned it to the ends of self-complacency—only to discover at last the old anthropomorphic self lurking behind each formula:

> For not to think of what I needs must feel
>   But to be still and patient, all I can;
> And haply by abstruse research to steal
>   From my own nature all the natural man—
>   This was my sole resource, my only plan:
> Till that which suits a part infects the whole
> And now is almost grown the habit of my soul.

[18] Correspondence in the *Manchester Guardian*, Nov.–Dec. 1937, quoted in Stebbing, *Thinking to Some Purpose*, 192–93.

II

The Social Revolution

This has been a century of vile bourgeoisie.

DUC DE SAINT-SIMON, 1715

1. 1859: The Critique of Political Economy

> In reality, it is impossible that commodities so widely different should be commensurable, but it is sufficiently possible to measure them with reference to wants.
>
> ARISTOTLE

> Labor, therefore, is the real measure of the exchangeable value of all commodities.
>
> ADAM SMITH

The second half of the nineteenth century unquestionably had every reason to recognize itself in the scenes painted by its Darwinian leaders. After the Quakerlike habits of the earlier period, the war drums suddenly (it seemed) struck up the beginning of what was to be a gigantic crescendo. First it was the new French dictator, Louis Napoleon, "the nephew of my uncle," who would certainly invade England with balloons, as the uncle had failed to do. Then the Russian Bear and the Sick Man of Europe fell out, and the Crimean War ensued, with the Charge of the Light Brigade as its sole compensation. In the heart of Europe, revolution was still alive. The failure of the German Assembly to make a nation, revolt in the Austrian Empire and in Italy, violence in Ireland, were symptoms of the European malaise. An infinity of cures were proposed, as before, but they now had a common factor: the use of force. For class, for nation, or for race, the war was on.

In the form of punitive repression war drove thousands, famous or obscure, to the distant haven, America—Carl Schurz, Kossuth, Francis Lieber—mingling with the many victims of Ireland's plight. Barring a few exceptions those who came here came to put Europe and its troubles behind them. For the agitators, exiles, and conspirators who still wished to take part in the making of European history, the place of refuge was England. Mazzini lived there, Kossuth and Garibaldi passed through and were acclaimed. Bakunin and Herzen—opposite symbols of Russian unrest—came and went, together with a sampling of Europe—Italians, Poles, Hungarians, Frenchmen—as little unified as their parent lands, for London was a cesspool and not a melting pot.

Into it came Karl Marx in 1849, escaping from Belgium and expecting to stay for a few weeks only, perhaps a few months. He remained in fact until his death in 1883. At first he was very much alone. The concentrated intellectual bustle of Paris had no counterpart in London. His coadjutor Engels was in Manchester, earning their living. A few, a very few, German exiles, like the poet Freiligrath and the docile Liebknecht, formed Marx's chief society, and in this new solitude Marx collected his thoughts.

It was a slow and laborious readjustment. He was poor, he was ill, he was depressed. He earned a few dollars by contributing articles on European affairs to Charles Augustus Dana's *New York Tribune*, a radical newspaper founded by American disciples of Fourier; he published a couple of topical pamphlets. But he and Engels had only one thought—when would the revolution come? Soon, or only after a slow heaping up of kindling? Hopeful answers alternated with gloomy ones. They rose or fell with the events of the day or the moods born of historical reading. Marx came to the conclusion that revolution followed economic crises. The slump of 1847 had brought on the uprisings of '48. Prosperity in 1851 had again set afloat the eternal ancient regime. A new depression came in 1857, but nothing happened except aggravated rumblings of Italian nationalism. Believing that these patriots' sentiments were illusory, and also despairing of a revolution tied like a kite's tail to the next business slump, Marx delved deeper into history and economics: they must be made to yield another, inescapable formula of prediction. In 1859, ten years after his arrival in London, he published the first part of that formula in the now famous *Critique of Political Economy*.

The Preface is dated January 1859: the *Origin of Species* was still ten months away. But the atmosphere surrounding the birth of both books was appropriate. The common thought was of the doings of the French Emperor, who in his New Year's greeting to his Austrian "cousin" had again alarmed Europe. The contrived ambiguity of Louis Napoleon's message was but the prelude to a little war which he and Cavour had planned to free northern Italy. Austria was made to appear the aggressor, the arbitration of a European congress was prevented, and the French armies invaded Lombardy with a sense that Napoleonic history was repeating itself.

Clearly the nationalism that Marx disbelieved in was justifying itself by works. But it held another lesson which was not lost on Marx—the lesson of "realism" which he and his generation first learned in despair, then taught in hopefulness. Napoleon III might be an idealist and Cavour at heart a liberal, yet their ways bore a new trade-mark. The monarchical policy of "principles" was dead. Divine right had descended to "the people" and in the form of nationalism was legitimizing the assertion of competitive wants and the virtue of cynicism. True, there was nothing new in the method, especially on Italian soil. But when the practice became the rule, and the rule was preached as a moral duty sanctioned by science—that was something new. It wanted a name and the period that was opening provided a choice of names: *Realpolitik*, the Survival of the Fittest, the Materialistic Evolution of History by Group Struggle.

It is for this historical materialism and for the authorship of *Das Kapital* that Marx is chiefly known. But it so happens that of the famous doctrine the famous book contains not an explicit word.[1] The theory must be pieced together from various passages, notably in the *Communist Manifesto* of 1848 and the Preface to the *Critique* of 1859.

As with Darwin's *Origin of Species,* Marx's *Critique* starts with autobiography. The author tells us that his first professional studies were in the law, but that he always gave precedence to his interest in philosophy and history. He traces back to 1844[2] his view that it is to political economy that we must turn in order to find the "anatomy of society." The familiar biological comparison is pursued: political economy is the skeleton of the social organism. If we wish to understand how the latter moves, we must first grasp how the former is put together. Further study led Marx to develop this view into a general theory of history which he and Engels applied, without referring to it as materialistic, in the *Manifesto* of 1848. In 1859 comes the explicit statement:

I was led by my studies to the conclusion that legal relations and the forms of the state could neither be understood by themselves nor be explained by what was called the general progress of the human mind, but were rooted in the material conditions of life. . . . Men, in the social production which they carry on, enter into definite relations which are indispensable and independent of their wills; and these relations correspond to a definite stage in the development of their material powers of production. The sum total of these relations of production constitutes the economic structure of society—the real foundation on which rise legal and political superstructures, and to which definite forms of social consciousness correspond.[3]

[1] Except in the Preface to the second edition of 1873.

[2] In *The German Ideology*—another parallel with Darwin, who wrote his first sketch on Natural Selection in 1844.

[3] French edition, iv–v.

Whole books have been written about this earnest paragraph in order to decide both what it states and what it implies. Obviously, it raises the question which has already crossed our path—of materialism and causation in society—and as a scientific and philosophical question it is of course older than Marx. What concerns us here is its form and its appearance in his work, at the precise moment when the century "gave up" Romanticism and Vitalism in favor of materialism and *Realpolitik.*

For Marx's theory of history is above all a theory of things, a distinction between the "real" base and the superstructure of appearance. Perhaps his specialization in the law heightened his sense of the unreality of the superstructure, since law is concerned with economic matters and its principles are embroidery upon interests. But Marx enlarges this insight into a general proposition: the way in which men earn their livelihood is fundamental to everything else. Political and legal conventions are reared upon it, and upon these all the rest of men's actions and ideas: "The method of production in material life determines the general character of the social, political, and spiritual processes of life. . . . It is not the consciousness of men that determines their being, but, on the contrary, their social being determines their consciousness. In the first view, one proceeds from the consciousness as the living individual; in the second, which conforms to real life, one proceeds from the really living individuals themselves and regards consciousness only as *their* consciousness."[4]

The mechanism is simple. From the socially established way in which man bakes bread or cobbles shoes, his conscious activity, however complex, could be explained. But Marx is less concerned with the individual than with the group—the class—and *its* mind is surely explicable by its material occupations. This genetic relation, moreover, has been true throughout history. Hence it is the clue to con-

[4] *Ibid.* and *The German Ideology,* excerpt in Marx, *Selected Writings,* Modern Library, 10.

temporary society and its future. There is a concreteness, a realism, about this view, which holds out a guarantee that we shall not get lost in the mists of fancy. It promises us hard facts and no nonsense. Marx never misses a chance of scoffing at the emptiness of "ideas." He repeatedly uses two words to make us feel his scorn: one is phantasmagoria, the other is ideology. Phantasmagorias are of course what goes on in people's minds about the basic material reality; the second term I need not define: how could we in the twentieth century dispute one another's phantasmagorias without that loaded word "ideology"? So many have capitulated to Marx's dogma that economic facts produce ideas, and have learned to accept, from him or others, the corollary of determinism. Men are not free agents; they "contract certain relations independently of their will"; and this is true for Marx not only when men feel compulsion, but also when they think they are acting from choice—voting for their candidate, believing in their creed, or living in their own way.

Taking this for granted, Marx can plausibly claim for his theory the title "scientific," for, as we saw, the contemporary scientist made the same assumptions. As he reduced the many-sided appearances to material motions, so did Marx reduce thought and action to material facts. Marx's example, drawn from the history of revolutions, shows the method: "When one studies these cataclysms, one must always distinguish between the material disturbances which upset the economic conditions of production and which can be measured with scientific exactness, and the revolution which upsets the legal, political, religious, artistic or philosophic forms—in a word the ideological forms—which serve man to become conscious of the conflict and to explain it. If it is impossible to judge a man from the idea he has of himself, one cannot judge such an epoch of revolution from the idea it has of itself."[5]

In an age of evolutionary faith, Marx could make a fur-

[5] *Critique*, v–vi.

ther claim to scientific precision. He could show that as he conceived it, history was the record of a measurable evolution, a clear progress: "A social state never dies before there has been fully developed within it the sum of all the productive forces that it contains. New relations in production, superior to the former ones, never come into being before their material reason for existence has developed in the womb of the old society. Humanity puts to itself only the riddles that it can solve, for on looking closely at the matter, one will find that the riddle is put only when the material conditions of its solution already exist, or are at least on the way to being born. As a general thesis one can consider the Asiatic, ancient, feudal, and bourgeois modes of production as the progressive steps of the economic formation of society. And the relations of bourgeois production constitute the last form of the productive process to be based on antagonism. . . . This antagonism will be resolved by the productive forces developing in the womb of bourgeois society, so that with this society ends the prehistoric period of all human society."[6]

One hears in this echoes of Hegel, Saint-Simon, and Comte. But Marx went one step further. He relied on the method of political economy, the only branch of social study which had as yet been accorded the name of science. It was the Dismal Science, to be sure, but perhaps all the more scientific on that account. Its flaws Marx meant to remove by this very *Critique* of 1859. In what, then, did it consist? Marx has told us that economics is the skeleton of society. But the economic ways of a society are not such simple and visible phenomena as they sound, and their cultural superstructure is an uncertain clue. The fact that the Greeks wore tunics and the mid-Victorians top hats does not at once disclose the ideologies of the two social groups, any more than it enables us to differentiate between the ancient and the bourgeois modes of production. It is the task of political economy to discover amid the welter of

6 *Ibid.*, vi–vii.

tangible facts the true elements of each stage of production. It must define them and find their laws. That is how we come to speak of Capital, Interest, Rent, and so on, which are not simple matters like bread and shoes, but abstract ideas referring to these matters. This is only another way of saying that scientific objects are not identical with physical objects, matter not the same as things.

We should expect, then, that Marx's *Critique of Political Economy,* though it starts with materialistic history, would deal with objects of common sense only for the sake of establishing certain abstractions. This is what we find. The book is chiefly concerned with one abstraction, that of Value; and since Marx's theory of value, first expounded in the *Critique,* is the starting point of *Das Kapital,* we may as well examine it in its later embodiment.[7]

About the Marxian value theory there has been unceasing and acrimonious debate. Economists have condemned it on economic grounds and philosophers on philosophical. Socialists have justified it on practical grounds, and some of them, who were both economists and philosophers, have interpreted it as a significant and necessary fiction. Whichever it be, as the cornerstone of Marx's whole "scientific" interpretation of society its tone and bearing are significant. I say tone and bearing because though it is possible and necessary to show how Marx was wrong, it is even more instructive to see why he felt he was right. In the economic science of his day he found many hints of the truth he sought but no correct system of value. This was due, according to him, either to the prevailing bourgeois ideology of those he called "vulgar economists" or, in the first-rate men, to the want of sufficient genius. Not sharing that ideology and not feeling this want, Marx pondered the problem until he had discovered, as he said, the solution to the riddle of the Sphinx.

[7] The *Critique* promises *Das Kapital* as a sequel, and *Das Kapital,* with one overlapping chapter, has *Critique of Political Economy* as its subtitle.

In ordinary speech the word "value" is applied to those things which in one way or another fill men's needs. We call these things goods or commodities, and the words themselves suggest what is good or commodious to somebody for some purpose. The worth or value of a commodity to the user is consequently called value-in-use. But this form of value is on the face of it difficult to assess or compare: is my use of a piano of greater value to me than your use of an automobile is to you? Or if I own both, which is of greater value to me? Though puzzled by this question, we soon notice that things difficult to compare are nevertheless exchangeable. We say that a piano and a certain make of car are both worth $2000, and anyone who has that sum can buy either. In the absence of money they could be bartered, which confers upon them a value different from value in use, namely value-in-exchange. Desiring as Marx did some uniform content of commodities which he could measure, he sought it in the analysis of value-in-exchange. If a pound of cheese has the same value in exchange as a dozen eggs (he argues) there must be some third thing which both the eggs and the cheese have in common and in equal amounts. Otherwise the exchange would be impossible. Marx cannot conceive an equation between eggs and cheese unless they both embody equal quantities of some other thing, which all exchangeable things likewise possess. "Each of them, insofar as it is exchange value, must be reducible to the third."

We see here the aspiring scientist at work. He has purposely disregarded the external qualities of things which make them of particular use and which are not reducible to a common denominator. Any given human being may loathe cheese or be allergic to eggs—their uses may have no value, but the power of exchange still resides in them. Marx abstracts this inner something, which will be the same whether we deal in eggs or pianos, and which will differ only in quantity. Quantity implies the ability to be measured, and measuring is the scientific aim par excellence. Marx's Value is thus at bottom identical with the Matter of the physicist—an absolute, homogeneous, measurable abstraction, which is imagined as lying beneath the surface qualities of things.

But on the market there is no way of manipulating goods to strip them of these surface qualities. How then can we reach the substance of value underneath? To answer this Marx asks himself what is indeed common to all values in exchange, and like a number of economists before him, he answers, labor.[8] Marx's difficulty is removed one step. He must now measure labor embodied in goods. We shall see later what is deceptive about these two ideas: one, that labor is the source of value; and the other, that value in exchange is the only measurable abstraction that can be made from objects of use. For the moment it is evident why labor is the true answer for Marx. He borrows it from the established "science" of Ricardo, and moreover, labor is a fact of common experience; it seems to give the abstraction of value a solid base in human brawn and sweat. To a prophet of the proletarian revolution a labor theory of value is bound to commend itself as both simple and popular.

But Marx still has to measure labor, a necessity which from this point on compels him to fashion one more abstraction after another. Ordinary labor which the eye can see is of course more vividly related to value-in-use than to abstract value. Labor makes shoes and coats—not value; to be of any use—as we say—labor must possess the concrete power of making one object for one purpose and another for another. It is not the same kind of labor. So Marx bids us assume the existence of an "abstract labor." He himself calls it an "unsubstantial entity, a mere jelly of undifferentiated human labor." All goods have value because this

[8] As Marx points out, Benjamin Franklin had already said that "trade in general being nothing else but the exchange of labor for labor, the value of all things is most justly measured by labor."/ In the century before Franklin, Sir William Petty had sought, much in the same way, a Political Arithmetick based on the laboring day as a unit [Note to the Second Edition.]

abstract labor has been expended upon them, and after being expended it lies within the objects as the component of value. Being labor it can be measured in the obvious way by hours, days, and minutes.

That is, it can be so measured as soon as we are sure that we have got hold of a truly uniform human labor congealed in equal amounts in commodities of equal value. And we cannot be sure of this until we have made one further abstraction, that of averaging all the different conditions of production into a "socially necessary labor time." Unless we do this, we are still in the workaday world where things are irregular, and not in the scientific world of uniform substance. In the workaday world, it is clear that a clumsy or ill-equipped worker will wreck all our calculations. He will put a great deal of labor time into goods that will turn out to have the same value as similar goods made in less time. Or machines may cut labor time in half. Will this machine-made article then embody only half the value of a less efficiently made article of the same kind? To forestall the paradox of more labor time yielding less value, Marx's theory requires the abstract notion of socially necessary labor time.

Thus refining upon the concrete aspects of both labor and goods, Marx felt that he was the first man in 2000 years to establish the true nature of value and consequently the first able to measure it. To reinforce the novelty of his theory, he gives in the *Critique* of 1859 an account of the history of value theories, which he did not republish in *Capital*. In both places, however, Marx's allusions to the work of the physicist and the chemist show that he thought of himself as a kind of Lavoisier or Dalton having just isolated an element and laid the foundation of a new science.

But Marx is all the while thinking of the connection between his abstractions and the materialism of his evolutionary history. Both imply that society is run by things, not men: "The social relations connecting the labor of one private individual (or group) with the labor of another, seem to the producers, not direct social relations between individuals at work, but what they really are: material relations between persons and social relations between things."[9] This obviously fits the earlier universal law of history: "Morals, religion, metaphysics and other ideologies, and the forms of consciousness corresponding to them, here no longer retain a look of independence. They have no history, they have no development, but men in developing their material production and their material intercourse, alter along with this reality of theirs their thoughts and the product of their thoughts."[10]

With the establishment of this view, Marx is sure, "begins the real positive science" which corresponds to "real life." "Phrases about consciousness cease, and real knowledge must take their place." On the "positive science" which measures value, at any rate, rests Marx's belief in the fatal evolution of capitalism. For upon labor value Marx rears the notion of *surplus* value, or that part of the value created by the laborer which is appropriated by the owner of capital. From this appropriation follows the resentment which animates the particular class struggle of capitalist society; while from the competition among capitalists and the laws of capital accumulation follows the concentration of wealth in a few hands, making it ultimately possible for the workers to expropriate the owners in their turn and usher in the communist state.

This chain of propositions will be gone into a little more closely later, for Marx, though holding on to one end of it whenever he wrote, did not exhibit it at full length in any one place. He unfortunately did not live to give the three volumes of *Das Kapital* a thorough revising, and the *Critique* itself ends abruptly on the word "*etc.*"—a symbol of the half dozen years to elapse before its resumption.

Meantime the responses to the *Critique* were few and unimportant. It was not until the Marxian movement had

9 *Capital*, I, Everyman ed., i, 46.
10 *German Ideology, loc. cit.*

gathered momentum about the turn of the century that a second edition and foreign translations were called for. But one early American review in a German-American newspaper did give Marx an opportunity to express himself in characteristic fashion.[11] The reviewer, it appears, was willing to grant the supremacy of material interests in the contemporary world. He was ready to accept Marx's economic interpretation of society. But he thought that the same interpretation would not apply to the Middle Ages under Catholicism, or to ancient Greece and Rome where politics swayed the state. There ideas and faith, not things, seemed to him to have the upper hand. In this criticism, Marx found only the strange supposition that he could be ignorant. He reasserted that the "secret core" of the history of any epoch is economic and he capped it with one of his familiar allusions to Don Quixote: knight errantry is compatible with certain economic forms only, and the Don's ignorance of this certifies his folly.

There can thus be no doubt that in Marx's mind economic interpretation and evolutionary history in distinct stages are synonymous terms. This is important because if we replace ourselves in Marx's London of 1859, before the *Origin of Species* and all the sociologies derived from it, we must ask, is Marx's sociology a new departure? If so why was an obscure American reviewer so ready to accept it; how much sprang from Marx's invention, how much was commonplace; and of these two sorts of contribution, how did Marx come to make a system which has moved the world as powerfully as Darwin's *Origin*? A system, be it added, which exists despite the fact that Marx never wrote it down in systematic form. Never the center of a world furore during his lifetime, never widely read, then or after, how did his hermetic doctrine interspersed among metaphysical analyses of economic ideas reach the public ear? Part of the answer is that his "system," like Darwin's, was borne on a current of pre-existing economic and revolutionary thought.

11 *Capital*, I, Everyman, i, 56–7 n.

2. The So-Called Utopians

> The capitalists will some day become a hated nobility.
>
> BALZAC, 1830

> This question, first of inherited property, and next of all private property, is to be handled in the nineteenth century and made to give its reason why the whole thing should not be abated as a nuisance.
>
> THEODORE PARKER, 1840

Though it simplifies things to speak of "the Marxian analysis of nineteenth-century European capitalist society,"[1] it is altogether misleading to suppose that this analysis was peculiarly Marx's own. Modern writers are inclined to make this mistake because they are accustomed to think that before Marx lived "Romantics," who saw the world through rose-tinted glasses, and in his own day "Victorians," who were "unrealistic" and complacent.

Even from the brief sketch I have given of Marx's views up to 1859, it should be obvious that the premises of his critique are borrowed ones. And I do not mean that he was preceded by the two or three little-known writers like Bray or Hodgkins who are usually mentioned as his "precursors." I mean that, like Darwin, he comes after most of the work has been done by others—by men whose ideas he often used without acknowledgment, or acknowledged condescend-

1 Leonard Woolf, *Barbarians Within and Without*, 1939, 7.

ingly as "petty bourgeois" or "Utopian." Unfortunately, his repetition of these contemptuous terms has made the epithets stick and added to the English language two more question-begging names which we could well do without.

The first arresting fact about the Utopians is that they were practical enough to try putting their ideas to the test of fact. Owing to the greater opportunities offered by a new country, many of these trials were made in the United States. The familiar names of Brook Farm, New Hope, New Harmony, New Enterprise, record these efforts, and the personalities of Hawthorne, Horace Greeley, Ripley, Albert Brisbane, Henry James, Sr., adorn a movement of ideas which continues to live, though in much modified form, in the modern world.[2] Contrary to usual belief, the actual settlements did not all come to an end from incompetence or quarrels or unworkability. Some even grew rich and became the object of their nonsocialized neighbors' envy. In the bulk they not only helped the spread of "practical" movements like trade-unionism and co-operatives, but they contributed a complete "analysis of nineteenth-century capitalist society."

This Utopian analysis itself had three roots—intellectual, social, and economic. By intellectual I mean all the complaints and ridicule which the Romanticist poets and artists heaped upon the bourgeois society of their day. From Byron's speech in the House of Lords on the condition of the hand weavers to Stendhal's dissection of bourgeois greed in *The Red and the Black*, there is hardly a Romanticist—Shelley included—who did not intermingle social criticism with his work. If any one school ever invented the social duty of the artist, and kept its critical eye on the contemporary scene, it is the Romantic group of alleged stargazers.[3] The spur to their social imagination came, of

[2] See the renewed interest in Utopian Socialism expressed by Lancelot Hogben, *Dangerous Thoughts*, 15; George Catlin, *Story of the Political Philosophers*, passim; and, most important, the writings of J. M. Keynes.

[3] For further detail, see below.

course, from the French Revolution. As for the technical studies of nineteenth-century capitalism before Marx, their inspiration goes back on the one hand to the ideas of Rousseau and the Physiocrats, of whom Du Pont de Nemours is the best known in America; and on the other to the doctrine of English political economists like Locke and Adam Smith. To these last two belongs the labor theory of value, made famous by Smith in the year of the Declaration of Independence.

But, it has been argued, all the economists before Marx were really apologists for the *status quo*. Marx alone was critical, and his genius lay not only in making his old teacher Hegel fall upon his feet, but in turning the classical economists upon their heads. This view will not bear scrutiny. Adam Smith was no apologist, but a reformer. Though he advocated what we now contemn as economic freedom, it was freedom from an outworn system, and he tempered his new one by warnings which show how clearly he foresaw the evils of unchecked competition.

After him, Godwin—Shelley's father-in-law—Charles Hall, Bray, Thompson, and Robert Owen, all in the three decades between 1793 and 1825, piled criticism upon criticism of the existing economic order. All of them tended to oppose large-scale industry as destructive of liberty, equality, and property for the craftsman. The moral principle which Marx will take for granted a quarter of a century later, that a man is robbed if he does not receive the full value of his labor, is here not taken for granted at all but demonstrated by example and reasoning, from explicit political principles.

Owen, the most famous of this group, was moreover a philosophical materialist and an active Utopian,[4] whose

[4] When only twenty-eight he had become resident manager of the New Lanark Mills, and shortly thereafter had introduced and carried out welfare measures of the most advanced kind: decent dwellings, education, sanitation, and high wages—all this at the same time as he paid a 5 per cent dividend to the shareholders. His colony on the banks of the Wabash failed in part through lack of his supervision.

successful management of both business and social welfare gave him great opportunities to advertise his methods and aims. Pleading for a *New View of Society* two years before Waterloo, he advocated first of all a patient investigation into the facts of social organization and human behavior. In this he is somewhat of a mechanist: man's character is "without a single exception, always formed for him"; so that at first sight one might take Owen for a pure proto-Marxian. But he perceived that environment included tradition and education, which made him hopeful of training a new generation to co-operative ways.

This feature distinguishing him from Marx's thorough-going mechanism is also dominant in the work of the French Utopians, Fourier and Saint-Simon. Although Fourier erred in giving his ideas too systematic and symmetrical a form—another eighteenth-century survival—he never forgot the important fact that in any improved society, man must work in harmony not only with his fellows but with himself. As a young man, Fourier had conceived a deadly hatred of commercial practices, built as they were on pinchpenny greed and duplicity, and he saw that so long as work, or the conditions of work, remained repulsive to the individual, it was idle to speak of a better world. His particular scheme, proposed to Napoleon in 1808, was no doubt ill-adapted to a society that wanted to become super-commercial and industrial. But in its recognition of the need for individual acquiescence in labor through association, the Fourierist principle rested on a recognition of man's emotional life—a human fact which had no place in "scientific socialism" and which was hardly reasserted until Freud.[5]

To understand the Utopians' insistence on co-operation rather than force, it may help to recall that the men of the Romantic period were rather more familiar with force and its effects than their successors. Having seen it at work during the revolution and under Napoleon, they had measured

[5] *Civilization and its Discontents*, and *New Introductory Lectures*, 96.

its shortcomings, whereas the *Realpolitiker* of the fifties, and notably Marx, could only form exaggerated estimates of its constructive power from the much briefer outbreaks of 1830 and 1848. The rhapsodic state of pleasure into which the Dresden affray sent Richard Wagner[6] is as indicative as Marx's own polemical thirst for blood.[7]

But the fact that the Utopians generally favored harmony does not mean that they overlooked the "class struggle." They knew it existed and, in fact, were exercising their brains to get rid of it. Its discovery, or rather the discovery that in society economic interests conflict, is probably as old as Thucydides. It is certainly as old as Voltaire.[8] The French Revolutionists and the Fathers of the American Constitution referred to it, and even interpreted political divisions by its means—witness the *Federalist Papers*; but none of them thought of such struggles as a principle of progress. So that we must distinguish here, as in Darwinism, between two things that bear the same names: Natural Selection is a well-known *fact*; so is class conflict; but neither can form the basis of a theory—that is to say, neither can turn into a cause of progress. But the problem of every Utopia—Marx's included—is a problem of evolution, consequently a problem of history, which accounts for the transformation of the *facts* of class struggle into a theory of evolution by means of it, and justified by historical research.

Marx, moreover, came to sociology from the study of Hegel—an evolutionary historian, as we know—and he absorbed with the socialistic ideas of the Utopians the theories of race then dominant in French history. Now, in the

[6] See below.

[7] Of all the Paris agitators in the forties, Marx preferred Blanqui, the only apostle of violence.

[8] "It is impossible on our unhappy globe, that men living in society should not be divided into two classes, one of oppressors, the others of oppressed; and these two are subdivided into a thousand and that thousand contains still further shades of difference." *Philosophical Dictionary*, art. "Equality" (1764).

works of men like Guizot, Thierry, and Carrel, it is impossible to distinguish between race and class. To them modern history is explained by a long struggle between "races" dating back to the barbarian invasions of the Roman Empire in the fifth century A.D. In these historians the French Revolution is a conflict between "two peoples on one soil,"[9] and they think of the Third Estate, that is the bourgeoisie, as a conquered race slowly regaining its independence in the modern state. This race-class theory, curiously enough, was originally a conservative and aristocratic dogma. In eighteenth-century France, Count de Boulainvilliers and Montesquieu himself had used it rather to help bring back a former state of things than to promote novelties; but their successors, finding that going back is itself a form of novelty, did not hesitate to make it into a doctrine of progress.

How much Marx knew about this prolonged controversy it is impossible to say, though it had long been common property. It is moreover acknowledged that the reading of Guizot suggested to Marx this same motive power for historical evolution. So that by the time Marx came to Paris at the age of twenty-five he found ready to his hand an historical-genetic conception of class and a many-sided practical interest in social reform. For at least fifteen years the term "socialism" had signified a radical criticism of the existing order, and the purely political movement was even older. It had been associated in the public mind with the names of Babeuf, Fourier, Saint-Simon, Proudhon, Blanqui, Considérant, and even Comte. The doctrines had been religious, atheistical,[10] agrarian, industrial,[11] co-operative,

[9] Marx, commenting on the June Days of 1848, spoke of the French as being divided into "two nations." He attached no racial significance to the term but doubtless derived it from Sieyès, who probably did. Karl Marx, a Symposium, ed. Ryazanov, London, 1927, 63.

[10] Blanqui's motto was Ni Dieu ni Maître; Weitling, the German agitator whom Marx met and snubbed, was an atheist.

[11] Saint-Simon's scheme was a sort of Christian technocratic dictatorship.

anarchical,[12] and communistic.[13] What could make it "scientific"? Clearly, the grounding of the best of these ideas on the science of political economy.

Here again, most of the critical work had been done. Three writers among those whom Marx read had systematized the new facts of capitalist industry and their sociological effects: the Englishman Malthus, the German Rodbertus, and the Swiss Sismondi. A fourth might be added, namely Proudhon, but owing to Marx's personal attitude toward him, it will be better to deal with him later as an antagonist.

In many ways the economist Sismondi bears to Marx the same relation that Lamarck bears to Darwin. He stands in the background, receiving mention, when lucky, as the walker-on before the king. Obviously Sismondi is no Marxist, as Lamarck is no Darwinist. But the important thing is not to show that the image of the master appeared before the master himself. For all we know they may both be masters. The important thing is to show that a critique of political economy was in print when Marx was in his cradle and when the facts were harder to discern; so that if there is talk of originality, Sismondi, who was the first to make the breach, must be allowed the first claim.

Sismondi's economic ideas—for he was also a voluminous historian—appeared between 1803 and 1836, in half a dozen lucid volumes dealing with every aspect of capitalist society. For this reason, to summarize his work in a few lines is impossible. I can only enumerate certain of its salient features. Sismondi, it may be noted in passing, was the first to use the term "proletariat" to describe the increasing population of urban workmen. He also coined the term *mieux-value*, which really includes all that is defensible in Marx's *Mehrwert*, or surplus value, as a means of analyzing and explaining the industrial exploitation of the

[12] Bakunin's influence on Marx was real but is difficult to trace.
[13] The "materialistic communists" condemned in Paris in 1847 were advocates of violence and "direct action" but had no clearly defined doctrines.

worker. But he was not misled by any labor theory into thinking that only proletarians produce value. He could see that value is not simply embodied labor, but also a function of human wants, of supply and demand as well as the processes of social consumption; and in none of these guises is it measurable.

Always arguing against the abstractions of the classical school, Sismondi repudiates all notions of automatic progress. He belabors the economists for supposing that if only production can be speeded up the nation will grow endlessly rich. He was so well aware of the class division brought about by the exploitation and expropriation of the proletariat that he urged the political economists to investigate remedies. In his own words, "every man of the privileged class can count against him five individuals, not belonging to the privileged class, and between the two there is such an opposition that the rich can say to the poor, 'Our life is your death,' and the poor reply to them, 'Your death would be our life.'"[14] This is vivid enough for any firebrand.

But Sismondi is not content to stop at observation. To him as to J. S. Mill later, economic science is one thing, political economy is another. As a science, economics should establish facts and their laws; but the political economist is not to fall down and worship these abstractions as immutable. He must use this knowledge for human ends; consequently Sismondi urged what has since been called labor legislation, and he did it at a time when it was considered reactionary, unscientific, and immoral. It is here that Marx parts company with him, for Marx is with the strictest of the classical writers; Marx is, paradoxically, an apostle of *laissez faire*:[15] he has deduced the march of history, and trusting that history, too, has a sense of justice,

[14] *Études sur l'Economie Politique*, Paris, 1836, 2 vols., i, 337.
[15] In Marx, the list of measures by which the proletariat will "wrest by degrees all capital from the bourgeoisie" remains an isolated and self-contradicting proposal, at variance with the rest of the system. *Communist Manifesto*, Section II.

he is prepared to await the inevitable change for the better. All consideration of economics apart, who then is the naïve sociologist, Marx or Sismondi?

Besides his critique of political economy, Sismondi offers a method and a theory. His method is historical and tends always towards the concrete: "I am convinced," he says, "that one falls into serious error in wishing always to generalize everything connected with the social sciences. It is on the contrary essential to study human conditions in detail. One must get hold now of a period, now of a country, now of a profession, in order to see clearly what a man is and how institutions act upon him."[16] Hence he was able to read the danger signs when these were few and slight. The first to state the fact of "overproduction," he seemed to the men of 1830 an alarmist or a madman. Since he came from Protestant Geneva he was accused of being puritanical and of saying that man could have too many good things, whereas what he said, because he saw it, was the now familiar paradox of "starvation in the midst of plenty." Bringing fact under the light of theory and denying that goods as such meant welfare, he advocated the study of new ways of distribution; he combated the new dogma of unlimited competition and the old fallacy of "private selfishness leads to public good"; he urged the need of forestalling crises (which embitter life for the capitalist as well as for the worker), of studying the control of banking and credit, and of averting nationalistic wars resulting from the competition for markets.

Sismondi was clearly a socialist, but having little regard for automatic schemes and a high regard for individuals, he feared an overriding state capitalism equally with any proposed dictatorship of a class.

No more than Sismondi did the Reverend Thomas Malthus believe that economics is an exact science. It can "never admit of the same kind of proof, or lead to the same certain conclusions as those which relate to figure and num-

[16] *Op. cit.*, i, p. iv.

ber."[17] And yet his spirit of fatalism, his faith in the working of unchangeable laws, his pre-Darwinian views on population and food supply, and above all his repeated attempts—the first in England—to show that the contradictions of capitalist production were inherent in the "system,"[18] make him perhaps the most subtle influence among those that Marx absorbed from the classical school. Marx, of course, opposes the Malthusian view of an eternal necessity regulating the fate of the poor, and he speaks contemptuously of "medieval ideas" being applied to nineteenth-century economy. But apart from our knowledge of Marx's hopes for the working class, it is hard to see wherein his own system repudiates the same absolute necessity governing the poor. Granted that the two differ in their final outcome, that difference is only the difference between an eighteenth-century rationalist in his static world, and a nineteenth-century evolutionist in his progressive world, both worlds mechanical.

The well-known objection to almsgiving as making things worse is implied equally by both, and is certainly a familiar note in the Marxian literature of revolution-through-desperate-want. Nor is Malthus altogether as soulless as he has been represented. He hopes that the absence of "systematic and certain" poor relief and the spread of birth control[19] may in time alleviate the lot of the poor; Marx hopes that the steadily aggravating plight of capitalism will destroy it and in time alleviate the lot of the poor; which means that both prefer to face present suffering rather than imperil the "laws of economy" by social legislation.

Malthus, it so happens, did not avoid the pitfalls of the labor theory of value which Sismondi had sidestepped. Like Adam Smith and Marx's contemporary, Rodbertus, he got caught in its contradictions only to be refuted by De

[17] *Principles of Political Economy,* 1820, 1.
[18] *Ibid.,* 462 ff. At odds with his own theory of population, Malthus wished for a large idle class to take up surplus products and prevent crises.
[19] By education and moral restraint.

Quincey.[20] Labor is *not* the measure of value for the simple reason that there are valuable things which embody no labor, or which embody very little compared to their value. As one critic put it, "Pearls are not valuable because men dive for them, men dive for them because pearls are valuable." Hence labor expended can be no measure of value. It is noteworthy, however, that the desire to give the laborer his due generally leads to this as a favorite fallacy.

Rodbertus[21]—another evolutionary historian—was convinced as early as 1831 that the distribution of goods in the state was a matter of arrangement and not of natural laws. Therefore the laboring class was exploited: they were making things of which they only received a minor share. The proof of it and the remedy lay in showing that value was made and measured by labor. His proposal, like Marx's, required that we should discover the goal of historical development, but Rodbertus would have us prepare it by the exercise of our free will. To emerge from the present state, in which possession is lodged in one class and work in another, the state must control production, money must be abolished (in favor of value vouchers representing a "normal" workday), and science must be applied to all the problems of industry.

It may now be easier to see whence and why Marx deliberately adopted a value theory which was not of his own making, which had been repeatedly disproved, which Sismondi had avoided by showing that value had more than one aspect, and which consequently could only be supposed to serve as a scientific base by a man who was a priori unwilling to meet the patent objections to it.

There are, to be sure, good psychological reasons why

[20] Another "Romantic" with a logical head. See his articles on Political Economy, *passim.*

[21] Born 1805, died 1875, one of the first of German "national economists." His practical work in agrarian Prussia was destroyed by the revolution of 1848. His main theoretical writings appeared between 1842 and 1852, and were summarized in 1885 as *Das Kapital.*

Marx was drawn to such a theory, and even a curious kind of observational truth in it. In the factory system, the undifferentiated labor jelly corresponds very vividly to the extinction of human personality; and with his bias in favor of straight-line evolution, Marx assumed that industrial enterprise would grow ever larger and dwarf man in proportion. What he did not see was that no matter how far industrialization went, it could not change or get rid of the basic relation between man and the goods of life—that value, namely, is a price we set upon things when they satisfy our wants, and that it cannot be reduced to any common measure.

Beneath all this theorizing and scheming of the Romantic period, there lies in addition the great insight of Rousseau and the Revolutionists that in a good society men must be equal. It is not a matter of measuring aptitudes or merit. Equality is a social goal. In the essay upon the *Origins of Inequality* (1755) Rousseau said in detail what every subsequent reformer has implied, even while denying it.[22] Marx himself was far from denying it. Still speaking of value, he affirmed: "The riddle of the expression of value is solved when we know that all labor, insofar as it is generalized human labor, is of like kind and equal worth; but this riddle can only be unriddled when the notion of human equality has acquired the fixity of a popular conviction."[23]

For such a conviction to become popular, it must be iterated and reiterated in every guise and every context. This was the work of a generation that was particularly rich in prophets and reformers, criers down of one or another inequality, even when they were not advocates of its thoroughgoing opposite: Chartists, Christian socialists, so-

[22] In any reading of Rousseau, E. H. Wright's little volume, *The Meaning of Rousseau*, is indispensable. Not that Rousseau is not clear but that commentators have created in our minds a pseudo-Rousseau who generally obscures the original text.

[23] *Capital*, I, Everyman, i, 31.

cial novelists, historians of liberty and revolution, and moralists, individualists, anarchists—to draw up the roster is as unnecessary as it is impossible. It is enough to remember a few names who will suggest the rest. Saint-Simon's should lead, if only because he was so clearly thinking of equality in entitling his last work *The New Christianity*.[24] His lasting influence, particularly in England, helped wake Carlyle and Mill from their rationalist slumbers and made them propagators of the faith. *Sartor Resartus* was one result, which should help us to remember, in spite of all that can be said against the later Carlyle's desperate "realism," that he was the first who called the British entrepreneur a Choctaw and who denounced the mounting tide of poverty, disease, squalor, and vice, in words which make Marx's sneers look boyish in comparison.

Carlyle and the Chartists were not on good terms, but they both carried on an intense propaganda opening men's eyes to what was around them. Between 1830 and 1859 there is scarcely a single writer in England who does not in some way take account of the same Carlylean complaint. We are no longer in the realm of abstract political economy but of day-to-day politics. The panaceas proposed may seem foolish to our hindsight but the disquiet was general and profound. Far from being limited to so-called agitators, it goes right through society: Mill, the Comtists, Martineau, the Saint-Simonians, Sadler, Shaftesbury, Mazzini, Spencer,[25] Lewes and his *Leader*, Maurice, Reade, Kingsley, Dickens, Disraeli—Disraeli who found in the Parliamentary Blue Books, before Marx, the matter for a work about the unbridgeable gulf between rich and poor. He made it into a novel and called it *Sybil: or the Two Nations*, and we are not surprised that in a man for whom race had ever a mystical appeal, the notion of class conflict

[24] Published in 1825. Saint-Simon's desire for an executive composed of scientists and industrialists intended them to act benevolently for the good of the rest.

[25] Spencer began as a nationalizer of land on the plea that property is theft.

should seem equally fateful.[26] *Sybil* appeared in 1845. It was in that same year that Marx read his new friend Engels's small book *The Condition of the Working Classes in England in 1844.*

Inspired by both Carlyle and Chartism, its solid mass of facts helped, with other circumstances, to turn the current of Marx's life into new channels. So far he had been concerned with the philosophy of social evolution, with materialism, and with the Utopian critiques of the existing order. He had argued all night with Proudhon in Paris and despaired of making a Hegelian of him. But Marx's period of preparation by discussion was drawing to a close. Exiled to Brussels, he indited a book against Proudhon—*The Poverty of Philosophy*; returned to Paris, he and Engels summed up their disapproving views of current socialist doctrines in a call to action—the *Communist Manifesto*; forced to leave once again, Marx now turned his steps to England, where with English facts drawn from the famous Blue Books, he would establish the scientific theory of capitalist exploitation.

[26] He ends on the note: "The claims of the Future are represented by suffering millions."

3. How the System Works

> Many sweating, ploughing, threshing, and then the
> chaff for payment receiving.
> A few idly owning, and they the wheat continually
> claiming.
>
> WALT WHITMAN

The whole point of contrasting "scientific" socialism with
Utopian is that, whereas the latter is a plan depending on
the good will of men to carry out, the former represents
the inevitable course of history. The economic base having
been made measurable through the labor theory of value,
Marx now explains through the related theory of surplus
value how exploitation occurs under capitalism. Whereas
Sismondi makes *Mieux-value* stand for what is now called
the undistributed increment of association,[1] Marx makes
Mehrwert fit his initial labor theory with deceptive mathematical exactness. He asks himself, Granting that in the
market all values exchange at the correct ratio—that is,
equal amounts of labor embodied in different goods—how
is it that capitalist profit is possible? Or in other words,
how do the rich, paying for things at their correct value,
get richer while the poor stay poor? That is the riddle

[1] I.e., the "surplus" which comes from the fact that a hundred
men working together create more than they would if each
worked independently at the same trade. This surplus is what **is**
appropriated through ownership.

capitalism propounds. Marx's answer is that whereas a capitalist exchanges the correct value for all his raw materials, machinery, and so forth, when he comes to paying wages to his workers a special situation arises. Under competitive conditions, as classical economy had shown, the worker gets paid at the rate that will maintain him and his family and no more. The excessive supply of laborers drives their wages down to the lowest level compatible with life. (This is the other side of Malthus's proposition that population presses to the limits of subsistence.) The worker gets the equivalent of what he needs to repair his tissue, shelter himself, and maintain his family at the bare minimum that he can stand. Now the equivalent of that minimum, according to Marx, it does not take the worker very long to produce. The first few hours of his working day suffice. Supposing he earns a dollar a day, and that his labor adds a value of twenty cents an hour to the materials he works upon, then at the end of five hours he has earned his keep. But in his bargain with his employer he agreed to work a full working day of, let us say, twelve hours, which means that in the last seven hours of each day, the worker creates a dollar and forty cents' worth of value which the employer pockets. The amount is the surplus value due to the unique nature of human labor power. When a capitalist buys raw materials he gets no more than he pays for, but when he hires a man, he gets the use of a surplus of labor time capable of creating value over and above the actual cost of feeding and clothing its provider. Surplus labor time creates surplus value.

This plausible explanation has been refuted many times. It might have been done sooner and more effectively if Marx had not taken many pages of intricate and ill-organized metaphysical distinctions to propound it. The distinctions are of course due to Marx's honest desire to correct some of his own difficulties, and when these multiplied under his hand in the third volume of *Capital*, posthumously published from notes left by him, he virtually abandoned his theory.[2] But the amount of these difficulties would have warned a less pedantic and self-willed mind that the theory was very likely based on erroneous premises. True, we find Marx casually giving up the main point of his basic-value theory when he adds the comment that of course the labor which gives us the measure of value must be *useful* labor.[3] Marx pursues surplus value through an intricate study of prices—where we need not follow him— in spite of the relatively simple observation that would refute it. If profits come from surplus value taken from the worker in the last hours of his toil, it should follow that the most profitable enterprises would be those employing the most workers. We find, on the contrary, that labor-*saving* machinery increases profits. A completely mechanized factory—like certain new brickworks employing only one man as watchman—still yields profits, greater profits, in fact, than those earned by hand labor.

Nor is it that mechanization permits the capture of the whole market and so changes the "socially necessary labor time." Suppose the single watchman dismissed, and still these bricks, into which no human labor has directly entered, which certainly no surplus labor time has created, would still have value and bring profits. At bottom the same facts which refute the labor theory of value refute the theory of surplus value. Labor is not the source of value, and profits do not come from the last seven hours of the working day. Which does not at all mean that the workingman necessarily gets his due: the problem is to decide what his due is, and the odd thing is that starting with the Utopians' ideal of giving the laborer the fruit of his labor, Marx is compelled by his theory to substitute an "average" labor time which would work hardships on innumerable workers, and to ultimately abandon individual labor as a measure of what is clearly produced collectively.[4]

[2] *Capital*, 1894, iii, 181.
[3] *Ibid.*, I, i, 44. Shaw has compared this to saying that all liquids are deadly to man and casually adding, "Of course the liquids I speak of are poisons."
[4] Marx's notions of what an average is are rather hazy. He

Nevertheless, as instruments of social agitation, as "scientific" proofs of social injustice, his theories both of value and of surplus value possess unlimited power. So many simple facts seem to support the idea that labor time=value ("things difficult to make cost a lot"), the notion merges so insensibly into the idea that if you hoe a row of carrots you are entitled to eat them, or if you make yourself a chair it is yours by natural right, that one is not surprised at the ultimate success of Marx's notion of a "capitalist system" ever grinding the faces of the poor by direct, outright robbery.

The success of Marxian "science" was of course aided by the labors of those who had the patience to unravel and recast in simpler form his somewhat tangled account of these matters; but this merely broadcast, it did not repair, the flaws in the theory, which was no sooner widely known[5] than shown to be untenable. Certain acute readers like Benedetto Croce, finding that facts contradicted it, concluded that Marx was knowingly describing a world that did not exist in order to cast light on the one that did. But certainly no hint of this was dropped by Marx himself nor by Engels, save once. Marx's scientific analogies, his insistence on the physiological fact of labor, on the reduction of individual labor to its "socially proportional measure," by a "coercive influence like an overriding law of nature," his discovery of the "secret hidden away behind manifest fluctuations in relative values," were taken literally as true descriptions by the political and intellectual socialists of the late nineteenth and early twentieth centuries.

---

speaks of an average value for all commodities, which is the negation of value, and he does not seem to recognize that if there is a "socially necessary labor time" for making any one article, the workmen who cannot meet this "average," for whatever reason, will be penalized instead of getting their true deserts. The Darwinian survival of the fittest seems to be implied here.

[5] Vol. iii of *Capital* was not translated into English until 1894; vol. i had been available since 1886. Vol. iii attempts to answer the paradox of surplus value increasing with the use of machinery, but does so by sacrificing the truth of individual exploitation which is insisted on in vol. i.

Bent on measuring purely material things under all the "appearances" of commercial society, Marx here again slid in as a joker the very element he had tried to exclude. Why is it that a special situation exists with respect to the purchase of labor as a commodity? Why does the laborer allow himself to be exploited? Obviously he has no choice. He is one against many. He competes against his fellows and therefore cannot struggle against his master. This was pointed out *ad nauseam* before Marx, even by the Classical Economists. But this predicament depends wholly on human consciousness: the worker, we say, is free to make a contract or starve. Being a man he will not choose starvation, will not choose it for his family. If he were a commodity, failure to compete successfully would not affect him. Goods that do not sell stay on the shelves quite happily or spoil at leisure. If he were a machine he would simply not function without adequate care and fueling, and it would not have been possible for Manchester to use up three generations of workers in the space of one. As a living thing, labor power *prefers* to make a contract which results in the creation of surplus value; for the characteristic of factory industry is that work can be done only on the employer's premises with his machinery and raw materials, that is to say, on his own terms.

Marx was not blind to this, far from it, but he pushed it into his formula through the back door, the front being inhospitable to the element of human consciousness. Let us, however, follow him in his further analysis of the capitalist system in evolution. The employer, though he has a wider latitude of life than the workman, is also caught in the net of "materialistic relations between persons and social relations between things." He must compete with other employers, he must weather crises, he must face a constantly lowered rate of profit, and he must find new markets.[6] In this many-sided Darwinian struggle, which Marx is at his best in depicting, many entrepreneurs perish. The

[6] Lenin added, He must wage imperialistic wars for their sake.

result is that capitalistic enterprise is more and more concentrated in a few hands. Each enlargement of a business
makes it easier for it to crush competitors; while the shrinking market in relation to production makes crises more frequent and severe. Unemployment grows, and with it greater
unrest and the impossibility of restoring equilibrium. This
goes on until the fully dispossessed proletarians are able, by
concerted onslaught, to recapture their own from their masters and to institute the classless state in which the means
of production are owned in common. Thus does Marx predict the fatal evolution of bourgeois society. First anato-
mized in abstract economic terms, it ends in a revolution
that is to make the whole past Prehistory.

All questions of life and death aside, there is grandeur
in the view. Standing above the inferno one can feel a sort
of Dantesque pleasure in witnessing the downfall of a civilization, a Wagnerian emotion before the Twilight of the
Gods. Coming down again to concrete experience makes us
tell a different tale. In the first place the self-acting process
by which the Marxian drama unrolls is not convincing: how
should the proletariat know when and how to reorganize
the complex industrial world for the benefit of their class?
Why should not the whole structure crash without any
aftermath, leaving all classes, that is to say, all men as individuals, to struggle helter-skelter for the dwindling remains?

The answer is that the Marxian process is almost, but
not quite, automatic. The minds of men are conscious now
and again, and explain to themselves the period of revolution. The further inference is that among such minds Marx
is the only one able to explain the new forms which the
present society holds "in its womb."[7] Marx undertakes to

[7] If he were not the only one, other socialists might be right.
And only he is right, because he is a scientist. As early as 1843 he
wrote, in the name of anti-dogmatism, "We will not [say] . . .
here is truth, kneel down here! We expose new principles to the
world out of the principles of the world itself. . . . We explain

predict on the basis of what he sees happening—the true definition of a prophet as well as the definition of a true prophet—and he proposes to make his prediction come true by arousing the minds of other men—the proletariat—to a sense of their future role. So here is an interaction of mind and matter which jars with the causation from below and which no amount of juggling with words can remove.[8] We cross the inner threshold of the Marxian temple and pass from the strictly materialistic and evolutionary purlieus of history to the inner sanctum where the revelation of class consciousness and class struggle makes right belief essential, intense propaganda imperative, and ruthless political action a moral duty.

These two supplementary ideas—class consciousness and a directed class struggle—are too familiar to require extended treatment. Many accordingly think that Marx's greatness lay in devising the tactics of modern revolution at a time when the best minds had no inkling of the true method. Without a doubt, Lenin and Trotsky were fed on these Marxian ideas and applied them successfully in Russia. But this was no Marxian prediction.[9] No concentration of capital brought about the revolution; on the contrary, the capitalist class of Russia was neither large nor powerful. Marx had predicted the revolution for Germany, where a long course of development had led to the ripe "stage." There, presumably, a class-conscious proletariat, well-led by a Marx-inspired minority and applying the vio-

---

to it only the real object for which it struggles, and consciousness is a thing it must acquire even if it objects to it." Quoted by Bernstein, *Encyc. Brit.*, 14th ed., art. Marx.

[8] E.g., Engels's letter to Mehring, July 14, 1893, about his (Marx's) "failing to stress enough" the "formal side" or the way in which "notions come about." It is not a question of more stress, and certainly not of a "formal side," whatever that may mean. It is a question of making or not making all phenomena derive from ultimate matter as a cause.

[9] True, he said late in life that if Russia had the chance, through internal troubles, of passing directly from a nascent agrarian individualism to communism it should not miss it.

lence needed to make the change permanent, would usher
in the new synthesis—first in the form of a dictatorship,
then as a classless state, finally as complete statelessness or
the perfection of anarchy.

This last stage was so far in the future that we need not
call upon Marx to explain how the political state would disappear. Even the motive must remain obscure, for people
living in the second stage would have no intelligible reason
for changing their classless bliss into a classless-stateless
condition that might conceivably endanger the industrial
basis of the bliss. Perfect anarchy has always been the
dream of some philosophers and it would be the act of a
kill-joy to insist that the way in which the word "anarchy"
has come to mean chaos implies a human prejudice that
may easily cause the thing it fears. It is rather more legitimate and useful to delve into the meaning of the classless
state. Why classless? Two answers are open to Marx: one is
that when the proletariat has seized the means of production the "other" class will be no more. Two minus one
leaves one. This view dates rather from *Capital* than from
the *Critique*, where Marx distinguishes not two but three
classes—capitalists, landowners, and workers. Land of course
is "a means of production," which would have to be seized
too; but the reasons that concentrate capital do not necessarily concentrate land, and the peasants might give trouble
as in fact they did in Russia.

But in this part of his system[10] Marx is really not thinking of his economic and material laws. He has become an
ordinary political writer with a strong moral bias. The
bourgeois liberal state is for him but a committee of the
ruling class, governing solely in their interest and replace-
able only by a working-class dictatorship. All other changes
would be illusory. Which suggests the second answer to the
question why the classless state? Marx desires it because it

[10] Particularly in *The Civil War in France*, 1871, though there
are fragments of the future society in the *Poverty of Philosophy*,
1845, the last chapter of *Capital*, I, and the *Communist Manifesto*.

seems to solve the old problem of how to make private interest coincide with public good. Marx is so sure action springs from class origin that, he thinks when all classes are reduced to one, each person's "natural" desire will contribute to the good of the whole.[11] The permanence of criss-crossing interests as a result of the mere number and diversity of human beings Marx did not contemplate, for opinions, ideas, prejudices, temperaments—these things come under "ideology" and the "crowd of phantasms." A new form of owning the means of production would change all that.

Moreover, the "racial" assumption of "once a worker, always a laborite" seemed to take care of the danger that the dictatorship might turn into a bureaucracy with privileges denied to the workers. The same holds true for the possible reduplication of capitalist tyranny in the new state—where after all there would be only one employer with unlimited power: the descendants of a common proletarian stock would angelically forbear to oppress one another, even after the term "proletarian" had ceased to have any meaning.

To skepticism on these points, the Marxists answer that it is based on a false idea of the unchangeability of human nature. But it is Marx who in this respect is trying to have it both ways. At one and the same time he thinks that existing material conditions will bring about a change in the character of men, and that a new order of production is nevertheless not going to change the original proletarian brotherhood. As in Hegel and Comte and Saint-Simon, evolution goes so far and no further. We may note in passing that while the schooling by which Marx hopes to mold a fighting force consists in hatred and merciless antagonism, these same proletarians are to maintain loyalty, devotion, and sweet comradeship towards one another. Marx, who was better endowed with the first qualities than with the last, doubtless imagined that in ordinary men the two sets

[11] Rousseau, who is so often accused of naïveté, shows why no form of government can rely on this assumption. *Social Contract*, ch. iii.

could go together and be controlled from above for the achieving of the revolution.

This is to put a heavy burden on the conscience and self-awareness of man. But no sooner has class consciousness been brought into being than we are asked to rely once more on automatism. The revolution over, Marx's communist society gets itself established by sheer historic necessity. Communism comes without any special plan, for plan makers are Utopians. Hence Marx contents himself with a pair of formulas: common ownership of the means of production; and, when production has become abundant, from each according to his abilities, to each according to his needs. These two formulas, which may be admirable for party platforms, are in truth little more than riddles. It is impossible to tell whether Marx advocated equal or "equivalent" incomes.[12] But, as he says, society never puts riddles to itself until the material means of answering them are ready. Consequently scientific socialism, starting in measurable values, teaches a consciousness of present injustice, spreads it by propaganda, brings about the final revolution of history and stops on the brink of eternity. The full solution of the riddle is on the other side of the line. No doubt the handwriting on the wall for capitalism is matched by an as yet unknown and more cheerful message for the proletariat on the other side. Prehistoric society has crumbled from its own inner strains, and when these are resolved, the human will has played its five-minute part forever.

Faith in the momentum of history reminds us of Weismann's idea that a new form appears only when the conditions are ripe to let it survive. It is also an echo of the Hegelian trust in the timely appearance of the World Historical Character, but without the character. Perhaps if Marx had allowed himself to think concretely of factories and ships and power plants he might have had doubts about

[12] There are definite suggestions of graduated rewards, and at one time socialists seriously debated whether intellectuals were producers in the Marxian sense.

the ease of the Great Passage. To re-create society upon a new basis requires something more than "social relations between things and material relations between persons." It requires new purposes, new practices, and above all, new habits. To supply the want of this psychological reformation, which would be contrary to his system, Marx had a faith in a special feature of the natural laws, a form which material action always took. I mean the dialectic.

Of recent years much has been heard about this principle which is as old as the Greeks and in some respects as irrefutable as the wetness of water. But it is susceptible of so many interpretations and misuses[13] that it might be well to find another word for the sound core of the idea. The crudest misuse is of course that which endows the dialectic with personality and power, like the dormitive power of opium. Some people speak of *the* dialectic bringing about an event as they might speak of the dumb-waiter bringing up the dinner. Needless to say, the dialectic is originally and inexpugnably an abstraction, a way of conceiving of things. In Hegel it means the process by which concepts or ideas pass into their opposites. Think of "All generalities are false" and you cannot help seeing that it implies "except this one," which denies it. Without wasting more time and words than human business will bear, it is impossible to get rid of constant self-implying contradiction. This insight leads to the belief that truth can only result from a view of two related contradictories.[14] Their relation yields dra-

[13] Though in his *Reason, Democracy and Social Myth* Sidney Hook denies all validity to dialectic, his essay is indispensable to an understanding of the subject. Some readers may feel that if there are seven sorts of dialectic, they would rather do without any.

[14] For Samuel Butler's clear statement of the matter, see *Luck or Cunning?* ch. iii, and also pp. 100, 130, 134, of the *Collected Works*, vol. viii. He says among other things: "When facts . . . melt into one another as the colours of the spectrum, so insensibly that no one can say where one begins and the other ends, contradictions in terms become first fruits of thought and speech. They are the basis of intellectual consciousness, in the same way

matic unity as in a dialogue where we need two persons to make clear one situation.

But contradiction, except to Marx, is not in things. Take that amusing novelette of Voltaire's[15] which begins "Memnon one day conceived the insane idea of becoming wholly reasonable." Armed with this morning resolve, Voltaire's hero sets out. At nightfall he finds that he has lost his money, had his eye put out, got drunk and had his estate distrained upon; yet he has only done throughout what seemed reasonable at the time. Hence reasonable behavior must lead straight to unreason. If we do not want the two terms to nullify each other we must find a new concept—say wisdom—where each of the two primary truths has its place. This would be the famous synthesis which merges the thesis and its antithesis.

In propounding the dialectic of history, Marx's master Hegel was thinking less of human than of metaphysical ideas, which he views as the motive power of human evolution: the moving finger writes and having writ moves on. Without going into the question how history embodies ideas we can return to Marx, who says to all this: Nonsense! History moves dialectically, it is true. But the dialectic is in the material stuff itself. Consequently, out of the present class antagonisms—and this is why he sees only two classes —must come the desired, unifying synthesis. Marx thinks of his Dialectical Materialism as putting Hegel right side up, for in his age and in science to talk of Matter is to be positive: this inversion of Hegel seemed a victory of common sense over airy speculation. But Marx continued to use Hegelian terms while nowhere explaining what he meant by matter. He assailed the "crude materialism" of Feuerbach, so that Marx's followers still show contempt for those who take Marx's materialism "mechanically," but it is nowhere shown how dialectical materialism differs from the

that a physical obstacle is the basis of physical sensation." Op. cit., 33.

[15] Memnon ou la Sagesse Humaine, 1747, clearly a first sketch for Candide.

nineteenth-century scientists' description of particles in motion.[16]

Yet Marx had not always been blind to other possible views; he had made himself so. In 1845 he had written: "The chief defect of all hitherto existing materialism—that of Feuerbach included—is that the object, reality, sensuousness is conceived only in the form of the object of contemplation, but not as human sense-activity, in practice and subjectively." One would think that this "conceiving of matter subjectively" and also "in practice" would make Marx an empirical pragmatist; but it does nothing of the kind. Like the evolutionists he chooses to make history rise from nature rather than conceive nature as a concept arising in human experience. Mind therefore remains outside as an epiphenomenon, "the glow of the corporeal furnace." With the whole physical world, with all of animal evolution, with all our economic life behind it, the momentum of history cannot but be tremendous. History points only one way and it is the right way. We need have no doubts, we need not even wonder that this resistless torrent should lay down its burden forever in the Union Terminal of the classless state. The dialectic of things acting like the "coercive influence of a law of nature" has made that synthesis materially secure.

[16] In a dispute by correspondence with a young admirer of his named Kugelmann, Marx explains the application of the dialectic to current events. It was 1870 and Kugelmann could not see why Germany should turn her defensive war against France into an aggressive and imperialistic war. Marx replies that the dialectic consists not only in opposing another force but in overcoming it and so fusing the two elements. Then he writes to Engels: "When a man attacks me on the street, according to Kugelmann, I have only the right to ward off his blows; to strike him in return and knock him down would be, according to him, to become an aggressor. It is clear none of these fellows understand anything about the dialectic."

4. The Sage of Soho

He saw further, deeper, and faster than the rest of us. Marx was a genius, the rest of us, at best, talented. Without him the theory would not be what it is today. That is why it rightly bears his name.

ENGELS

No man is great because he preaches a particular doctrine.

R. B. HALDANE

When Engels, speaking at his friend's grave and using Marx's favorite image of himself, called him the Darwin of sociology, the parallel may have seemed presumptuous, for Marx was then but little known. Later, when he had become a world figure, some of his admirers did not hesitate to proclaim him the Aristotle of the nineteenth century. But this muddles everything: if we recall Darwin's right to be the Newton of Biology, bringing Aristotle and Newton cheek by jowl through their alter egos, Marx and Darwin, leaves the biographer agape for other great names to dignify other great men.

The Darwin-Marx comparison was on solider ground from the start. "Just as Darwin has discovered the law of organic development, so Marx has discovered the law of human development in history, that is to say the simple fact, hitherto masked by the rubbish of ideologies, that before he is able to concern himself with politics, science, art, and religion, man must first eat, drink, house, and clothe himself."[1]

The truth in this extract is not that Marx discovered that people eat first and think afterwards—the ancients had already captured this elusive fact in the motto *Primum vivere deinde philosophari*. It is that, like Darwin, Marx thought he had discovered the law of development. He saw history in stages, as the Darwinists saw geological strata and successive forms of life. The scientific law that each sought for was that of the motive power within a world which everybody agreed was a dynamic one. Materialists and systematizers both, they put forth seemingly complete theories which, when they precipitated great movements, became justly known by their names. The delay of thirty years which made Marx's influence follow a whole generation after Darwin's is from this point of view an accident.

But there are even finer points of comparison. In keeping with the feelings of the age, both Marx and Darwin made struggle the means of development. Again, the measure of value in Darwin is survival with reproduction—an absolute fact occurring in time and which wholly disregards the moral or esthetic quality of the product. In Marx the measure of value is expended labor—an absolute fact occurring in time, which also disregards the utility of the product. Both Darwin and Marx tended to hedge and modify their mechanical absolutism in the face of objections. When hard-pressed they made room for ideas and feelings and their judgments similarly implied a moral standard. But in their "last analysis" the gap between fact and value would soon close over, leaving only a naturalistic or an economic interpretation. In describing "evolution" both supposed that in a world of struggle nothing good is really lost; things happen automatically and for the best—another way of saying that their work owes the same debt to the nineteenth-century science of economics. We might indeed infer it from their relation to one man—Thomas Malthus.

[1] *Karl Marx, a Symposium*, ed. Ryazanoff, London, 1927, 43.

It is also true that both relied on a multitude of predecessors. They were not pioneers in the strict sense—men who are the first to explore uncharted lands. Rather they were intellectual imperialists who absorbed and made their own the holdings of others. This they did in a large measure by instinct and not calculation. They refused to know, or did not like to admit, how much they had borrowed without acknowledgment. Marx particularly, since he had personally met most of those who furnished ready-made parts for his doctrine, comes before us as an eclectic by reflex action. Looking back upon him from so short a distance as seventy-five years, we are naturally inclined to feel that being Somebody he must have contributed Something; and it is that something which makes the flattering Darwin-Marx parallel even more meaningful. Like all men who are great by acclamation rather than by analysis, their chief virtue was to come at the right time and to do what was wanted. To them applies Pope's couplet about "what oft was thought," though it does not follow that what they said was supremely well expressed. It suffices that it was expressed with the right sort of words and in the right sort of mood. And for both of them, we know, the words were "science" and "law," and the mood materialistic evolution.

Marx, for one, hardly had to seek out these ideas from among a contrary set of prevailing notions. Born just too late to share the hopes of the liberal and romantic revolutionists, he was turned thirty when the outbreaks of 1848 put an end to those aspirations. By that time, he had acquired from his elders and contemporaries all the elements of his doctrine: from Hegel and Feuerbach, the dialectic and its material contents; from the English economists and Sismondi, the language of the dismal science and its critical antidote; from the French historians and socialists, the notion of class struggle and communism, with an odd lot of practical measures. Atheism, science, and evolution were in the air, like the awareness of spreading industrial misery—intellectual property common to all. Exiled from his native

Germany, but carrying away from it an unsatisfied passion for revolt and dominion, Marx was ideally situated to lead socialism away from the small-scale experiments of Owen or Fourier, to inject venom into the theory of class struggle, and to become the prophet of a militant religion.

At the same time the suffering, impatience, sense of weakness, and trust in numbers that the revolutions of 1848 had bequeathed to the second half of the century, were creating a temper favorable to all programs of force. We may wonder that it took so long to raise Marx from obscurity. Though his enemies died early—Lassalle in '64, Proudhon in '65, Herzen in '70, Bakunin in '76—it was not until the nineties that Marx became a real power, posthumously. No doubt the delay was due in part to obstacles over which he had no control. But his own aims and temperament supplied the other part. It was one task to preach a violent class struggle to the proletarians of Europe and organize an international labor movement. It was another and a contradictory task to be the Sage of Soho—a scientific student of capitalism and socialism, toiling at the metaphysical riddle of Value. When Oedipus guessed the secret of the Sphinx, she helpfully jumped into the sea and left him free to deal with practical politics. When Lassalle turned popular leader, he had all his legal and philosophical research behind him. But Marx was ever in both worlds. It was a necessity of his character, which is reflected in his works. It accounts for the presence of scholarly abstractions in the *Communist Manifesto* and of soapbox invective in the treatise on Capital.

With his longings for power, Marx was not content to remain the leader of a small group of conspirators awaiting the moment for action. Not only was he rather unsuccessful at the game, but seen from London, that chance of a winning play steadily dwindled. Marx therefore applied himself to the statement of his sociology. But alas, there was something uncongenial about that too. *Das Kapital* became "the damned book" and never took final shape beyond the first volume. So Marx never found a clear enough channel, neither in agitation nor in scholarship, to drain his abundant energies.

Thus divided in his work, so was he in his person. He was one man to his family and another to the world, and this not with the mild duplicity of convention. In the bosom of his family, there was no more warmhearted husband, father, and host than Karl Marx. Idyllic scenes of play with his children, instances of his lifelong tender respect for his wife, and later for his grown daughters, have been preserved in the memory of witnesses and conveyed to posterity. But this man of feeling and consideration at home never made or kept a friend outside the charmed circle. Engels was a slave, a good man Friday, and only thus a friend—as Marx showed in his self-centered behavior towards him. As for the rest, the acquaintances and colleagues of the Paris or London days, the testimony is nearly unanimous.[2] Carl Schurz summed it up when he said: "I have never seen a man whose bearing was so provoking and intolerable. To no opinion which differed from his own did he accord the honor of even condescending consideration; every argument that he did not like he answered either with biting scorn at the unfathomable ignorance that prompted it, or opprobrious aspersions upon the motives of him who had advanced it. I remember most distinctly the cutting disdain with which he pronounced the word bourgeois; and as a bourgeois—that is, as a detestable example of the deepest mental and moral degeneracy—he denounced everyone who dared to oppose his opinions."[3]

Nor was this a mere first impression. It never wore off, because Marx, thinking himself always among enemies, never relaxed his vigilance. Bakunin was not venting a grudge but assessing a relationship of long standing when he wrote: "Mr. Marx is immensely malicious, vain, quarrelsome, as intolerant and autocratic as Jehovah, the God of his fathers,

[2] The chief exception is Liebknecht, a mild man whom Marx and Engels tolerated rather than loved. In his later years, of course, Marx received very amicably the adulation of younger men.

[3] *Reminiscences*, i, 139–40.

and like him, insanely vindictive. There is no lie, no calumny, which he is not capable of using against anyone who has incurred his jealousy or his hatred; he will not stop at the basest intrigue if, in his opinion, it will serve to increase his position, his influence, and his power. Such are his vices, but he also has many virtues. He is very intelligent, and widely learned. In about 1840 he was the life and soul of a very remarkable circle of radical Hegelians—Germans whose consistent cynicism left far behind even the most rabid Russian nihilists."[4]

Like Richard Wagner in this respect, Marx found in each new acquaintance only a fresh mind to suck dry, contradict, insult, and add to the ever-lengthening list of fools or scoundrels which, trailing behind, enables us to trace the progress of the thinker. Coarse abuse, childish sarcasm, and imputed vice were the normal expressions of his sense of superiority, and possibly of the common enough fear of being grateful. It would be unfair to imagine that he was hardhearted or that he enjoyed his own malice. He was entirely sincere. His cunning was sanctified by his cause, which in turn was indistinguishable from his own interests of the moment. The double standard was, so to say, his second nature. When he flatly contradicted himself, as he did about Proudhon,[5] that was a scientific correction of his earlier views; when another was inconsistent, that was a sign of a weak intellect. When a class-conscious agitator like Wilhelm Weitling had no definite program for the proletariat to follow, Marx stamped out of the room shouting "Ignorance has never yet helped anybody"; when his own program wobbled from action by a revolutionary elite to evolution by political methods, that was "realism"; when some form of emotion—national, religious, or artistic—moved a Bakunin, a Louis Blanc, a Lassalle, they were

[4] Quoted in I. Berlin, Karl Marx, 1939, 106. I omit from this paragraph the suggestion of cowardice, which is patently untrue, and which Bakunin does not give on his own authority but merely reports.

[5] See below.

branded with Marxian fury as sentimental and unscientific. But Marx's own moral indignation at the lot of the poor, his passion for the good life, his quotations from the poets and his idealization of Greek art—these must have been true learning and right thinking.

With his sturdy energetic nature, full of repressed resentments, lacking the imagination of the real, and hence ignorant of the feelings of those not living under his own roof, it would have been surprising had Marx been more just to others or to himself. He was bound to consider every opponent at once a fool and a knave—a fool because he could not see the light, a knave because he would not follow it. Though the light might appear flickering to others, for Marx it cast an unmistakable shadow. He was drawn to Blanqui because of his genuine love of force, but he never really understood the far different powers of a Bakunin. As a moving orator and a Russian, Bakunin must be twice a fool. Lassalle, a nationalist and a lover of women, was a menace to socialism. Proudhon, as an easy-going French peasant, was but a petty bourgeois.

Such a lack of comprehension of men and their motives makes a poor politician. Without funds and without power of persuasion, only one weapon was left—the bludgeon, verbal or physical. Hence Marx's "organizing" consisted principally in destruction. He erected his weakness into the principle, excellent as far as it goes, that destruction is a mode of construction; and, despising cowardice, was ready to admit that his happiness lay in fighting.[6] Marx accordingly gave the majority of his works the form of attacks on particular persons—Proudhon, Karl Vogt, Feuerbach, Bruno Bauer, Louis Bonaparte, Palmerston, among others —and Engels continued the tradition with his so-called *Anti-Dühring.*

Meantime, lacking heads, Marx mowed down plans, platforms, and reputations instead. His public appearances in

---

[6] See his answers to the game of "Confessions" reprinted in *Karl Marx, a Symposium,* and the account of his interfering in a London street incident on behalf of the injured party, *ibid.*

socialist circles left the audience with a sense of irresistible brawn and brain. His language, mixing the professorial with the unparliamentary, withered away whatever group of men it touched. The longest-lived of his organizations, the First International, he did not create. It grew out of a visit of Continental workingmen to the London Exhibition of 1863. Marx captured its council the following year, then successfully coddled it for a few years, but in the end had to purge it in the best style of Molière's doctors, until it perished, an emaciated corpse, at the Philadelphia Centennial in 1876.

A characteristic trait is revealed in the comment Marx made on revising its original program. He found in it the words, "All societies and individuals connected with the association acknowledge truth, justice and morality as the basis of their behavior among themselves and towards all their fellow-men without regard to color, creed or nationality." These words, "truth, justice and morality," Marx allowed to remain, he said, in a context "where they would do no harm." In this simple scorn of "bourgeois ideals" and confidence in a "tough-minded realism" we may measure how far Marx was ahead of his time. Only five years had elapsed since the *Origin of Species*, and the Social Darwinists had not yet made commonplaces out of it.[7]

Marx, tormented by all he had seen and felt, no less than by his personal ailments of body and purse, began to lose the sense that words and things, and means and ends, cannot be merged into an idol for men to worship as Struggle. Granting his objection to the platitudinous use of abstract ideals, it should not have made him believe that the "behavioral facts" behind truth, justice, and morality were also platitudes. Such words as: "the struggle for the emancipation of the working classes does not imply a struggle for class privileges and monopolies, but for equal rights and

[7] K. Timiryazeff in his laudatory article on Darwin and Marx speaks of Darwin as "the founder of the new realistic school of ethics." *Karl Marx, a Symposium*, 173. Surely Marx was a "realist" of this stamp before reading Darwin.

duties and for the abolition of all class domination" are no more "scientific" than "idealistic." A longer life might have opened his eyes. Party verbiage about the need for "industrialized nationalization" and the "disindividualization of capital" became as stereotyped and meaningless by the end of the "realistic era" as "truth, morality, and justice" may have been at its beginning. The difference between emptiness and meaning can only be tested by the concrete consequences that follow. And since Marx was unwilling, after 1848, to commit scientific socialism to a detailed program beyond violent revolution, we have the paradoxical result of discovering in Marx an apostle of both equality and hierarchy, violence and reform, ruthless language and innocuous abstraction. Like Darwin, he can be quoted to many purposes, though the prevailing cast of his mind, at least in public, leaves uppermost his scorn for moral obligation—a scorn which others have found only too easy to carry out in numberless concrete ways.

Marx's ideas are said to form a scientific system. But it is clear that despite his quick and restless mind, Marx was not a system maker—neither an Aristotle nor a Newton. His Communifesto, if we give back most of it to its chief inspirer, Victor Considérant, seems slight; and if we do not, it remains a rousing succession of dogmas about history and a call to mass action. The *Critique of Political Economy* twelve years later is, as we saw, an interrupted fragment reembodied in the first chapter of *Capital*. The first volume of *Capital*—which I shall return to in a moment—Marx found difficult to write and unsatisfactory when written. The remaining volumes he could never bring himself to finish. Engels found the notes for them in a much worse disorder than he had expected, and this in spite of the fact that the last fifteen years of Marx's life were passed in relatively easy circumstances.

As these fragments stood, moreover, they endangered some of the positions taken in volume I: the right of the worker to the full product of his labor, the correspondence of the value theory with facts, the relation of surplus value to profits. Of other works written by Marx alone or with Engels, the most complete and sizable are *The Holy Family* (a critique of German philosophy), *The German Ideology*, and *The Poverty of Philosophy* (a critique of Proudhon's ideas). On none of these works nor on any of the political tracts can a claim be based for Marx as a great architect of ideas or a methodical scientist. It was Engels who in *Anti-Dühring*—to which Marx contributed very little—gave their historical materialism a full treatment, just as it was by piecing together pamphlets and boiling down *Capital* that Marx's followers gave Marx's doctrine to Europe at the end of the century.

There remains to consider the first volume of *Capital*. Setting aside later contradictions, is it in any sense a perfect fragment, a corner of an unbuilt Parthenon worthy of our sympathetic and imaginative admiration? Those who presumably know it best, namely the Marxists who have tried to explain it by editing or commentary, generally agree that it is badly written, ill put together, lacking in order, logic, or homogeneity of material. Benedetto Croce, one of Marx's most sympathetic critics, and a trained historian and philosopher besides, says of it: ". . . The strange composition of the book, the mixture of general theory, of bitter controversy and satire, and of historical illustrations or digressions, and so arranged that only Loria (fortunate man!) can declare *Das Kapital* to be the 'finest and most symmetrical' of existing books [is] in reality unsymmetrical, badly arranged and out of proportion . . . resembling in some particulars Vico's *Scienza Nuova.*"

So that while certain devotees see in it a literary masterpiece, more candid Marxists reject all pretense that it is intrinsically a great book. Extrinsically considered it has been a powerful source of emotion, discussion, and controversy; it has in a measure become the "Bible of the working classes" and the oracle of a great nation; and its name and associations will not soon be erased from men's minds. But when we are considering not men's minds but Marx's mind, and go to the first volume of *Capital*, we find it falling very far short of a classic.

It seems as if written in part by a living man and in part by a Hegelian academic with "a style . . . par excellence profound and scientific, where a reader is tormented to death by the narcotic effect of long-spun periods without a single idea in them."[8] Marx's effort to be painstaking and scientific often results in tautology. There are pages and pages in the work of which the significance is no more crystallized and tangible than in the following extract:

The simplest form of the circulation of commodities is C–M–C, the transformation of a commodity into money, and the retransformation of money into a commodity; selling in order to buy. However, side by side with this form, we find another, which is specifically different. We find the form M–C–M, the transformation of money into commodities, and the retransformation of commodities into money, buying in order to sell. Money that circulates in the latter way is thereby transformed into capital, is already potential capital.

Let us examine this circuit M–C–M more closely. Like the simple circuit C–M–C, it passes through two antithetical phases. In the first phase, M–C, purchase, money is transformed into commodities; in the second phase, C–M, sale, commodities are retransformed into money. The combination of these two phases is the aggregate movement thanks to which money is exchanged for commodities and these commodities are exchanged back for money, commodities being bought in order to sell them again—or, if we ignore the formal distinction between buying and selling, we can say that money buys commodities, and then commodities buy money. The upshot of the whole process is the exchange of money for money, M–M. If for £100 I buy 2,000 lbs. of cotton, and then sell the 2,000 lbs. of cotton for £110, I have,

[8] Schopenhauer's description of the Hegelians' style before Marx wrote. *Sämmtliche Werke*, 1891, vi, 552.

in the end, exchanged £100 for £110, money for money.[9]

After which follow some four or five further iterations, such as "He only parts with his money for the sly purpose of getting it back again,"[10] ending up three paragraphs later with: "The circuit C–M–C starts with one commodity and finishes with another, which falls out of the sphere of circulation and enters the sphere of consumption . . ."[11] giving us at the end what should have sufficed for the whole. As with Darwin, the weight of the apparatus—facts, citations, footnotes—and the truth of the outlying portions befog the main ideas, the simple utterance of which might have led to their revision. This is not to say that *Capital*, volume I, is as adroitly argued as the *Origin of Species*, though there is an interesting parallel between Darwin's successive alterations of his text and Marx's gradual withdrawals in volume III. No. The *Origin of Species* is poorly written, tautological, and hesitant; but compared with it *Capital* is as undigested as the ingenuity and patience of a German Ph.D. could make it. Marx could write tersely and directly when he chose, as in his polemical "calls to action," but as to many an author of dissertations, something happened to him when he approached scholarship and science.

In thus judging of the style of a philosopher of history, we are not judging mere externals, but the very substance of his thought and its effectiveness. In the descriptive chapters of *Capital* Marx is at his freest and best, despite an excess of quotations from the famous Blue Books. Little good can be said of his much vaunted sense of humor and powers of irony. Marx was no Swift, and in the difficult context of appalling misery related in his pages, his efforts strike one like feeble jesting out of place. He quotes, for example, a physician's report: "They are so ill-fed that assuredly among them there must be many cases of severe and injurious privation." Marx adds: "There is also priva-

[9] *Capital*, I, Everyman, i, 131 ff.
[10] *Ibid.*, 133.
[11] *Ibid.*, 134.

tion on the part of the capitalist. He deprives himself of the privilege of paying a sufficient wage, a wage such as his hands need for the barest subsistence!"[12]

Marx also interlards his descriptions with attacks on Malthus or Sismondi, always personal, yet often it is their words which make his point, without gratitude from him: "Finally, hear Destutt de Tracy, the cold-blooded bourgeois doctrinaire, who bluntly tells us the truth: 'In poor nations the common people are comfortable; in rich nations, they are generally poor.' "[13] Why cold-blooded? Why the assumption that Destutt will not tell the truth if he can? Marx seems never content with merely refuting, he must contemn and communicate his contempt. This literary irritability—always greater as the print at the bottom of the page becomes smaller—is sometimes so prurient as to obscure his meaning. Thus we are told about William the Third's alleged sexual perversions—a well-known monopoly of the crowned bourgeoisie—as somehow relevant to the land grants in Ireland.[14] Burke is ridiculously accused of having been "bought" by American interests to plead their cause and by royalist henchmen to attack the French Revolution.[15] It is curious that Marx should have required the other side to be always corrupt. The common fault is to judge others by oneself, but Marx, who was patently incorruptible, never seemed to think it likely that other men could resist temptation: there is always a ten-pound note from Bismarck peeping out of their pockets.

Corruption may be for Marx the mere outward sign of cynicism, and it is then by his own that he judges theirs. For as an amateur *Realpolitiker* he thinks he must scorn principles and disregard all claims upon his sympathy. Hence when it is not personal, Marx's contempt is national or racial. Until late in life, when the spread of his ideas and a devoted following in Russia helped him change his

[12] *Capital*, I, Everyman, ii, 725.
[13] *Ibid.*, 716.
[14] *Ibid.*, 801 n.
[15] *Ibid.*, 843.

mind, Marx was sure that the Russians were an inferior race deserving extinction. Throughout the life of the First International, Marx's hatred of the French was outspoken —sometimes based on the Proudhonian allegiance of the French workers, sometimes on the general ground of France's corruption. The Czechs were strong nationalists; therefore they ought to be trounced. This passion for vicarious trouncing led Marx to espouse Bismarck's cause as his own when war was declared in 1870. A Prussian victory would mean that the German proletariat would become dominant in the world, and this dominance "would mean at the same time the dominance of our theory over Proudhon's."[16]

Six months after Engels had agreed that "it would be absurd to make anti-Bismarckism our only principle," Marx has had another change of heart. Bismarck is now a "donkey" and France "fights not only for her national independence but for the liberty of Germany and Europe."[17] Restlessly Napoleonic, Marx had an imperial reluctance to thinking in particulars. Classes, races, political groups, lived in his imagination as entities stuffed with people but not composed of them. He would have liked to move them en masse, like huge pawns. And contrariwise, individuals took on in his eyes the massive importance of whole groups. The savage attack on Proudhon in the guise of an obituary notice, the treachery to Bakunin when the latter was engaged in translating *Capital* into Russian, even the callous indifference which wounded Engels when he imparted to Marx the news of a deep personal grief—these show that in Marx's eyes the men surrounding him were instruments of policy, useful or dangerous, for or against him, but neither human beings nor opponents to be tolerated, for in the struggle of classes quarter must be neither taken nor given.

We touch here the heart of the Marxian psychology

[16] To Engels, July 20, 1870.
[17] Letter to the *Daily News*, Jan. 16, 1871.

which has had such a powerful influence in our day: in a bourgeois regime—the proletariat excepted—everyone is necessarily corrupt. Redemption is only possible by faith in the Marxian revelation. All other motives are class—and therefore crass—motives; all significant actions spring from the baseness of the base—the material fact of property holding. This is Marx's form of the genetic fallacy. One need not ask how he, living on Engels and Engels on Manchester cotton, could escape the universal taint. A prophet's garments are pure from the very fact that he is a prophet and cries out. What we must ask is how in a scheme in which truth, morality, and justice are "ideology," anyone can be corrupt; how, further, anyone can be a prophet. Commentators are right when they say that Marx's system does not mean that men act only from greed. That is a Marxian imputation quite outside his system—or rather, it is hidden inside his own emotional system. For surely it was out of a passionate hatred of injustice that Marx spoke of exploitation. Otherwise why was not capitalism perfect as it stood? The social Darwinists were more consistent: if struggle is the law of nature and if classes are bound to prey on one another—and Marx tells us this is the sum total of history— why lecture the world about it? Why are the crowding, the pain, the anguish, the toil, and the death of countless millions to be deplored? In a thoroughly naturalistic scheme it is as idle to pity them as it is to pity the poppy seeds that are trodden down and never flower. The strength of Marx is precisely that he shared the feelings of the downtrodden, that the prejudice of equality was in his very fiber, joined to the ambition and jealousy of power, which made him ready to destroy the present moral order in the name of a higher that he saw.

"He never condescends," said Shaw four years after Marx's death, "to cast a glance of useless longing at the past: his cry to the present is always 'pass by: we are waiting for the future.' Nor is the future at all mysterious, uncertain, or dreadful to him. There is not a word of hope or fear, nor appeal to chance or providence . . . nor any other familiar sign of the giddiness which seizes men when they climb to heights which command a view of the past, present and future of human society. Marx keeps his head like a God. He has discovered the law. . . ."[18]

This is the public Marx, the hero with a single purpose which he would have wished posterity to remember. Like other men he fell short of his image of himself, and the circumstances of his life did little to sustain him in a role that he never assumed even in private. His domestic tastes were on a modest scale. His origins, his habits, his commonplace dealings with neighbors and with children, his admiration of his wife's noble birth and noble character, his tender feelings for his father-in-law, the devotion of the faithful nurse 'Lenchen—all show him as a good-natured and somewhat helpless paterfamilias. Indeed, a modern Marxian interpreter, given these facts anonymously, might do worse than guess: petty bourgeois. But this omits the intellectual side. No creator and no artist, he was a cultivated mind, even a learned one, yet always unaffectedly fond of great literature. Spoiled by early addiction to academic philosophy, he endured the torments of a scholar who is torn between the study and the soapbox, and who, constitutionally active, is plagued with the ills of sedentary life. Beyond the range of these many earthly ills, his intense spirit also suffered the cramping limitation of never having known himself.

[18] Bernard Shaw and Karl Marx, a Symposium, ed. Ellis, 1930, 114–15.

5. The People's Marx

> But history in the nineteenth century, better under-
> stood and better employed, will, I trust, teach a
> civilized posterity the misdeeds of both these bar-
> barous ages.
>
> BURKE, *Reflections on the
> French Revolution*, 1790

Just as Marx's gift to social thought has been the materialistic conception of history, so his message to the masses
has been the idea of the Class War. The *Communist
Manifesto* of 1848 has remained for all popular and practical purposes the chief, the only, embodiment of Marx's
philosophy. Overcharged with theory though it is in parts,
its effective "nonscientific" rhetoric about struggle, chains,
and the need of banding together to cast them off has
proved to be the true "People's Marx." This is not to depreciate the several popular works which go by that same
title, and which attempt to make *Capital* shorter and
easier to read. But these restatements of Marx's "science"
could never form the basis of a popular movement; their
usefulness has been spent on intellectuals who were not
economists or metaphysicians, yet who wanted to know
what Marx had said besides the simple arguments of the
Manifesto.[1] *Capital* may still be called the Bible of the

[1] In answer to a question about important books, Clifton Fadi-
man answered: "I suppose our generation has been more influenced by Marx than by any other single writer, yet very few of

Working Class, but it is a Bible that is seldom opened, being, like many a book of Revelations, too symbolical to apply.

Similarly, from the rest of the Marx-Engels writings, only what fits the simple idea of class war could help active socialists. The bare words "exploitation," "surplus value," "capitalist system," "labor the source of all value," were enough by themselves to supply texts for inflammatory speeches and arouse proletarians to the meaning of their experience. In an age of social Darwinism, the combination of the ideas of struggle, of historical evolution, and of progress, proved irresistible. The Marxists became simply a sect in the larger church, a sect whose special tenets addressed the individual somewhat as follows: The struggle for life is universal; human history shows that progress comes from the conflict of classes; since your masters exploit you, you are bound to fight them; if you do not, resistless evolution will take its course, leaving you behind in its wreckage. Hence you must gird your loins and help bring it about, for the fight is to the strong and the race to the swift; and you are both, because, independently of your individual will, the next stage in history is the abolition of capital ownership and the dominance of the proletariat. Workers of the world, unite! You have nothing to lose but your chains!

In urging these lessons, Marx and Engels set the pattern of all subsequent Marxist polemics by using what may be called the evolutionist's double standard: When you do it, it's wrong, because you are the past; when we do it, it's right, for we are the future. The mood—borrowed from science—is that of a mighty ruthlessness. History, like nature, is tough. Thus, "during the conflict and right after the battle, the workers must to the fullest extent possible work against the bourgeois measures of pacification, and compel the democrats to carry into action their present terroristic phrases. They must work to prevent the immediate

us—certainly not myself—have really read much Marx." *Books That Changed Our Minds*, 1939, 16.

revolutionary excitement from being promptly suppressed after the victory. They must keep it going as long as possible. Far from setting themselves against so-called excesses, examples of popular revenge against hated individuals or public buildings with only hateful memories attached to them, they must not only tolerate these examples but take in hand their very leadership."[2] At the same time, dealing with the Commune and looking back to the June Days of 1848, Engels wrote in apparent surprise: "It was the first time that the bourgeoisie showed to what a mad ferocity of vengeance it can be stirred up, so soon as the proletariat dares to stand up against it as a separate class with its own interests and demands."[3]

Marx wanted the proletariat to outdo its enemies in "mad ferocity," and then to build the new order which would end all class wars. But when the leaders of a revolution begin by sowing suspicion of mankind and imputing vile motives to a foe whom they have just proved to be historically determined in his acts, they must expect the return of the boomerang sooner or later and be themselves ready to face the firing squad or the assassin's knife. That is to say, they must carry on a new war for their own skins, now identified with the evolution of history.

As an historian of revolutions and *coups d'état*, Marx must have known this. One therefore wonders by what secret mechanism he expected that in *this* case men goaded to destruction and sadism would settle down into artisans of peace and order. His optimism ("Force is the midwife of Progress") tided him over the difficulty. The only guide to constructive action which he offers is, as we know, the ten points of the *Communist Manifesto*, revised, of course, in the light of changed conditions. The proletariat, having wreaked its vengeance on the exploiting classes, goes back upon its tracks and dispossesses them little by

[2] "Address to the Central Authority of the Communist League," 1850.
[3] *The Civil War in France*, Introduction to the German Edition, 1891.

little through nationalization, the abolition of inheritance, and so forth. Nowhere does Marx's imaginative weakness and inconsequence appear more clearly than in this mish-mash of bloody revolution with reformism. The reform is carried out, to be sure, by a dictatorship of the proletariat,[4] but here again we are never told whether it comprises the whole working class acting through democratic elections or only the compact minority of ruthless leaders who have just led the rest to final victory.

Meantime of course, the idea of class war is clear and simple enough to fit the obvious facts in a world of rich and poor. H. G. Wells, who never was a Marxist doctri-naire, who, on the contrary, finds Marx his *bête noire*, has given an excellent account of the state of feeling to which Marx in his popular incarnation appealed. "There would have been Marxists," says Wells, "if Marx had never lived. When I was a boy of fourteen I was a complete Marxist, long before I had heard of Marx. I had been cut off from education, caught in a detestable shop, and I was being broken in to a life of mean and dreary toil. I was worked too hard and for such long hours that all thoughts of self-improvement seemed hopeless. I would have set fire to the place if I had not been convinced it was over-insured."[5]

Such a state of mind, born of economic exploitation, should indeed have made Marxists at mass-production rates. The trouble was that when Utopia through fighting is preached to people whose condition inspires revolt, the result is not two groups of which one is the historically elect, but rather fifty groups of which none has any real chance of exterminating the rest in due theoretical form. Even in theory, Marx and Engels had to introduce distinc-tions in order to preserve the face-to-face antagonism of two classes from denial by facts. Besides the real proletariat they discerned a *Lumpenproletariat*, or rabble; and besides the real bourgeoisie, a petty bourgeoisie. Clearly, propa-ganda was needed to make all but the bourgeoisie, which

[4] *Criticism of the Gotha Program*, 1875.
[5] *Russia in the Shadows*, 1921, 85.

is so by nature, class-conscious. And since the conflict between these two ultimate groups still leaves the peasants out of account, Marx was obliged to borrow an idea from that eminent bourgeois Macaulay, who had said that the middle class was the natural representative of the general interest. Marx merely changes the terms and says of the working classes that they are the "natural trustees" of the peasant interest. The principle of each class for itself, determined to war by its economic condition, has to be eked out with strangely "moral" group solidarity and mutual trust between two classes, one of which ceases to behave as a class and acts for another.

The result of this contradiction in practical politics is energy wasted in quibbles over dogma and the consequent splitting up of revolutionary parties over purity of intention and belief. You then find socialists and communists of every hue, some calling themselves nationalists, some racialists, some possibilists, others anarchists or syndicalists, each group believing itself the only true embodiment of the future and each, in virtue of its own supreme principle, subdividing itself into a fine dust of agitated particles, ready to annihilate all the others if it could only find a point of vantage in the chaotic whirl. The small band of "self-appointed saviors" emerges by a process of Natural Selection which itself inspires an endless struggle for survival. The tactics by which Marx triumphed over Bakunin and Proudhon,[6] by which later Lenin became head of the Bolshevik Party, and by which Stalin overthrew Trotsky, have indeed produced powerful survivors, but it would be hard to show how this differs from the worst of bourgeois politics, and how it produces any greater fitness for organizing, governing, and improving mankind.

Until late into the nineteenth century the Marxian socialists, even with converted Anarchists added, remained without influence on the masses of the European popula-

[6] Principally by intrigue, "confidential communications" behind the backs of colleagues and rivals, and electoral "purges."

tion. A good many intellectuals, particularly the Russian victims of Czarist oppression, like Lenin, Stalin, and others, found relief in the promise of wholesale and speedy revenge which Marx's creed held out to them. It is not for those who did not suffer their wrongs to judge them. But other intellectuals who seemed to adopt violence as a tonic—in complete ignorance of its effects—were really not contemplated in Marx's theory as forming anything more than the early guides of the genuine movement from below.[7] And this movement predicted by Marx never manifested itself anywhere at any time under the banner of strict Marxism.

The truth is that the spread of socialism as a doctrine in prewar Europe was no more due to Marx's direct political efforts than to the persuasiveness of his abstractions.[8] It was the followers of Proudhon, Louis Blanc, and Bakunin who, with a handful of Marxists, formed the First International. And if anyone can claim as his own handiwork the transformation of modern socialist ideas into a truly popular movement, it is the much-reviled Ferdinand Lassalle. It is usual nowadays to belittle his role in German history and to depreciate his mind and character. Marx, who could not bear rivalry, started the fashion. He always referred to Lassalle opprobriously, sometimes as the Jewish Nigger. Except for the religious and social background which they had in common, Lassalle was everything that Marx was not —a judicious scholar, an artist, and a man in whom, despite appearances, logic and enthusiasm combined with a rare degree of balance. He was above all a born leader of men

[7] Many meetings of the First International debated whether intellectuals were workers. Tolain, a French artisan, maintained the logic of the class war and moved to exclude all but manual workers. Though his motion was lost, Marx was very much hurt. (To Engels, Sept. 20, 1866.)

[8] He thought any unprejudiced reader of Capital would understand it and be convinced by it. The Russian censorship knew better and allowed the book to enter on the ground that it "is unlikely to find many readers among the general public." I. Berlin, Marx, 237.

and a natural master of politics. At the age of thirty-nine, after two years' campaigning, he had built up in the teeth of opposition by the government, the industrialists, and the humanitarian liberals, a German Workers' Party. In those two years of indefatigable activity—1862–1864—he spoke to thousands throughout the Germanies, he published twenty volumes on political and social questions, carried on an enormous correspondence, and organized "sections" wherever his pen or his person could reach.

His force, magnetism, ingenuity, oratorical power, knowledge of people and of history, were lavishly expended in a way ruinous to his health, but which created what had never existed before: a party of the Fourth Estate growing almost simultaneously with the industrialization of a great European power. It was this party which a decade after Lassalle's death joined the Marx-controlled International to form the great German Social Democratic Party.[9] The two who might have been his allies—Marx and Engels—kept an aloof silence while he spent his strength and resources upon the task. Lassalle dead, they collected the fruits of his labors and expressed their relief at his removal by insulting his memory.

The Social-Democratic Party, then, which forced Bismarck and his successors to steal so much of its thunder worked presumably in the name of Marx, but actually on Lassallean principles. It was national, for, as Lassalle perceived, a German national state was the first demand of all Germans after the failure to unify in 1848, nor could economic problems be handled otherwise than nationally in the European system of sovereign states. It was political and not revolutionary, for the German working class wanted tangible benefits together with security of life and limb— another lesson remembered from 1848; lastly, it always tended away from Marx's theoretical materialism to Lassalle's practical idealism. As a political party doing a politi-

[9] Marx's criticisms of the famous Gotha Program of 1875 would have wrecked this union, hence Liebknecht did not transmit them.

cal business, it could not overlook the part of mind and theory in action, and its leaders very soon replaced Marxian materialism by a neo-Kantian philosophy which Lenin was later to attack. Meanwhile, what remained of Marxian fatalism was throughout a hindrance to its natural development,[10] and even contributed to its final downfall before the active antideterminism of Hitler.

Lassalle was seven years younger than Marx, but he had been brought up in the same Hegelian school of thought and had, independently of all Marxian influence, taken a somewhat similar path. When Marx published the stillborn *Critique of Political Economy* in 1859, Lassalle was giving to the world his extraordinary study of Heraclitus the Obscure. Lassalle's concern with the Greek philosopher who reduced the whole world to the motion of particles marks the practical materialistic tendency of the decade. But unlike Marx, Lassalle did not let materialism darken the Hegelian insight into the function of mind. All three— Hegel, Marx, and Lassalle—stressed the historical mode of treating all social questions. But the dialectical process was not for Lassalle a piece of machinery embedded in history. It seemed to him rather the natural way of conceiving motion and change. Fully as early as Marx, he stressed the social and practical origins of legal systems and constitutions, but faithful to Hegelian thought, he never supposed that they were mere offprints of a self-existing material reality. "Long before barricades can be raised in the outer world," he told the Court of Assize in 1848, "the citizen in the world of mind must have dug the pit which will swallow up the forms of government." Consciousness was a logical and necessary part of his sociology, not an embarrassing illusion as in Marx.

Whether in the courtroom or on the platform, Lassalle's studies in law, history, government, and philosophy made him a formidable debater, but they appear at their fullest

[10] See Rosa Luxemburg's article in the Marx Symposium already cited.

and maturest in his written works. In strong contrast to Marx's crabbed polemics and tortúous erudition, everything in Lassalle is lucid, generous, and orderly. There is but little oversimplification, yet simplicity is the result, unmarred by any attempt at original profundity if it happens that at this point he is neither original nor profound. In economics, Lassalle accepts the classical labor theory of value as reinterpreted by Rodbertus, and when he borrowed from Marx the doctrine of surplus value to explain the formation of capital, he was careful to make full acknowledgment.

For the rest, Lassalle draws on the same general fund of socialist ideas which we know to be due in the first instance, not to Marx, but to Fourier, Saint-Simon, Hess, Sismondi, and other socialists of the first half of the century. The conclusion so often insinuated, that Lassalle was a hasty and incomplete popularizer of Marx, is thus groundless, another instance of the desire to rewrite history in the victor's favor.

With the quick spread of democratic institutions in the last third of the nineteenth century—in France, England, and Germany, in Italy and in Austria—and with the increasing power and liberty of trade-unions, it was possible to combine the Marxian spirit of class war with the immediate demands of the enfranchised working class. General and local strikes, general and local elections, lent themselves to dramatization on the pattern of war and conquest. For although "ballots not bullets" distinguishes genuine from false democracy, it is also true that the feelings behind the casting of ballots ape those behind the shooting of bullets. Candidates campaign; electors rally. Victory and defeat, denunciation and defiance, indignation and contempt, are the stock-in-trade of parties and factions, down to the last "challenge" of the registered voter at the polls. Nor is it the vocabulary alone that is martial. And yet, in spite of this and in spite of Marx, the large socialist parties formed in Europe before the World War all tended to become "Reformist," "Revisionist," parliamentarian—in a word, flatly non-Marxian in their tactics. It was always *Tomorrow*, the

International brotherhood of man and the death of the Capitalist system. It is easy to ascribe this fact to the "betrayal" of party leaders and to sow dark hints of corruption. History does not support the view that significant events, particularly similar ones occurring independently in many places, are the result of conspiracy. Even when treachery can be shown, the further reason for its success needs to be pointed out.

As an alternative explanation, it can of course be said that the failure of Marxism between 1890 and 1914 was due to the inherent sheeplikeness of men. But then what becomes of the inevitable evolution of history based on class antagonisms? When it suited him, Marx reserved the sheeplike qualities for the Christian bourgeoisie and made fun of its traditional religious symbol—the Lamb of God. The proletariat on the contrary was supposed to be fierce, atheistical, heroic, long-suffering, and infallible. It would not hesitate to strike when the hour itself had struck. But neither struck.

The fact was that although popular Marxism was in tune with the Darwinian struggle for life, it overlooked two things. One, the irreducibly individual perception of that struggle insofar as it exists, which meant an unwillingness among the masses to risk life until the victory was reasonably sure; the other, the inheritance, by tradition, of a hundred different forms of association other than class. The scientific farmer joined co-operatives and made politics serve his needs. The backward peasant stuck to his wooden plow and hated the city laborer; the city laborer stuck to his bottle or his game of bowls, and refused to be the heroic artisan of the future; the active, the intelligent, the political-minded among the workers, joined trade-unions and political parties that would give them immediate concrete benefits through social legislation—shorter hours and more pay—the materialistic conception of history expressed in consumers' goods; the religiously inclined followed the lead of their churches—all of them engaged in social betterment and securing it in the form of free education, shorter hours, and labor insurance.

Moreover, as voting citizens who had been educated at public expense, and who were more and more sedulously courted by politicians, peasant and proletarian began to take an increasing interest in national destinies. Nationalism and imperialism became intense passions which the new yellow press was not slow to exploit and to satisfy. Fed on vicarious prestige, diplomacy, and colonial politics, the new masses often outstripped their leaders and did as much to foster the "New Imperialism" and the race for armaments as the sinister economic influences tending in the same direction. To these forms of partisanship, racialism lent a pseudo-scientific aura, its doctrines seemingly borne out by plain facts whenever war or the competition of cheap foreign labor piled its burdens upon existing evils of local origin.

Whichever way the late nineteenth-century world is examined, Marx's single proletarian class waging a single combat against its hereditary enemy appears as a dimmer and dimmer abstraction. It was an idea which might have come true, if the masses who were to form the class and wage the war had been simply and directly taught by a leader of genius, very different in mind and temperament from the propounder of the theory; or again if the masses had remained illiterate as they were in 1850; or if, desperate and religiously inspired, they had had faith enough in progress through the Martyrdom of Man to sacrifice themselves and the present benefits of unionized bargaining to the Marxist Utopia; or if, getting poorer and poorer instead of becoming in so many cases "petty bourgeois" of the most unrepentant kind, they had begun a slave revolt against a mere handful of plutocrats.

Since none of these things happened, we are obviously left with too many if's for any theory to withstand. Marx had without a doubt helped to crush Utopian socialism, he had poured scorn on the principle of co-operation to the right of him and on the anarchical ideal to the left; he ultimately had his name, his catchwords, his picture, and his books widely circulated among the political groups concerned with improving the lot of the worker. But neither the lightening of class bonds nor the concentration of capital in a few hands, nor international unions across frontiers, nor the "next step" in historical evolution, came as he predicted it, where he predicted it, or for the good of those to whom he predicted it. The hopeless splitting up of international socialism at the outbreak of the war of 1914; the occurrence of the communist revolution, not in Germany where it belonged, but in Russia, where a conspiratorial group of Marxian type, relying more on "ideas" than on "conditions," rose to dictatorship over an overwhelming agrarian country; finally, the mystical-nationalist form of "the revolution" in Germany and Italy—are as many witnesses to the failure of popular Marxism.

One thing only did Marx contribute to the revolt of the masses in our century. In insisting upon group violence for alleged economic ends under the aegis of would-be scientific theories, Marx was in step with all the cultural forces of his age and fastened his grip on the future. But this means that like many another religious success, his has been that of temperament expressed through scattered aphorisms, and not the working out of predictions based on scientific system.

6. His Majesty's Opposition

> I cannot admit that facts fatal to a theory can be
> rendered innocuous to it by a simple statement that
> the author "never doubted them for a moment."
>
> G. B. SHAW on *Bluffing
> the Value Theory*, 1889

> Deny the validity of Property and you do not
> thereby establish the validity of Communism.
>
> PROUDHON

Long before Lenin and his twenty-seven conspirators
crossed the border into Russia and so galvanized Marxism
into a new burst of life, the system of the master had un-
dergone severe criticism. Like Darwinism and about the
same time, it was attacked on technical as well as general
grounds. Among other things, Marx's failure to publish the
last two volumes of *Capital* had created, from the time of
his death and particularly in England, a doctrinal situation
whose comic side did not escape the rising Fabian George
Bernard Shaw. The predicament of the would-be orthodox
socialist was this: Marx had set forth a theory of surplus
value which seemed to fly in the face of facts—the more
laborers were employed the greater should capitalist appropriation be; but capitalists all preferred to install machinery
and dismiss laborers. A blind adherent like the co-founder
of the British Socialism, Maurice Hyndman, kept repeating, with his eyes shut, that Marx had fully taken care of

every objection and that his work was "tested science." But as Shaw and other critics pointed out, Engels himself recognized the apparent flaw in the theory, and held over everybody's head the revelations contained in the unpublished chapters left behind by Marx. Hyndman and the doctrinaires were being more royalist than the King and taking their science on faith. This was about 1887, and one reason why the question arose to plague nascent Marxism was that a revolution in economic theory had taken place throughout Europe in the seventies.

It was not aimed especially at Marx but against all previous theories of value, from Locke, Adam Smith and Ricardo, down to Rodbertus and the Marxists. The latter, indeed, were still without much influence, so the renewed attack on the old theory of value had little to do with the fear of socialism or with an interest in Marx's works. It paralleled, rather, the distrust of thoroughgoing materialism in science and contained the seeds of twentieth-century immaterialism in both science and sociology.

The men who put forward the new views were Jevons in England, Cournot in France, Walras in Switzerland, and Carl Menger in Austria. It is also worth noticing that when the new school had made some headway it rediscovered a forerunner in Gossen, whose work back in the fifties had necessarily been overlooked as contrary to the dominant trend.[1] Technical differences in assumptions and method should of course prevent us from lumping together all these men, but their differences matter less than the sharp change of direction they imparted to economic thought.

The classical and Marxian views were that value arose from the labor embodied in goods. The new view asserted that value arose from the human perception of comparative usefulness in a world where goods are scarce. Value was a psychological as well as an objective fact. As Whately had said much earlier in a short refutation of Ricardo, men

[1] Even earlier opponents of the labor theory, like McCulloch, Senior, and Bailey, became better known with the return to favor of the idea of utility.

dive for pearls because they are valuable; pearls are not valuable because men dive for them. This was certainly still true forty years later, but it did not solve the problem of political economy, which was not merely to define value, but to measure it. In Marx, value was proportional to labor time. Time was measurable, labor was tangible; economics could therefore grasp the very substance of value and become indeed a science. But Marx purposely neglected the uses for which objects are made by labor, and while whisking by the problem of scarcity embroiled himself in the inconsistencies between his proposed measure of value and the common measure of it in the form of price.

Volume I of *Capital* appeared in 1867; as early as 1871, Jevons and his Continental colleagues, unknown to one another, were publishing their works. The old attempt to measure value was not given up—far from it. The result was the so-called theory of "marginal utility." This expression implies a calculation which Economic Man presumably goes through when he decides that he would rather buy a book than keep his five dollars. According to the marginalists, such a man may be regarded as making a mental division of an object's utility into a number of units of decreasing utility, the last one of which, or final increment, actually determines the choice. Knowing the last degree of utility represented by spending his money for some other want, he is matching it with the last degree of the book's utility. Experience tells us that when we are hungry every succeeding mouthful of food diminishes our want, until a point is reached where, if we had to make the slightest exertion to obtain a further mouthful, we should decline the opportunity. Similarly, say the marginalists, the value to the individual of any portion of the available supply of a uniform commodity equals the significance attached by him to the least intense bit of satisfaction he can derive from a single portion of the supply: the utility of the marginal unit acquired or consumed. The whole supply will then exchange at this value until the market is so well provided with the commodity that its psychological utility de-

creases and the price falls. This will happen regardless of
the amount of labor which may still have to be embodied
in the cheaper goods.

Marx had argued that since uses were diverse it was impossible to abstract from them any common stuff to measure. Labor looked to him much more concrete and uniform,
hence more adapted to measurement. But he found that
labor was far too concrete and diversified also. He had to
squeeze from the separate acts of labor the "abstract jelly"
of "socially necessary labor power." And he did this without
seeing that separate concrete utilities could just as easily
jell into an "abstract utility." By showing that values on the
market expressed in objective form various degrees of this
abstract utility, the marginalists corrected the error and
opened out a new field of factual and theoretical investigation.

For one thing it seemed clear that with the new definition of value the balance of supply and demand could be
neatly deduced. If many consumers desire watches, the
supply's total utility increases, the price goes up; watchmaking will attract capital and the market will be supplied with watches to the point where the steadily diminish-
ing want for them discourages further manufacture. All
these operations, beginning in the head of the customer
and ending on the jeweler's tray, could be mathematically
expressed and graphically plotted. Consequently the new
value theory was felt to be the first and only basis of a true
economic science; and that phrase itself ultimately replaced
the older name Political Economy.

Again, under the labor theory, it was impossible to establish true formulas of economic exchange. Marx's inaccurate use of the word "average" in "average labor time"
and elsewhere betrayed his own lack of interest in actual
measurement. He could never define "socially necessary
labor time" or truly reduce skilled labor, as he wished, to
units of simple or unskilled labor. Marx was in fact content
to show that with time and labor congealed in things, the
measurement of their value was possible. And he made use

of it only for showing how through surplus value the employer appropriates the excess labor time given by the worker.

It is true that as measurements the new formulas of the marginalists were not perfect. They often conflicted with statistical facts, but the discrepancy might prove to be no more than the error which a scientific law encounters when applied in the real world. The significance of utility was in any case reaffirmed. Things have value because we want them. Their value to us is their use value as compared with other use values. Things of course need not be useful in any narrow sense: a swig of prussic acid for the suicide, a pink paper cap for the reveler, a bread pill for the imaginary invalid—all have utility. And they may have it while a steam calliope, embodying months of socially necessary labor power, approaches the limit of inutility and valuelessness. Utility, in short, is Hamlet's "there is nothing either good or bad, but thinking makes it so." Mind was creeping back into the world of things, and the active preaching of socialism in England by the Fabians was to be done in the name of Marx's Utopia but with the aid of Jevonian economics.

By the old guard, Gossen, Jevons, and the rest were naturally accused of subjectivism and other horrible practices forbidden in science, but in truth they were only adding a psychological perception to the old Benthamite assumptions about human behavior. They assumed that man acts from pleasure-seeking motives, that he knows what the final utility of a watch or a book actually is for him in the moment of choice. But what if man acts from habit or social compulsion, not from rapid calculation? Or again, Jevons's law of indifference, which states that any portion of a commodity on the market is as want-fulfilling as any other of the same kind, will apply (for a jaded palate) to all commodities of similar price, or to two commodities of different price. Utility will then hardly exist as a measure of value.

Besides, the theory assumes an equality among purchasers which does not really obtain. If I must have an alarm clock in order to reach my new job on time and it costs me half my present supply of funds, my yardstick for measuring clock utility differs widely from that of a man in the same need but who has an income of two hundred times the price of the clock. Consequently, although our effective demand from the market is faithfully recorded in the same way—the taking up of one clock—the calculations that led to it are not comparable. And there is worse. The beauty and delicacy of a market mechanism self-adjusting to human needs not only presupposes equal pulls upon it expressed in equal dollars—which is false as we have just seen—it presupposes also the complete lubrication of the parts, so that when watches are needed, capital will go into watchmaking and manufacture will stop in time to avoid a glut. This lubricant is of course information, seconded by the power to act economically. But as it happens this is precisely what an actual market situation precludes. The buyer knows but little about the wares he buys and less about competing prices. The manufacturer must guess about demand and fend off unexpected avalanches of supply; while the intermediaries slow up the self-adjusting processes in both directions—all acting in the most approved ways of economic men. The upshot of these well-known criticisms is that modern economics has no definition and no yardstick of value to show for its repeated efforts. It has destroyed Marx's theory, but has not replaced it by a tested "scientific" one.

Still it would be unjust to belittle the significance of the marginal theory of value. Into an excessively rigid materialistic scheme it reintroduced the variable factor of human wants; and into an excessively gelatinous scheme of labor-time products, it reintroduced the concrete usefulness of common goods. From Marx's invention of socially necessary labor time—a sort of headless monster whose decrees were binding on toiling mankind—Jevons and his colleagues returned to a consideration of the individual. True, they

made him too independent and canny by far, and they mis-
conceived or neglected some of his relations to other individuals; they may even have wished to justify an obviously
imperfect scheme of production and distribution, but in
seeing man in the midst of a market, choosing wares made
by his fellows, and acting and acted upon through things,
they described what could be tested by experience and observation. Their science was faulty, but it made no pretense
to going below the surface of appearance to a real world of
hidden causes beneath. It could, in other words, be criticized in the light of its own methods, which had nothing
sacred or tortuous about them.

The new theories had of course no effect on Marx himself, who at the moment of their appearance was bringing
out the second edition of *Capital* in full confidence that
it held the formula of "scientific socialism." It was this faith
in the certainty of "German science"[2] which made him so
unrelenting an opponent of the man who, a generation
before the Marginalists, stood as the living denial of his
politics, economics, and sociology. I refer to Pierre-Joseph
Proudhon.

What the educated reader is likely to know about Proudhon is that he said "Property is Theft," and that Karl
Marx wrote *The Poverty of Philosophy* as a reply to Proudhon's *Philosophy of Poverty*. Two such pieces of information are enough to "place" a man, but they hardly suffice
for understanding him. There are signs, however, that with
the decline of the third, or American, wave of Marxism,
Proudhon is being examined anew. If this is done at all it
must of course be done not in the scales of Marxian truth,
but in his own terms.

To see the two men in historical perspective, we must
remember that Proudhon's influence began with his first
memoir on Property in 1840, when he was thirty-one and
Marx was still an adolescent given over to Hegel and the
writing of tragic verse. That influence ended, not with

[2] Letters to Bolte, Nov. 23, 1871, and to Sorge, Nov. 5, 1880.

Proudhon's earthly life in 1865, but rather some ten years later, with the merging of the Marxian and Lassallean groups in Germany. The first International was largely composed of Proudhonians, and French socialism has never wholly abandoned his spirit.

What then is the Proudhonian spirit? Some might say a priori that it must be the well-known French logic and clarity. Nothing could be further from the truth. Proudhon's writings are uneven, inconsistent, and often misleading. Nevertheless, his meaning is less subject to dispute than Marx's, its development is less encumbered with academic baggage, and its temper makes it readily translatable into our twentieth-century idiom. Proudhon's central thesis is that the present social system is a mass of contradictions, chiefly economic, and that the task of the nineteenth century is to create an order embodying the ideas of 1789. The contradictions prevent Liberty, Equality, and Fraternity from being more than words engraved on public buildings; yet the possible realization of these ideals is what social reform must achieve if revolutionary chaos and decadence are to be warded off.

Like all the thinkers of his time, Proudhon is first of all a social historian. That is why he is hard on Rousseau though he really follows in his tradition—the romanticist tradition of diversity in unity and concreteness above all things. "Property is theft," to take an example, was no new axiom. Rousseau had said it in his *Discourse on the Origins of Inequality*, and Pascal—a romanticist out of time—likewise.[3] "Property is theft" does not mean that Proudhon wants all property held in common or redistributed by legislative fiat. It means only that in the present order, property does not yield the benefits that it is supposed to yield. It does not guarantee liberty; it is the negation of equality; and it actually prevents fraternity, or co-operation among men of one community. Nor is property an idyllic privilege of the rich which the poor should envy and snatch

[3] Herbert Spencer himself had conceded it early in his career.

away from them. It is simply an outworn and destructive institution.

Proudhon therefore feels like Fourier that communism is no solution. In both the extremes of individual property and of communism there is tyranny. In the former, it is the tyranny of the strong; in the latter, of the weak. "The injustices of communism are irreparable, it does violence to sympathies and repugnances, it puts free choice under an iron yoke, it exercises moral torture on the conscience, it plunges society into apathy (*atonie*)—in a word it enslaves in a stupid and gaping uniformity, the free active, reasoning, unsubmissive, personality of man."[4] If we are to escape this fate some other form of ownership—what Proudhon calls Possession—must be instituted in place of the self-contradictory modern property.

This demand is of course what Marx attacked as Proudhon's petty-bourgeois ideal; yet he did not do so before learning from his later *bête noire* a good deal about the "contradictions" of capitalism.[5] In 1843 Marx was pleased to write: "Proudhon subjects the basis of political economy, property, to a critical examination, and it is indeed the first decisive, rigorous and scientific criticism of it that has ever been made; it is a great scientific step forward which revolutionizes political economy and permits it for the first time to be made a true science. Proudhon's *What Is Property?* has the same importance for modern political economy as Sieyès's *What Is the Third Estate?* has for modern political theory."[6] But Marx's tune changed as his ideas veered to communism and statism, by which time the same work

4 *Qu'est-ce que la Propriété?* 1926 ed., 325.

5 Marx's word play on the title of Proudhon's book makes us forget that it reads in full, *Economic Contradictions*, or *the Philosophy of Poverty*. When a noted writer asserts that "many an economist who today analyzes the contradictions of Capitalism does not stop to think that these ideas stem from Marx," he should perhaps stop to think how much of Marx "stems" from Proudhon—and Sismondi.

6 Quoted by Bourguin, "Des rapports entre Proudhon et Karl Marx," *Revue d'économie politique*, March 1893, 177–78.

of Proudhon's had become "a piece of writing which in a rigorously scientific history of political economy would hardly be worthy of mention."[7]

One source of misunderstanding between the two men grew out of their meeting in Paris when Marx went there in search of economic and social knowledge. Marx was then preaching Hegel, and Proudhon, who had had Hegelian friends earlier, was captivated anew by the notion of the dialectic. Yet his natural way of thought was rather Kantian than Hegelian, so that even while he thought himself indebted to Hegel he never did more than borrow a few of his terms. Thereupon Marx, forgetting about Proudhon's "rigorous and scientific" essay on Property, had an easy time showing that Proudhon knew nothing of Hegel at first hand—Proudhon himself said so—and that nothing he wrote could be "scientific."[8]

We know in what way Marx was Hegelian. By Proudhon's contrasting or Kantian way of thought I mean his perception that antinomies, or what he preferred to call contradictions, cannot be abolished but must be transcended. What Proudhon saw in Property, Capital, Labor, Value, Taxation, Competition, Monopolies, Credit, or War, was not entities existing by themselves and possessing a distinct, inalienable character. He saw aspects of things in movement, which the mind fixed by means of abstract names and mistakenly believed to be absolutes. Instead of personifying them as "enemies" to destroy, Proudhon regarded institutions as "historical categories." His aim, therefore, is not to foster antagonisms which will swallow the present and spew up an automatically improved future, but to change our uses of reality through ideas and laws in order

[7] Letter to the *Sozial-Demokrat* on the occasion of Proudhon's death, 1865.

[8] The German socialist writer and politician Eduard Bernstein admits that in the *Poverty of Philosophy* written in 1845, Marx attacks Proudhon's words rather than his thoughts. The neo-Kantian tendency of German and Russian socialist leaders like Woltmann, Bernstein, Vorlander, and Lunacharsky is an interesting return to some of the Proudhonian assumptions.

to create new social relations of a more satisfactory kind.

The opposition of capital and labor, for instance, is such a relation, which the Marxian materialist, however much he may deny his mechanistic interpretation, is bound to promote as a class war, trusting that the extinction of the one will inure benefit to the other. Proudhon shows that Capital and Labor, though at daggers drawn, are not antitheses. Labor becomes capital; capital feeds and furthers labor, and the two are the beginning and the end of one human process, falsely abstracted into two warring principles. Marx naturally calls this sophistry, because he thinks that Proudhon is blinking the evil effects of accumulated capital upon poverty-stricken labor. But as a self-educated cowherd of the poorest class, Proudhon knew a good deal more than Marx about the poor workman's lot in France, and he felt no need to "prove" the evils of the Capital-Labor relation, no need of two theories of value.[9] Nor was Proudhon original when he described those evils: they were admitted on all hands, even by the Classical Economists.[10] They were a shocking novelty only to Marx emerging from a study of Hegel and Jurisprudence.

Unlike Marx's, Proudhon's solutions are always purposive, nonviolent, pluralistic. His is never a "brooding one-ideaed thought." He repudiates by anticipation the Marxian view of a single class emerging on the wreck of all the others and remaining single through an eternity of bliss. He wants his followers to transcend class ideas, not to embitter themselves by seeking mass power in a spirit of self-righteousness. In his political journalism, Proudhon always wrote with the points of view of all classes in mind, for in virtue of his strong moral sense—almost as puritanical as

[9] On the subject of value, Proudhon points out that value in use and value in exchange are also contradictory abstractions but really inseparable. Unthinkable apart from each other, they can negate each other, as when a producer who oversupplies the market becomes richer and richer in goods as he becomes poorer and poorer in exchange value or its equivalent, money.

[10] The class antagonism is implicit in the Wages Fund Theory of their school.

Marx's but more aware of itself—he saw that no workable society could arise from mere aggressiveness, "expropriating the expropriators" or "liquidating" inconvenient groups. It was Proudhon's influence which in 1864 compelled Marx to retain the "Truth, Justice and Morality" clause in the statutes of the First International, for Proudhon—brought up on the Bible and the French *Encyclopédie*—knew that men cannot live by cynicism alone. Proudhon was as conscious as Marx of the hypocrisy which can lurk behind the mouthings of morality, but he was not so naïve as to think that getting rid of the words and acting in a perpetual maze of lies and irresponsibility could lead to a better order. And fittingly enough, the men who learned from Proudhon as he had learned from history and the Gospels never tried to make his writings into Holy Scripture, whereas the atheistical Marx, with his tyrannical temperament, has left us a Bible of the Working Class and a host of fanatics.

Believing that life was activity, creation—"anti-death," as he called it—Proudhon dwells on his philosophic and moral axioms, and thereby speaks more persuasively to us than can any propounder of economic "science." The history of Marxism itself has taught us that men are not machines and that the practicability of a new scheme depends on human beings' developing new habits and desires. Marx thinks he refutes Proudhon on this point by saying: "The windmill will give you a society with a feudal overlord; the steam-operated mill will give you a society with an industrial capitalist."[11] But this is the egg-and-hen debate, unless one takes the Proudhonian view that change is slow, difficult, and must be prepared, that it takes the action of ideas to affect both the superstructure and the base. In the Marxian dialectic the antithesis destroys the thesis and the synthesis swallows what survives. In Proudhon the contradiction is wholly accepted, *as* a contradiction, but it is made tolerable by arrangements which mitigate the conflict. His Utopia will not be frictionless, it will not be

11 *Misère de la Philosophie*, 155–56.

bureaucratic perfection, but it will presumably be an improvement over the present state of neglected contradictions. Hence Proudhon's motto—obscure unless expanded: "Universal conciliation through universal contradiction."

But how did Proudhon propose to bring about the transformation of so contradictory a society as his own? Did he mean to follow the middle road of tinkering? Far from it. The middle of the road he considered "treachery and intellectual dishonesty, the soldering of half an idea to the other half of another idea."[12] His resolution lay through mutualism, anarchism, and what might be called today "social credit." As in Marx, anarchism, or the absence of political government, was something in the future. It may therefore be canceled out as a common quantity in both doctrines. Proudhon's mutualism implied small, self-sustaining geographical units. Contracts and civil laws both within and without the unit would provide the necessary sanctions to assure the production of human goods.

Proudhon, it is true, neglected to provide for the growth of giant industries and the raising of huge armies. He died before seeing either of them established on French soil. This deficiency was Marx's strongest and best argument against his erstwhile friend and teacher. But the applicability of Proudhon's desideratum remains regardless of his views on size, as is shown by the fact that when big industry had conquered France the syndicalists who preached a federation of democratic industrial units claimed Proudhon as their guide. And today when industry shows signs of having reached the high point of unification, Proudhon's "cellular" idea may again seem suggestive.

As for Proudhon's reliance on contract and "mutualism" it is a new expression of Rousseau's idea that a good society must depend not on coercion but on good will. The social cement is mutual interest and mutual aid, not laws and policemen. Here Proudhon undoubtedly overstated his

[12] *Création de l'Ordre,* 214.

case, but his sense of the relation of possession to independence and to co-operation is acute and meaningful to us at a time when totalitarian control threatens to achieve half the aims of socialism at the expense of the reason for achieving them. The making of goods is at the root of the trouble but the tree of evil has more than one root. Proudhon saw this and insisted on possession, including the right to work and the minimum wage.[13] The present scheme of property denies the individual the possession of what he makes or helps to make. Hence Proudhon took the theory that labor is the source of all value not as a description of what is, but as a description of what ought to be. This relation is not yet a fact, but it is an intelligible goal.

Proudhon's financial proposals—including the plan and the failure of his People's Bank—would take us too far into the details of a past beyond recall. Suffice it to say that, as modern manipulations show, Proudhon was farseeing in his view that credit, finance, and the use of paper bore some relation to economic health. It is untrue that he relied exclusively or even mainly on paper tricks to make all things new. In any case Proudhon's importance does not rest on what he planned for immediate use a hundred years ago; it rests on his critique of property and on his principles of social reorganization. Far more than Marx, who concentrated on economic theory and revolutionary tactics, Proudhon attended to the gross facts of social life in his century. He discussed the capacity of the working classes; the psychology of riches and poverty; the nature of revolutions; the problems of war and peace; the dangers of nationalism; the limits of sociological laws—to say nothing of the place of ethics and religion in the present and the probable future. To each of these topics he devoted whole volumes.

[13] Speaking to Finance Minister Goudchaux in 1848, he exclaimed, "Well! if you concede the right to work, I'll concede the right to property." *Le Droit au Travail*, ed. 1850, 13. It is not necessary to underline how much modern legislation and theory— see the Webbs and J. M. Keynes—have followed Proudhon's precepts of a century ago.

Well might Prince Metternich say with double meaning that Proudhon was "the natural son of the Encyclopedists." The very size of his output discourages the modern reader; but there are rewards for overcoming this discouragement. In spite of obvious declamatory passages, Proudhon's prose is sinewy and full of life. Like Rousseau, he often gives the impression of being abstract and legalistic when in truth he is concrete and hardheaded. Like Samuel Butler he takes pleasure in paradoxes, but it is his enemies and not himself that carry them to inept lengths.

On certain points he is, like Marx, undecided and misleading if opened at random. Certain passages in the early Proudhon suggest that he began as a materialist, even as a strict economic interpreter of history. As late as 1865 he said: "What governs the modern world is neither a dogma, nor a faith, nor a tradition. It is not the Gospel, nor the Koran, nor Aristotle, nor Voltaire; no more is it the Constitution of 1852 or that of 1793. It is the Great Ledger whose pages carry only two words in large letters: on one side Debit, on the other, Credit."[14]

This must not be made to mean more than it says. All his life Proudhon dinned into the public ear the importance of economics, but when mechanistic materialism was sweeping Europe he took his stand against it. In particular he opposed the two forms of political materialism that were gaining ground during his last days—the principle of nationalities and the principle of natural frontiers. He prophesied that they meant war, like all mere agglomerations of things and people organized for a one-sided purpose. He foresaw likewise that "the jurisdiction of war" would not solve a single economic problem. An economic code was needed to recognize and to justify economic interests in conflict, as political treaties could not do. He scouted the talk of a League of Nations or other purely political federation of Europe, and he analyzed its futility as if he had lived to see one.

[14] Guerre et Paix, 462–63.

His predictions had, however, nothing "scientific" about them. "History," he affirmed, "is the mode according to which any creation occurs . . . it is the general picture of the development of all the sciences; it is an exposition, a testimony. The diversity of its subject matter prevents it from being a science. It is only material for science. . . . Fatality does not govern society . . . there is a life, a soul, a liberty which defies precise and fixed measurements of the kind that applies to matter. As regards society, materialism is absurd."[15]

[15] *Création de l'Ordre*, 357.

7. After Marx: What Is Social Science?

The establishment of socialism, therefore, on any
national or race basis, is out of the question.
　　　　　　　　　E. BELFORT BAX on *The*
　　　　　　　　　Religion of Socialism, 1886

Socialism will be a dictatorship with racial selec-
tionism or it will not succeed.
　　　　　　　　　VACHER DE LAPOUGE on
　　　　　　　　　Social Selection, 1896

It is customary to date the rise of fascist theory from the
turn of the century. Pareto and Georges Sorel come to mind
as the outstanding figures who "prepared" the advent of
Mussolini and Hitler and in some way began the "retreat
from reason." This view is the result of mistaken hindsight.
The turn of the century was not occupied with preparing
Mussolini any more than with making way for Lenin. Its
business in sociology was to examine, among other theories,
those of Marx, Rodbertus, and the Marginalists. And the
interesting point to note is that the criticism of Marx's
tenets came close upon the heels of their popularization.
Historical Materialism first became widely known in the
nineties and the reaction against it began before 1900.
Knowing how the current of opinion was setting in other
quarters—in biology, in physical science, and in philosophy
—we need not be surprised that Marx's victory *then* should
have been short-lived. He had competitors: the Proudhoni-

ans were not all dead or converted; the Anarchists and Nihilists of Bakunin's school were still plotting and preaching; the so-called Historical School of economists, re-established in Germany in 1872 and harking back to the men of the eighteen-forties, numbered many adherents.

In America, Henry George had begun his analysis of Progress and Poverty and his crusade against landlordism —a crusade directed at abolishing poverty through the confiscation of "economic rent"—and was supported by Alfred Russel Wallace in England and Colins in Belgium. George's influence as a speaker and writer on both sides of the Atlantic was far more immediate and widespread than Marx's; it was his fiery person and brilliant book that woke many a man, like Shaw, from rugged individualism, in a sudden and decisive fashion beyond Marx's power. In the same decade, a German-trained farmer's son from Illinois, Simon Patten, was beginning to teach at the University of Pennsylvania a generation of economists who no longer looked abroad for doctrine, but saw in the facts of American life the proof that the world was entering a new "economy of abundance." The old "laws" would no longer apply to it and the old institutions must be reshaped according to plan, so as to avoid the waste which the former "scarcity economy" had enforced through its makeshift method of unregulated competition. Another American, Veblen, by combining the evolutionism of Darwin with the anti-bourgeois bias of Marx in a way that brought the doctrines back into Lamarckian and "historical" channels, was beginning his painful academic career and creating by his publications the future Institutional School of economics. These were but a few of the ideas growing with or against the Marginal Theory and superseding the Utopian and Classical sociologies, even before *Capital* had been widely translated and discussed.

So that when Marx's principal critics—Pareto, Sorel, Croce, Sombart, Böhm-Bawerk, Andler, Pantaleoni, Stammler, and others—did come round to his general and special theories, they were obviously more concerned with finding answers to the problems everywhere agitated than with getting rid of him as a menace. They could not foresee 1917, 1922, or 1933, and could hardly have dealt with Marx differently even if they had. Revisionism and Reformism had already begun to disarm the small socialist parties of the Continent, and as early as the mid-nineties Sorel and Andler could speak in a descriptive way of the *Decomposition of Marxism.*

The first difficulty that Sorel encountered in Marx was that of passing from the theory to the facts. The value theories, the concentration of ownership, the falling rate of profits—none of these had been borne out by experience during the thirty years since *Capital* had appeared. Moreover, in the face of an indifferent proletariat, the class war was beginning to show up as a mere tautology: historically, class struggles would take place when there were classes, when these classes had opposite interests, and when the classes were conscious of this opposition. As for "the" dialectic at large, advances in psychology, in statistics, and in other social sciences showed the behavior of matter to be more and more of a mystery.

If facts rebelled, it became necessary to inquire what Marx, the man of science, could have been talking about. The most likely supposition was that he had been writing "pure" science, which did not hold true of observed facts but, like the theory of gases, stated the limiting case. He would then be describing the sort of world where you can safely "neglect friction, the pressure of the atmosphere, and the weight of the elephant." Sorel and Sombart believed this for a time, and interpreted Marx accordingly. They even drew from Engels (shades of Concrete Matter!) the admission that it was exactly so. But it soon became clear that a "law" which not only failed to closely fit phenomena, but seemed rather to fit their opposite, was not even an "ideal" law. Sorel, for one, concluded that Marx's pronouncements about the Capitalist System were only meant to "cast a partial and indirect light on economic reality." Marx's Historical Materialism would then figure as "a

metaphysical instrument" yielding a metaphysics of economics. "Marx, like Ricardo, conceived a mechanistic society perfectly automatic, in which competition is always
at its maximum efficiency . . . he supposed that the various
sociological conditions are measurable in intensity . . .
hence in such a society, utility, demand and trade are the
results of the divisions of classes."[1]

This well-meant effort shows how desirous of salvaging
Marx were the leading sociologists of fifty years ago. In
their eyes "the only scientific sociology" was still venerable.
Croce agreed with Sorel that Marx's economic ideas were
not "laws" in a descriptive or physical or ethical sense. They
are laws in a Marxian sense. Croce, who wished even more
than Sorel to rejuvenate Marxism, and who incidentally
had the merit of refuting Pareto from the start, was forced
to conclude that Marx had worked not with one but with
two abstract hypothetical societies—one in which labor
would be the source of value and automatic adjustments
would provide justice; another in which the private ownership of capital led to the appropriation of surplus value and
made for injustice. Neither of these was the factual society
of nineteenth-century Europe and America. It followed
that Marx had not provided socialists with a solid basis
in the present or the historical past; rather, by proposing
these two hypothetical societies and contrasting them, he
had inspired the labor movement to struggle for the just
society. Marx also showed the true method—historical materialism—and there he was to be taken in the crudest and
most literal sense. Taken all in all he was the "Machiavelli
of the working class movement."[2]

In saying this, Croce made it clear that he set no store
by Marx and Engels's researches into the origins of the
family, their idea of inevitable evolution through unskip-
pable "stages," and all the imposing apparatus of historical
proof. Similarly, according to Croce, Marx's philosophical

[1] *Journal des Economistes*, May 1897, 222–31.
[2] *Historical Materialism and the Economics of Karl Marx*,
N. Y., 1914, 117.

kinships did not bear inspection. Not only was the Marxian terminology perversely inappropriate, but historical materialism had nothing to do either with the true materialistic tradition or with the Hegelian dialectic. These were mere ballast for a doctrine whose basic purpose was practical, whose origins lay in the French Revolution, and whose technique was simply *Realpolitik*. Croce felt that a brutal outbreak of the masses would nevertheless not occur, because he did not see whence the indispensable religious leadership would come. He apparently believed that further study and the spread of socialist aims might yield the fruits desired by Marx, but through peaceful evolution. More impatient, Sorel gave his mind to the problems of a new proletarian group, the industrially organized Syndicalists. But soon weary of their bickerings, he went one step farther towards paternalism with the French royalists, and lived long enough to admire Lenin and receive from Mussolini unexpected credit for a supposed influence on his Caesarism.

Meantime from the camp of the pure economists came Vilfredo Pareto, a free trader, trained in science and mathematics, and ready to follow the results of his researches wherever they might lead. In controversy with Croce and others, he freely admitted the waste and inefficiency of the unregulated "liberal" market. But he also urged the immense practical difficulty of socialism—not the political obstacle of getting it accepted, but that of running it economically once adopted. While in this poised frame of mind, Pareto was led to question the Marginalists' psychological interpretation of Utility. Utility, they alleged, determined choices and controlled the market. Hence the less the market was manipulated from outside, the more total satisfaction it would yield. Pareto showed that in truth economics knows nothing of utility or value as it appears to the individual. It can only point to acts of choice. He constructed curves showing how various quantities of two ordinary wares could be combined to yield the same satisfaction, or lesser, or greater, in complex permutations. The market seemed no longer to hold the secret of a free man's happiness and Pareto asserted what Mill had said a good many years before, that economic laws are neutral. The kind of society we have results from a choice which we make independently of science. This was the germ of Pareto's attempt at a general sociology dividing the rational from the nonrational factors in human conduct and so paving the way—we are told—for fascist unreason.

This modern criticism of Pareto misses the mark, and Croce, in two letters dated 1900, showed the true mode of attack on Pareto. Insofar as Pareto discovered by his own devices that science cannot yield a set of directions for the march of history, he did an excellent job. He was sloughing off the mechanical Spencerian monism in which he had grown up. Indeed he was doing in his field what hundreds of other Europeans were doing in theirs, going upstream against mid-century scientism and groping towards the corrective which the Romanticists in their day had applied to the same rationalist error of the eighteenth century.

Where Pareto went astray was in imagining that man could be split like a pea into two halves, one logical, the other nonlogical; or that experience could be correspondingly split into reason and emotion. Croce pointed out to him that this was a division for purposes of thought, not a division possible in fact. Economic science is not a self-sufficing realm of independent things. Like any subject matter it is an aspect of experience, related to other aspects and set apart only by men's minds. In Pareto's "pure economics," for example, the objective "scale of preferences" is not something existing apart from the human acts which indicated these preferences. It is a way of talking about them, a useful metaphor. It is true that we cannot infer from the mere act of choice how much Jones values a new radio-phonograph above the old player piano. But this does not split off the act of choice from the feeling of Jones. Indeed, Jones never does measure the two objects on a scale: and only in a figurative sense does the rejected article contain an amount of something called value. If Jones chooses the phonograph, the other is simply a non-value. More abstractly, values exist in relation to man, and emerge only in the act of choice. The gap between the needs, the desires, and the interests of a conscious creature on the one hand, and the things counted by any science on the other, is not bridgeable in such a way that by counting the things you can measure the choices. The living experience that includes both scientific objects and human values is *one* experience, not a Jekyll-and-Hyde manifestation in which you can grasp the character of Jekyll by grasping the coattails of Hyde.

But these arguments of the year 1900 did not at once spread to the larger public that forms what is politely called public opinion. We have only to recall that Pareto's ideas began to be talked of on these shores about 1930. Between Croce's debate with him and this date there occurred the Russian Revolution, which meant a second boom of Marxism, heightened by the world-wide depression which followed a decade later. The connection between Marx and the Revolution is plain, but what portion of his teachings did the event justify? Certainly not the prophecy of an urban, proletarian uprising either in England or in Germany. Marx had also spoken of Russia's possible return to communism before thorough industrialization. If Marx the prophet was right, were not his critics premature in speaking of the disintegration of Marxism? Or was Lenin—the hero of the Communist Revolution—the Machiavelli whom Croce discerned in the teachings of the master? In any case, Lenin was the spiritual reincarnation of Marx. He was philosopher, pamphleteer, and tactician, and his influence on all those who have ever given allegiance to Marxism has been due to his ability to restate the doctrine in simpler, more modern, and more explicit terms, while denying that he was in any way altering the text.[3]

[3] Lenin's *Imperialism*, according to Granville Hicks, has been

Lenin began his political career in the late nineties by attacking the Social Democratic reformers and revisers in the name of the *Communist Manifesto* of 1848. Overlooking its one lapse into reformism, Lenin from the outset preached revolutionary action—a human interference with the historical process which jerks forward the inevitable. To prod the hesitant, Lenin continued the Marxian polemic of personal abuse, quarrel, and expulsion within agitators' groups. Living not very far from Marx's former lodgings in Soho when this century began, Lenin carried on the work of his predecessor by struggling over the control of the obscure newspaper *Iskra* which he had founded in Munich for Russian refugees; beating down the Menshevik policy of participation in the Russian Duma or Parliament; and trying to build up an "aristocracy of revolutionists."

In those days even Trotsky did not escape abuse and ostracism, but it so happened that fifteen years later Trotsky was head of the Petrograd Soviet Military Committee whose force Lenin needed for his Marxist coup. He purchased its help by abandoning his "tactics" and proclaiming a temperate and "democratic" platform suiting the wishes of the already formed Soviets and their leaders.[4] Lenin had of course no intention of abiding by the promises of this conversion. It was all "democratic nonsense," just like the half measures which followed his seizure of power in November 1917. Domestic enemies had to be fought off, peace had to be made with Germany, and an administration created out of whole cloth. In such straits no theory could hope to be applied intelligibly. Even after peace and order had been won, famine, lack of communications, general stupidity and mental resistance postponed anything like a thoroughgoing communism. Lenin's recognition of failure in the premature application of strict doc-

the usual introduction of American intellectuals to Marxist thought. *Books That Changed Our Minds*, 13.

[4] It should be remembered that the Bolsheviks did not overthrow the Tsarist regime but the six-months-old "liberal" government then led by Kerensky.

trine led to his New Economic Policy, which in his own words was "capitalism plus socialism."

Then, for the sake of popular prestige, or else as a result of fatigue and bad judgment, Lenin embarked on a plan for the electrification of Russia—a country as ill-provided with water power as can be found in Europe. Socialism was redefined as "Electrification plus Power to the Soviets" and a naïve admiration for American methods seemed to compete in favor with the expectation of thorough communism. Materialism, perhaps, was working on the Russian leaders in a different sense from the philosophical. In 1924 Lenin died as the result of overwork and a wound received in 1918. Trotsky, absent on a duck-shooting trip at the time, lost grip on the reins of power, and Stalin made his way to dictatorship. Materialism plus nationalism, plus partial collectivism, plus balance of power politics, became the Russian reality—interspersed with the purges inseparable from revolutionary dictatorships. And throughout, the double Marxist-Leninist theory remained the source of endless argument, abuse, proscription, and death.

As a philosopher, Lenin always insisted on a strict materialistic monism. Arguing from geology that nature is prior to man, he concluded that man's consciousness is a late evolutionary product of no fundamental significance. He attacked Kant and the neo-Kantians for their insistence on the human subject as indispensable to the act of knowing. He attacked Huxley for his candid admission about the untranslatability of sensation into matter. He attacked Henri Poincaré for his critical awareness of the limits of science. He declared, quite rightly, that the "new physics" was irrelevant to the question of materialism, and gave it as his reason that if matter is redefined as energy, it is still that something outside us which is "primary." We "copy" it with our minds and thus it rules history. Lenin claimed descent from the school of Diderot—evidently without reading him thoroughly—and called everything else "bourgeois reaction"—evidently forgetting how bourgeois the eighteenth-century *philosophes* were. For him their liberating doctrine was slowly being corrupted by a return of bourgeois religious thought in the guise of philosophy and science. He blamed Berkeley for a part of this latter-day revolt against matter—a remote action at a distance, surely, even for a Bishop. In the light of a priori atheism, the force of Berkeley's argument escaped Lenin, and he fastened materialism as a creed upon art, thought, and speech, in a Russia which was simultaneously growing mystical over its new heroes and saints.[5]

It would be hard to exaggerate Lenin's part in shaping the Russian revolution and in spreading Marx's ideas. But these two functions form no consistent single role. Now one, now the other is distorted, sacrificed, palliated. Lenin won power by abandoning his tactics and lost communism in the shuffle for that power. Political necessity, which he was a master at divining, explains his lightning changes of mind, so distant from the stiff economic interpretation of history which he was at such pains to inculcate. The happy or wretched series of accidents which brought him to Russia at the moment when the United States entered the war, which gave him control of the Petrograd telephone exchange in November 1917, which drove a bullet through him in August of the next year and then sent Trotsky duck-shooting at a critical juncture six years later, is hardly "explicable" by any analysis—"first" or "last," material or spiritual. It can only be contemplated as a whole made up of infinitely interrelated parts in which cause and effect, and condition and result, cannot be separated into economic base and ideological superstructure.[6]

[5] According to an official hymn composed in 1935, Stalin has "brought man to birth, purified the earth, and restored the centuries," while also causing "the spring to bloom and the musical chords to vibrate."

[6] By what formula of dialectical irony, for example, could the tough proletarian leader be brought to write on Jan. 4, 1923, the famous complaint about Stalin's lack of bourgeois virtues: "He is too rough-mannered, and this defect, which is quite tolerable among us Communists, becomes intolerable in the function of

Yet the reader will only have to search his own mind in order to discover how "natural" and convenient this sort of economic interpretation has become. It is not only natural in the sense of familiar; it is also naturalistic, and shines in comparison with the supernatural or political or intellectual explanations. This adoption of Marxian ways of thought is obviously not all due to Marx himself. We associate it with his name, but it drew reinforcements from Darwinian biology, behaviorist psychology, and popular medicine—all at one in asserting that whatever human beings think or do or want or say is due "in the last analysis" —that refuge of the hard-pressed—to some material cause. And of all material causes the social or economic, being closest and most common, is the most persuasive.

This is not to deny the importance of economic fact and economic motive in human life; and the point of anti-Marxian criticism is not to banish all economic interpretation in favor of some other kind; rather, it is to discover its meaning and assign its limits. As a revelation of "the secret" of history, it is no better and no worse than any other single-answer system. As a verbal substitute for "events" it is, like all verbalisms, a distortion and a bad habit. Its correct application requires a careful fitting of economic fact with human motives. For it is the truth of the much-decried economic motive which can give to economic generalities a place among concrete events. When Webster and Calhoun both argued the preliminaries to the Civil War with appeals to self-interest, they were not only following a venerable tradition, but using what they knew would move men to action. The word "motive" enshrines this fact of experience. A human motive is economic when the possession of goods forms a part of the purpose in hand, as when Homer, some centuries before Marx, in mention-

---

General Secretary. That is why I propose . . . nominating in his stead a man who in all respects is distinguished from Stalin by being his superior, that is to say, more patient, more loyal, more considerate towards his comrades, less capricious, and so on." Quoted in Catlin, *Story of the Political Philosophers*, 617.

ing the Greeks' desire to recapture Helen of Troy invariably adds: *and all her wealth.*

The difficulty of this form of interpretation lies in showing the motive to be present. Consider how an American historian who was never a Marxist varies in his meeting of this difficulty. In dealing with the onset of the Civil War, Charles A. Beard begins by telling us: "The fighting was a fleeting incident. . . . The core of the vortex was in the flowing substance of things limned by statistical reports on finance, commerce, capital, industry, railways, agriculture."[7] And so on in this vein for many pages which are, quite literally, non-sense. Four years of war are not and can never be "a fleeting incident." Those particular four years generated passions still alive, still at work throughout the land; whereas the "core of the vortex" is an unreality which no reference to commerce can make concrete. The historian's task is not to dismiss either the abstract or the tangible but to connect them before our eyes. This Beard does successfully when he forgets the hocus-pocus of war "foreshadowed" by "the economic flux" and brings us face to face with motives and conditions: "The sentiments," he says, "the patterns of thought, linguistic devices, the social psychology, of regional leaders, sprang mainly from divergences in the necessary adjustment to environment: labor systems, climate, soil, and natural resources."[8] This is intelligible, and all the more acceptable that he denies any exact mechanical alignment of groups according to geography or economics. He shows that a momentous event like the Dred Scott decision was affected by personal ambitions and passions, and in giving due weight to the Abolitionist crusade, he declares that its sources, like those of most moral crusades, are still wrapped in mystery. In short, the nature of the great conflict was complex, not simple.[9]

This pluralistic interpretation, which includes the economic, stands in sharp contrast to the orthodox Marxian's. Here is no "last analysis" which makes history unroll by

[7] *The Rise of American Civilization,* ii, 54.
[8] *Op. cit.,* i, 663.
[9] *Ibid.,* i, 667–68, 698–99; ii, 19, 36.

means of a hidden mechanism below. The highly important "economic factor" is not a base but rather one among
many competing "ideologies."[10] It implies human purpose
and allows for human error. A Southern planter may oppose slavery or favor it for many reasons, even in spite of
his own interest or that of his class. Opinion, tradition,
propaganda, are thenceforth not superstructures floating
above the "core of the vortex" but real agents of change.
Fact and idea interweave in a seamless pattern of which
no historical analysis can unravel the main thread, for there
is none.

It was precisely to avoid this pluralism and this human
teleology that Marx made it clear he did not mean economic motives when he said economic interpretation. He
distinguished between the forces of production and the
modes of production in order to bridge the obvious gap
between the windmill and the feudal lord which it "produced;" he added an Ideology to embrace the feudal lord's
urge to build Lady chapels; but he found it impossible to
observe these distinctions. In argument, Marx leaps over
his own fences and cites simple human greed to explain
events: the repressors of the Paris Commune had "secured
a consideration of several millions" on a national loan and
distributed it among themselves.[11]   At the same time the
Commune itself is forced to figure as the rising proletariat,
although its members were in fact neither class-conscious
nor proletarians. Distrusting the concrete as superficial,
and seeking large abstractions as alone worthy of the dialectic, the Marxist historian has to swing between the in-
vidious and the metaphysical. In the end, forces and modes
give place to the bare "dialectical process," and it in turn
to "History."

Yet it is not History that produces a windmill but some
man. Every novelty occurs first as an idea in a human
brain. Because its embodiment and its effect are not at

[10] For an excellent example of the interweaving of motives in
matters of great economic interest, see Dwight C. Miner, *The
Fight for the Panama Route*, 1940.
[11] *The Civil War in France*.

once visible in the chaos of things, we may think of "forces of production" or "stages of development" as independent entities spinning out fates by themselves. But our inability to sort out the tangle beyond a certain point does not warrant our selecting one of its striking features as "primary"; and we should perhaps not be tempted to do so if we did not want to found a "social science." We have inherited from Marx and his fellow scientists of the mid-century the faith in social control through things. We want to understand, not by familiarity with verified facts but by formulas derived from them. We mistake conditions for causes and tie them together in chains. We know that *Uncle Tom's Cabin* was not written with a view to making the cotton mills of New England more prosperous, but we find economic forces determining cultural modes and these expressing themselves in a "class ideology" which in turn produces the state of mind of the novelist and her public. This links the economic with the social interpretation and disposes of art, but at the cost of making life an illusion and men purposeless.

Still, if one believes that history and society are made up of constituent factors, some of which are "fundamental" and others superficial, it follows that sociology must set to work to discover them. Hence for many Marx is undoubtedly the first scientific sociologist. Others, remembering the fallacies of his two interlocked value theories, judge that he has failed. They conclude that the "Capitalist system" of which we all speak in imitation of him is, so far as his showing goes, no system at all. If surplus value does not arise as he says, the exploitation of the workers is not the result of a "system" but is a by-product of industrialization. If labor, however essential to the creation of many values, is nevertheless not their scientific measure, any more than Utility, then economic science had better give up its title, and resume its more descriptive name of Political Economy.[12]

[12] See Barbara Wootton, *Lament for Economics*, 1938, 306–07.

Again, if there is starvation in the midst of plenty, it is not because the state is a conspiratorial tool of the ruling class, sharpened on the grindstone of classical economy, but rather because of the market-and-price institution which has been jammed by the rapidly changing powers of private property. Lastly, if the word "capital" is dissociated from its -ism and the compound term from its imaginary "system," we may find again that capital is not our old enemy the "given stage of development" that will breed an equally ugly antithesis, but one of the conditions of large-scale manufacture. The capitalist system then becomes simply privately owned capital; and though as such it still carries its evils on its face, it loses its Marxian character of a Bastille which can be stormed and taken with the assurance that out of its ruins will automatically sprout the fair harvest of a fully equalitarian society. Historical automatism in fact disappears with system, and the task of men resumes its eternal form of choosing ends and finding means in a complex world.

III

The Artistic Revolution

If natural causes be more known now than in the time of Aristotle, because more studied, it follows that poesy and other arts may, with the same pains, arrive still nearer to perfection. . . .

DRYDEN, 1668

1. 1859: Tristan and Isolde

My task is this: to bring revolution wherever I go.
. . . I shall write a peppery article on the theatre
of the future. . . . If my money gives out too soon,
I am counting on another source of help, that of
the social republic which sooner or later is bound
to come in France.

RICHARD WAGNER, 1849

While Karl Marx was fleeing the continent in 1849 to take refuge in England, the thirty-six-year-old conductor of the Dresden Opera, Richard Wagner, was sharing popular excitement on the barricades of that city and helping with pen and voice to conduct . . . the revolution. The opera house where he had lately led Beethoven's democratic Ninth Symphony had gone up in flames while he watched with undisguised pleasure; with so much, in fact, that he was accused of having fired it.[1] But his fire at the moment was mainly internal. He was ecstatic, he was drunk with crowd sensations, with freedom from responsibility, and also with vindictiveness against the Philistinism of the opera-going bourgeoisie. His friends, the revolutionists Röckel and Bakunin, could not quite make out the reasons

[1] A Communal Guard who was also a musician shouted at him: "Herr Kapellmeister, der Freude schöner Götterfunken hat gezündet!" (The divine ray of joy has come ablaze.) An allusion to the lines of Schiller sung in the choral part of Beethoven's Ninth Symphony.

for Wagner's fever heat. His knowledge of politics was slight, and though he wrote incendiary appeals in Röckel's sheet and rang alarm bells at the risk of his life, his demands for a better future seemed somewhat contradictory: an *absolute* king ruling over a *free* people, without parliament or nobility.

The truth was that Wagner's interest in the revolution was highly personal. As he had already done in the Leipzig riots of 1830, he was above all eager to merge his excitable self in the chaotic motions of the mass, in what he called "the mechanical stream of events." Next to this, he was protesting against the tyranny of the bourgeoisie, typified for him by the difficulties of his life, even as the envied second-in-command at the Dresden Opera. It was not, he had come to feel, the royal tyrants but the comfortable Philistines who were the cause of all evil. Hence he deprecated parliaments and exalted the goddess Revolution, hoping that she would bring forth a leader who could lift the masses to power and, incidentally, to the heights of art and a new German national spirit.

When the Prussian troops finally entered Dresden, and Wagner too had to flee in a hired coach, it was on this theme, punctuated by cries of "Fight, fight, forever!" that he declaimed for hours in a demonic strain to Bakunin and two other silent companions. Once safe, the first fruits of this passionate mood was the tract *Art and Revolution*, in which the hope of a regenerated state is linked with a cultural revolution effected through the popular art of the theater. The poet being its high priest, he must hold the nation under the absolute dominance of art, seconded in his ministrations by the absolute king.

Dominated himself by these hopes, and driven by necessity to further wanderings, Wagner came for the second time to Paris. He felt that he had striven for the socialist state that was bound to come out of the Second French Republic, and that it would raise him to the pinnacle he had just assigned to the poet. The king was now forgotten, or rather, Wagner petitioned the German princes for a subsidy enabling him to carry on his artistic work. Franz Liszt, the well-connected pianist through whom the petition was to be made, took a more immediate view and, advising Wagner to drop his "socialist fiddle-faddle," urged him to seek tangible results through the writing and production in Paris of a solid grand opera.

Painfully short of funds and desiring any sort of public success that might lead to more, Wagner fell in with the suggestion. He abandoned his dramatic theories, sought out a regular librettist, and made plans for composing and placing this "Paris opera" within six months. But in order to do this, he preferred to live quietly in Zurich. He accordingly returned there and at once indemnified himself for his unhappy stay in the city of light without culture by writing *The Artwork of the Future* (anti-opera) and *The Jews in the World of Music* (anti-Meyerbeer).[2] He also continued to work at his play, *Siegfried's Death*, altering it to suit the expanding revolutionary scheme of his *Ring of the Nibelungen*.

Before he could return to his practical operatic plans, however, Napoleon's coup of 1851 put an end to his hopes of Parisian and revolutionary success. Again this loss was compensated, by the production of *Lohengrin* at Weimar under Liszt's competent direction. This spurred Wagner on to the completion of the *Ring* poem, and shortly to its private printing and distribution. Wagner had not composed a note for six years, but confident in his social theories of art and in their just completed dramatic embodiment, he awaited the verdict of his friends.

Their response was distressingly cool. Even Liszt, who had been much taken with the idea when first broached, was critical without enthusiasm. The *Ring* was a failure.

[2] I shall use throughout the neologism "artwork," which corresponds not only to the ordinary German word *Kunstwerk*, but also to the idea of a new form cast in one piece and different from a simple "work of art." In the other essay, Meyerbeer is not mentioned by name but alluded to in frequent and transparent expressions.

Wagner's spirit sank in despair, he complained in shameless letters, threatened to emigrate to America or, better still, to kill himself. The end of the "social republic" at the hands of Napoleon III and of the artwork of the future at the hands of Liszt seemed to change for the time being Wagner's whole philosophy. Nine months elapsed before he could compose himself to compose.

The new impulse came partly from the natural strength of the ego, partly from a reading of Schopenhauer in the spring of 1854. Hitherto Wagner had been, loosely, a follower of the German positivist Feuerbach. From him Wagner had learned that the best philosophy is to have none, and that the ideal way of life is the pagan materialism and cheerful individualism of the Greeks. Now in a chastened mood, Wagner gave himself over to a course of pessimism. Not Achilles or Siegfried—his earlier heroes—but Buddha engaged his affection. The spare existence of a Hindoo beggar struck him as the only fitting life, renunciation its keynote.

But in a man of his vitality and self-assertiveness, this denial of power, money, and success could only be temporary, while his restless credulity led him to ever-new solutions and salvations, both for himself and for his heroes. With a deft turn, the *Ring* was, so to speak, reaccented, making Wotan the principal figure as the god resigned to the doom of the present, and Siegfried secondary as the unrealized representative of the future. The poem followed Wagner's personal and political readjustment; but in his distress literary accommodation was not enough, any more than vegetarianism or the water cure. He must return to music, which he had always thought of as *das Weib*—the feminine draught of self-forgetfulness. He began to compose parts of the poem, but before long he found the *weibliche* solace in life itself. The result was a fresh interruption of the *Ring*, and the making of *Tristan*.

The story of Wagner's finding help and asylum with the Wesendonks and winning the love of Mathilde is too well known to need retelling. At her bidding, and in accordance with his new philosophy of renunciation, Wagner gave her up and went to Venice to finish the great work he had undertaken in her honor. There he wrote the famous second act, then returned to Switzerland for the last. Finished in the summer of 1859, *Tristan* marks not only the end of a theoretical and literary period in Wagner's life; it marks also the birth of what Wagner's contemporaries took to be a new form of art: the music drama. Under this designation it has long served Wagnerians and others to divide the artistic creations of the century. "Before and after *Tristan*" corresponds to the New and Old dispensations of the Darwinists and the scientific socialists.

Wagner himself felt that he had composed the poem and the music with as little conscious use of his expressed theories as might be and yet that it embodied them perfectly. Of all his works, *Tristan* represents Wagner at his most spontaneous, the artist working under a strong emotional impulse, enjoying the act of creation and striving to outdo himself. But what were those innovations characterizing the new form of art? *Tristan and Isolde* is first of all a musical work for the stage, though obviously different from the average opera of its day. It is in three acts instead of the usual five; each act is virtually continuous, not divided into "musical numbers"; the drama is not historical but legendary, and consists less in action than in mental conflict made evident in speech set to music, whence it follows that long portions of the work are given over to strongly underscored monologue and declamation, rather than to ensemble singing. Moreover, for dramatic and psychological reasons it utilizes the principle of the leitmotif, or recurring musical symbol.

The substitution of a prelude for the usual overture is likewise of significance, as bearing both on the public's reception of the first fragments of the work and on Wagner's musical system as a whole. But perhaps the most important elements of *Tristan* are the symphonic treatment of the music and the stuff of the story itself.

As a narrative it has been called the greatest love story ever told and Wagner has been numbered among the romantics, but it may be doubted whether Tristan's drama has anything whatever to do with so-called romantic love. It is rather with biological love that the catastrophe is concerned. For these lovers, "sex is the return, the complete forgetfulness. . . . There is no tenderness, no awareness of each other. . . . There is only the fierce impersonal longing for utter consumption. . . ."[3] Anything more remote from the true romantic's passion for awareness, for communication, for analysis and the sharing of intellectual pleasures, it would be hard to imagine. The romanticist longs for the completeness of experience, Wagner's figures for its annihilation. The "Love-Death" is spiritually a narcotic, scenically a verbose rendezvous, and musically a sexual encounter. The second act of *Tristan* enshrines, celebrates, *is* the biological act. The argument for its immorality depends on the standard one applies, but given the context, the argument for its realism depends on whether one uses one's eyes or one's ears.

Moreover the origin of the passion is external to the lovers. It is a force of nature, symbolized by a magic potion, that seizes them and ends by destroying them. Wagner himself declares that Tristan is "like Siegfried, the victim of an illusion which makes him unconscious of his deed." And the deed, socially considered, is simply the abuse of the confidence reposed in him by King Mark, whose bride unhappily turned out to be the woman which "a law of nature" had evidently destined for Tristan.[4] Everything is fated, and the fatalism is gladly accepted by creatures weary of their will.

The subject of the new work therefore wears a double aspect. As a legend, it is the symbol of a fatalist philosophy; as a play, it is—beyond its autobiographical reference —a bourgeois drama of adultery, of which King Mark un-

[3] Paul Rosenfeld, *Musical Portraits*, 1922, 8.
[4] Wagner, "An Account of the Circumstances Surrounding the Composition of *The Ring*."

folds the implications in a famous harangue. Wagner's concern with sexual morality was constant, and successive legends from *Tannhäuser* and *Lohengrin* before *Tristan*, to the fully developed *Ring* and *Parsifal* later, embody his ambivalent—and very modern—feeling that physical love is at once sin and salvation. Legend rather than history was clearly the proper medium for carrying this "real" problem to the stage and moving the spectators to a pitch of participation while leaving them enough psychological distance not to feel preached at. The music drama is therefore a contemporary drama with a precise message; it is not an entertainment or a spectacle whose effect on mind and heart can be allowed to remain indirect and diffuse.

But this drama is also musical, and music, though precise, is not articulate. It does not state or inform, but rather impresses or conveys meanings. Hence the leitmotif is the device systematically used by Wagner to link the two parts, visual and auditory, of his creation. The six notes, for example, to which the meaning of Desire is attached in *Tristan* incessantly recur in every act, in almost every scene, and in two preludes out of the three. This confirms the listener's suspicion that desire is the driving force behind every character, that *Tristan* is a drama of desire. Again, when Tristan in his delirium asks Isolde, "Where are we?" she replies, "Near the goal," but these words are sung to music which has previously accompanied the remark, "Head destined for death." The system is clearly capable of infinite and unmistakable suggestion.

In order to use this device, however, a symphonic treatment of voice and instruments is imperative, that is to say a treatment in which short phrases, meaningless in themselves, can be repeated, interwoven and developed over long stretches of time. With the contrary method of set numbers—arias, duets, choruses, and so forth—the repetition of Wagner's themes, intrinsically unimportant as musical ideas, would be tedious, if not completely obscured by the longer independent melodies which the set forms require. But by Wagner's system of an endless musical stream—somewhat misleadingly called "continuous melody"—it is possible to unite the musical tags, the accents accompanying the utterances of the characters, and the general atmospheric effects of orchestral color, together with that other resource of the composer: imitative figures. I mean, for example, the "waving" figure in the orchestra which accompanies Isolde's waving of her veil at the approach of Tristan.

The beholder is thus assailed from all sides. He sees, hears, follows thematic material and interprets legendary symbols in a complex synthetic experience. It is almost a mechanic reconstruction of the world across the footlights. Each spectator, according to Wagner, is supposed to lose himself in the "bottomless sea of harmony" and to be made anew by the submersion as the Greeks presumably were by attending *their* theater, where poetry, song, and show were also made one.

But Wagner's scheme presented difficulties which the Greeks had not known. For one thing, Wagner's message in all his works is the need for salvation through some form or other of self-destruction. Somewhat according to the Marxian pattern, his revolutionary anarchism made him an apostle of the Utopian idea I have called the Martyrdom of Man: destroy the evil at the cost of self and the good will spring up of its own accord. Consequently Wagner would have his audience emulate his heroes and throw themselves into the faith which he thinks at the moment central to the universe: love, death, the curse of gold, or the birth of the superman. And as we have just seen, the listener must also plunge headlong into the music. In order to do either or both he must take extraordinary pains to know precisely what is going on, and this in a highly technical way. He must know the German language and the meaning of the legend as reworked by Wagner; he must learn the principal motifs, and he must follow in one comprehensive act the deeds, words, objects, and musical details of the performance.

This means that the material base of the Wagnerian art

engages the whole of our attention. We need a guide to the music and a commentary on the philosophy. Which accounts for the well-attested fact that the first performances of the Wagnerian preludes meant absolutely nothing to those who heard them. The completely ignorant might receive a vague nervous thrill—and Wagner, like Darwin, professed to prefer this lay appreciation to all others—but in proportion as one possessed musical sensitivity one grew bewildered, for the things, persons, and ideas to which the musical elements of the Prelude referred were lacking.[5] In other words, music drama, the new art, was program music—the first to be programmatic in the full sense of the term, with the program intelligible in two steps: the musical program visibly objectified on the stage instead of printed and set aside; and the full dramatic program embodied in the philosophical commentary, and not simply in the libretto.

Tristan was completed in the summer of 1859, and shortly afterwards the bourgeois drama in the Wesendonk household came to a sudden end. Wagner was compelled by the injured husband to leave his benefactors' city, which set him once more on the road to Paris. He arrived there in September, his wife Minna soon rejoined him, and as part of a new campaign they set up an attractive establishment in the Rue Newton, near the Etoile. To it came the distinguished friends and fashionable acquaintances of Liszt's daughter Blandine and other well-wishers: Emile Ollivier, husband of Blandine and leader of Napoleon's repressed opposition; Frédéric Villot, head of the Imperial Museums; Jules Ferry, also in politics; Carvalho, Director of the Lyric Theater; Liszt's younger daughter, Cosima, with her husband Hans von Bülow, fresh from the salon of Lassalle in Berlin and from other pianistic triumphs throughout Europe; the painter Doré; Gasperini, an influential physician; the poet Baudelaire, and likewise Berlioz,

[5] Wagner ultimately supplied programs to accompany his most important Preludes.

the composer who had helped Wagner on his first visit to Paris twenty years before, and whom Wagner had especially courted recently when they were both in London, conducting rival orchestras.

With the aid of Carvalho, three concerts of Wagnerian excerpts were given in the early months of the new year—a dead loss financially, like all performances of new music in the capital, but an excellent advertisement for Wagner and a real *succès d'estime*. Berlioz was seen at the concerts vigorously applauding the pieces, some of which he had before praised in print—all but the new *Tristan* Prelude which he conscientiously declared unintelligible.[6] Beyond the circle of those who came and heard, there was already much talk of the great though obscure theories which lay behind all this "difficult" music. Wagnerians were beginning to be formed, even before the complete works had been properly produced and heard. Everywhere, to be sure —in Zurich, in Paris, in Brussels, in London—the *Tannhäuser* overture produced a great *physical* impression, particularly, as Wagner was glad to learn, on the women. And women were perhaps the first to give him their unbounded admiration. "True musicians," said the passionate Madame Vilbort, "from this moment on take sides with Wagner against all others, present and future."[7] The Princess Metternich, wife of the Austrian ambassador in Paris, was also a believer in the new master and she it was who persuaded Napoleon III—eager after the late war to soothe Austrian feelings—that he should order one of Wagner's works for performance at the opera.

This led to the famous and extremely useful fiasco of *Tannhäuser* in March 1861. The enormous expense, the rehearsals protracted through nearly a year, the pandemo-

[6] Musically speaking, of course. Its atmosphere he understood well enough, characterizing it, without irony, as "a long moan"; which the later Wagnerian Kufferath says is exactly the right description. *L'Art de Diriger*, 1911, 73.

[7] Juliette Lamber Adam, *Mes Premières Armes Politiques et Littéraires*, 1904, 239.

nium set up by the whistles of the Jockey Club members who had been defrauded of their usual ballet, the controversy in the press, the publication of Wagner's four plays, with a letter on music drama, the estrangement of former friends over the music of the future, the opportunities for Wagner's characteristic misbehavior towards fellow artists, friends, and rivals, the nationalist indignation in Germany at the fall of the opera—all these sources of talk and high feeling helped form the growing legend of the Coming Man.

Already the Emperor of Brazil had commissioned an opera for Rio de Janeiro; a young British diplomat, Bulwer Lytton, the son of the author of *Rienzi*, was translating *Tannhäuser* into the blank verse "lately brought to perfection by Tennyson"; Baudelaire and Gasperini were issuing pamphlets; little knots of Wagnerites began to be heard of even in the unmusical French provinces—one at Bordeaux and another at Marseilles, to which Zola and Cézanne belonged. Weimar was of course a stronghold through Liszt, and London had begun to respond, with Queen Victoria showing gracious favor to the enemy of Mendelssohn and the revolutionary fugitive from justice.

But all this is retrospect, an invisible growth of little aid to the composer at the time. Wagner retired from Paris seemingly defeated and with his most intelligent critic, Berlioz, not properly initiated. Hurt, Wagner had made his protest directly to him in a confusing and unjust Open Letter; yet before printing it, he had also sent him the first copy of his newly engraved score, with the inscription, "To the great and dear author of *Roméo et Juliette*, the grateful author of *Tristan und Isolde*." Berlioz had grounds to doubt the gratitude, but the written words, sincere or not, acknowledge the only one of his many artistic debts that Wagner ever tried to pay. For like Darwin and Marx, he was a heavy and long-insolvent borrower from the immediate past.

2. The School of Romanticism

You may speak of Wagner, but he learnt from
Liszt, and Liszt learnt from Berlioz.
BERNARD VAN DIEREN

"Few composers," says Cecil Gray, "have actually invented
less than Wagner."[1] This patent fact has made many of
Wagner's critical admirers see him as a wonderful summary of a whole period of music which was itself wonderful—the Romantic period. And there is enough truth in the
observation to make it plausible. But as we just saw in passing, the conception of love in *Tristan* is not a romantic
conception, and this, though slight, is a clue to Wagner's
position in the century.

Twice before, with Darwin and with Marx, we have been
confronted with imposing work built almost wholly on the
half century preceding, yet hailed as new, and indeed
steeped in a spirit alien, reactionary, to that of romanticism. With Wagner the discrimination of similarity and
difference has never been made sufficiently clear, perhaps because music, opera subjects, and ideas about art
seem more fluid things than scientific and economic theories. Nevertheless Wagner repeats the pattern: his personal
and musical relations leave no room for doubt, and his
example even throws added light on that of Marx and
Darwin.

[1] *History of Music,* 207. See also Paul Rosenfeld, *op. cit.,* 10.

When Wagner first came to Paris in 1839 at the age of twenty-six, he was poor and friendless, accompanied only by his very small wife and his very large dog. When he left three years later, his worldly prospects were not much brighter, though his writings had made him better known. But he had had, according to his own testimony, one great revelation: the dramatic symphonies of Berlioz, particularly *Romeo and Juliet*. The personality of the French composer, the polish and precision of the orchestra led by him, the form and substance of the new compositions, opened out to Wagner "a new world of possibilities which I had not then dreamed of." He followed the performances of other Berlioz works with unabated interest.

This is not to say that Wagner had any temperamental liking for the music. He was, as he said, strangely moved, full of eager recognition of the strokes of genius, but often baffled and even wearied; and this remained throughout his life his ambiguous attitude towards the French master —he could never forget or dismiss him entirely and neither could he become his disciple.[2] He helped himself liberally to the treasures he fancied among Berlioz's orchestral and melodic ideas, the most famous that comes to mind being the main theme of the *Tristan* Prelude, which is lifted bodily from the opening of *Romeo and Juliet*, Part II.[3] But it is not unfair to say that just as Berlioz could not see in 1859 what Wagner was driving at in the fragment from his new music drama, so Wagner twenty years earlier could not fathom the intention of the new dramatic symphony. Nevertheless, the experience of *Romeo* worked powerfully on Wagner's spirit and stayed in his memory to the end.

Meantime the relations of the two men were most cordial. Berlioz, who was Wagner's senior by only ten years,

[2] In one of his confessional moments, Wagner wrote to Liszt: "There are only three of us fellows that really belong together these days, because only we are our own equals, and that's you—he—and I." Quoted by E. E. Taubert, *Die Musik*, iii, No. 5, 385.

[3] See "The Influence of Berlioz on Wagner" by Gerald E. H. Abraham in *Music and Letters*, v, 239 ff.

was already established in the critical world, and he enabled the younger man to place some paid articles, gave him personal encouragement, and as soon as he heard them wrote some highly favorable notices of his works. But their differences could not be glossed over by the mutual appreciation of their inessential parts. The open break of 1859–1861 was already implicit two decades earlier: it is the break between Romanticism proper and the Wagnerian world.

What one notices from the outset in Wagner's objections to Berlioz is that he invariably tends to programmatize Berlioz's music, and then to complain that the program he has imagined has not been carried out. In the adagio of the *Romeo and Juliet* Symphony, a purely instrumental piece bearing the mere title "Love Scene," Wagner seems determined to find representations of nightingales and "events" which have no place there, either musically or dramatically.[4] The musical unity of the piece, which depends on melodic transformations rather than on the usual development of a short theme according to the German symphonic pattern, escapes him entirely. So that what Wagner apparently learned from this and other Berlioz works was fragmentary and external. He took themes, orchestral subtleties, dramatic or poetic ideas—such as the piping of the shepherd at the opening of the third act of *Tristan*, evidently borrowed from the third part of the *Symphonie Fantastique*—and in an important but general way systematized Berlioz's attitude towards the dramatic expressiveness of instrumental music.

This attitude was of course not peculiar to Berlioz. It was characteristic of Romantic music, beginning as far back as the late works of Mozart and Haydn. It was a faith in the power of music to embody with precision certain parts of human experience which no other art can express. It was

[4] This was Wagner's habit with other composers too, though he did not always complain. He thought, for instance, that Beethoven's C Sharp Minor Quartet represented an actual day in the composer's life. *Gesammelte Schriften*, ix, 118.

based on literature only to the extent that poems and stories furnished a common fund of situations that could be used as starting points for new and nonliterary creations. Just as Bach used the Christian Epic and the Protestant ritual to create a religious dramatic music—the bulk of his work—so the Romanticists used the secular literature of their own time. Beethoven, Schumann, Weber, Mendelssohn, Chopin, and Berlioz belong together as independent representatives of a musical *Zeitgeist* which though new for its time had had historical predecessors in the sixteenth and seventeenth centuries.

Unfortunately these simple facts are obscured by the word, even more than by the idea of, Program. And to take Berlioz's outstanding case, the fact that he wrote a program for the first performance of his first dramatic symphony— the *Fantastique*—has overshadowed the other and more important fact that he soon entirely suppressed it and never wrote or thought of another. More strictly than anyone else, he maintained that music has nothing programmatic about it: it does not recount stories, it does not represent events, it does not follow a prearranged literary pattern; it is an independent art. In inditing his program after the completion of his symphony, Berlioz was only following the unfortunate example of his teacher, Lesueur, and of his admired contemporary Weber,[5] for the sake of helping the public. This whole question is of course the one that Beethoven tried to settle by saying that his own Pastoral Symphony was "the expression of feelings and not scene painting."[6] But apparently for those to whom the language of music is difficult, the confusion between the two will always remain—and remain associated with Romanticism.

[5] The program of the latter's *Konzertstück* is more elaborate, perhaps, than any other traditional program.

[6] When bothered by the programmatic scribblings of a musical revolutionist, Beethoven added these decisive words: "If expositions were necessary, they should be confined to characterization of the composition in general terms, which could easily and correctly be done by any educated musician." Thayer, *Life of Beethoven*, iii, 37.

The true distinction, however, is not between program music and absolute music; it is between pattern music (e.g. a nondramatic fugue) and dramatic music, some pattern music being dramatic in effect and vice versa. Nor is this distinction upset by the fact that all musicians without exception occasionally use imitative patterns—the horse's hoofs in Bach's *Farewell to His Brother*, the storm in Beethoven's *Pastoral*, the "wave" motif in Mendelssohn's *Hebrides* Overture or Wagner's *Tristan*.

Now we come to Wagner's position in the face of this tendency dominant in music by the time he began to think of esthetic problems. Strongly attached to the theater— much more than to music as an independent art—Wagner felt that his elders, including Beethoven, had missed the right path to the elaboration of a new and popular art. The old opera, Italian or French, was of course condemned without appeal as upper-class frivolity. Even Mozart's relation to music was, for Wagner, "at bottom frivolous." Beethoven represented an advance in seriousness and in technical approach to this new dramatic art, though the Ninth Symphony, which one might have thought fulfilled all Wagner's requirements, was strictly (and respectfully) "non-sense." Weber had been nearer the mark, for in *Freischütz* he had combined a popular legend with music somewhat freed from the set forms of the old opera. So it was in the Weber tradition that the answer to Wagner's problem must be sought: the new work of art must combine theatrical means, German inspiration, symphonic music, and dramatic effect. For this last, the great expansion of the powers of the orchestra through mechanical inventions and the experimentation of numerous composers made a whole new world possible—as in Berlioz. But the new art must be revolutionary, popular, national; hence Berlioz's dramatic symphony, relying on familiarity with the language of music and appealing to the imagination through the ears alone, was the wrong answer. "Our eyes, the strongest witnesses," as Dryden says, must be brought into play and given something material to work on while the symphony works on the beholder's feelings and the words on his mind. The so-called music drama is the outcome of these considerations.

Set forth in this way, the idea of music drama possesses great logic. Given the aim of teaching the people through a musical and theatrical show, these means and no other must follow. Yet Wagner does not seem to have arrived at his conclusions through logic so much as through absorption. When he came to Paris, he was a comparatively raw young man, of uncertain education and limited artistic experience. He was moreover undecided—as he was his whole life long—whether he was destined to be a dramatic poet or a musician. Thus, although we think of him as a composer contemporary with Schumann, Chopin, and Berlioz, he was not really so; he only gradually became Wagner when his great predecessors were gone. The music drama *follows* the era of musical Romanticism.

Still, the persistence with which in his public and private writings Wagner returns to the problem posed and solved in one way by Berlioz shows that Wagner never wholly burnt his bridges. The steadfast isolation in which the French master had to work in a world that was becoming less rather than more musical may have been an inspiration to the equally struggling Wagner. But while the latter hesitated between two careers, he made good use of the musical creations of the period that was passing: the harmonic system of Chopin, with its iridescent chromaticism and its constant search for tender nuances, contributed to making the Wagnerian "sea of harmony" a kindred chromatic sea of enharmony. The perpetual soft sliding, the enveloping caress of edgeless sounds, which is at first so enchanting in Wagner is Chopin reduced to a system and orchestrated. And Wagner's scoring, fine as it is and full of borrowings from the more truly orchestral masters, retains always the character of conception at the piano: it is significant that Wagner truly foretold how his success with

the musically learned would come through the piano tran-
scriptions of his operas.

These operas, moreover, did not spring full-blown from
a mind that weighed the relative merits of Weber and Beethoven's "methods" and then took an evolutionary step beyond them. The music drama sprang very clearly from a
first-hand acquaintance with the works of the now despised
Meyerbeer. It was only after his first Paris stay that Wagner
began to move away from the usual opera form. But where
did he learn the art of conceiving musical stage plays in
broad symphonic tableaux interweaving the emotions and
summing up the musical effect of the preceding moments,
if not from the German master of the Paris opera in the
middle decades of the century? Where did he first see the
leitmotif employed with telling effect as an index of dramatic relations between characters if not in *Le Prophète*
and *Struensee?*

A modern composer and critic, disregarding the usual
uninformed abuse of Meyerbeer's "taste," has gone back
to the scores themselves and shown how close the essence
of the Wagnerian drama really is to the great scenes in
Meyerbeer.[7] Wagner systematized the former's innovation
of the symphonic tableau and wove his whole pattern out
of leitmotifs. He also tried to get rid of the repetitions of
words which presumably make all grand opera ridiculous,
but as a matter of fact the short alliterative lines which
Wagner gives to his figures produce, less frankly, the same
effect. Van Dieren's example, drawn from *Tristan,* is conclusive. While the symphony goes on its necessary way (as
in Meyerbeer) the singers are forced to repeat themselves:
*"Uns're Liebe?/ Tristan's Liebe?/ Dein und mein/ Isolde's
Liebe . . . Ewig einig/ Ohn' Erwachen/ Ohne Bangen/"*
etc., followed by a redistribution of nearly the same words
to Tristan and Isolde—a dialogue that no more carries forward the thought than the famous chorus "We go, we go,

[7] Van Dieren, "Meyerbeer," in *Down Among the Dead Men,*
1935.

we go!" carries the singers off the stage. "Yes, but you don't go!"

Meyerbeer wrote no theories, nor did he belong especially to the intellectual movement of Romanticism, yet in spite of his fashionable success, his career reflects the artistic conscientiousness of the period. It was only after Wagnerism got under way that Meyerbeer began to be looked upon as a Philistine tradesman in music. He made, it is true, certain concessions to the taste of the period—so did Wagner[8]—but far from being a slapdash purveyor of ready-made effects, Meyerbeer led a life of thoughtful retirement in which he slowly and carefully elaborated his dramatic inventions. He took the greatest pains with the librettos which Scribe and others wrote for him, setting the words with solicitous attention to accent and feeling, polishing the scoring and harmony to the last minute, and supervising through extra rehearsals, often paid for out of his own pocket, the acting, staging, decoration, and ensemble.

All this does not suffice to make him a great composer. Berlioz was as repelled by the bulk of Meyerbeer's work as Wagner himself, though he had the justice to admire Meyerbeer's execution of his own intent. And in the grand operatic tradition Meyerbeer must be recognized as having left his mark with a number of artistically successful discoveries which had entered the public domain before Wagner and Verdi made them commonplace. We may—in many cases, we must—dislike Meyerbeer's plushy gorgeousness, the big display of equipment and machinery and *Luxus* in his dramas, but we must not forget that these same features in Wagner are not disinfected from crass materialism by being attached to legendary subjects.[9] This is

[8] "Wagner's music, more than any other, is the sign and symbol of the nineteenth century . . . it is the century's paean of material triumph . . . even *Tristan* . . . and *Parsifal* are set in an atmosphere of heavy gorgeous stuffs, amid objects of gold and silver, and thick clouding incense." Rosenfeld, *op. cit.*, 3-4.

[9] Meyerbeer himself made a venture in legend with *Robert le Diable* in 1836.

particularly evident if we remember that the Wagnerian message was, at best, contemporary philosophy in the spirit of Feuerbach, and at worst, plain bourgeois drama in the spirit of Scribe. One would have thought that Meyerbeer was in truth the ideal, many-sided artist-dictator of the theater that Wagner longed to be; and Wagner must at times have thought so too.

There was, however, nothing exclusive about Wagner's self-education. He contemned the regular Italian opera, yet it is clear that from Spontini's great historical pageants, *La Vestale* and *Fernando Cortez*, he learned something of advantage, if only in the management and orchestration of stage marches. From Bellini likewise: the *Liebestod* idea, as distinguished from its Berliozian theme, is an expansion of the last scene of *Norma*. And to indicate his indebtedness to Weber would be to catalogue some of Wagner's most applauded innovations. *Oberon* and *The Flying Dutchman* were as obviously woven on the same loom as the interchangeable parts of any two of Wagner's own operas. Schumann saw it at a glance, long before Wagnerism had become an issue: "Wagner would be the privileged man of his time, had he as much power of melodic invention as he has intelligence."[10]

To those whom Wagner's music completely satisfies, these considerations naturally do not matter. But these happy persons can hardly ever refrain from holding over their opponents the additional claim of Wagner's greatness as a theorist. Alone in his century, they think, he saw broad and deep into the problems of art and life and brought his practice to public perfection. In this view Wagner may have taken his material wherever he found it, he alone could have fashioned it in accordance with the two great principles which all friends of culture should be loath to give up: the dominance of art in national life and the importance of the artist to society.

Unfortunately, here again Wagner is only a late fol-

[10] *Gesammelte Schriften über Musik,* iii, Aug. 7, 1847.

lower. Not only did his essays about *Art and Revolution* or *Opera and Drama* merely re-echo the familiar plaints of the Romantic School against bourgeois society,[11] but in the special domain of musical art Wagner came when most of the arduous campaigning had been done. Ever since the decline of the patronage system in the last days of the eighteenth century, the artist and his work had been at the mercy of a usually indifferent public. Music, being the least accessible, the least "universal" of the arts, had suffered most. Beethoven, who complained so frequently of neglect, was still comparatively well off. It is Weber who marks the true beginnings of the wholly independent artist, the self-sustaining host in himself who must be impresario, press agent, conductor, journalist, and diplomat in order at once to create and to found.

The necessity gave rise to theorizing about "the artist's place in society." Read Weber's literary works and you will find a lucid statement and solution of the problem.[12] He sketched once for all the needful, though even before his precept and example had been noised abroad, Berlioz had begun to tread the same obvious path. From the early thirties onward Berlioz did not cease from expounding and showing what the conscious artist of the nineteenth century must do to justify his existence and what society owed in return. He was the only musician, as Wagner noted with some surprise, who stood apart and would not work for commercial ends. Instead he inaugurated the practice of organizing independent concerts run entirely under his direction, he carried his musical message to Germany, England, and Russia, and he devised the "Festival" plan as a means of interesting a large public in the works of Gluck, Beethoven, Weber, and himself.

A year before Wagner came to Paris, Berlioz's opera *Benvenuto Cellini* had been composed and produced as a

[11] See above, "The So-Called Utopians" and "How the System Works."

[12] See the excellent biography of Weber by R. P. and L. P. Stebbins, *Enchanted Wanderer*, 1940.

sort of manifesto in behalf of the artist's need of independence, both from patrons and from outworn convention.[13] It failed, which was a demonstration in itself, but Berlioz kept on with articles, novelettes, and critical studies carrying the same burden. The "Bayreuth" idea—of a time and place set apart for the annual performance of serious musical works under ideal conditions and without thought of profit—was first sketched by Berlioz in the *Gazette Musicale* for 1844. He called the imaginary city where the art of sound was thus honored "Euphonia" and placed it in the Harz Mountains, on German soil. He returned to the theme and elaborated it in further writings, the best of which formed that witty collection of *Evenings with the Orchestra* published in 1852.

As for the utilization of music in popular or national occasions as against courtly or sociable ones, that is a tradition which Wagner inherited from Beethoven and—through Berlioz—from the musicians of the French Revolution.[14] After Gossec, Méhul, and Lesueur, Berlioz found it natural enough to devote his *Requiem* and *Te Deum*, some of his secular cantatas, and especially his Funeral Symphony of 1840, to public occasions. This last was written for the commemoration of the heroes of the July Revolution and it moved Wagner to write his only wholehearted appreciation of Berlioz: "It is noble and great from the first to the last note . . . a sublime patriotic enthusiasm, rising from the tone of sorrow to the highest summit of apotheosis, preserves the work from expressing any unhealthy excitement. . . . This symphony will last and will heighten courage as long as the French nation endures."[15]

[13] The subtitle of *Benvenuto Cellini* is "The Master Goldsmiths of Florence." In "Berlioz als Dramatiker," Kurt Mey says: "Not musically but in its contents, the opera reminds one in many ways of *Die Meistersinger*. Fieramosca is . . . like Beckmesser, etc." *Die Musik*, iii, No. 5, 340 ff.

[14] In the same spirit, Fourier had provided for "community music" in his system of phalanxes.

[15] *Europa*, May 5, 1841, over Wagner's pen name "Freudenfeuer."

Berlioz, it is true, saw no reason why all music should serve national purposes, and he wrote many more intimate works on a smaller scale; which again serves to emphasize the difference between Wagner's wish to systematize and the characteristic romanticist wish for diversity. The paradox in the situation is that Wagner's would-be "popular" works require a complex, even learned, preparation and must be performed indoors under Bayreuthian conditions, whereas from the Revolution through Berlioz, the music for national occasions was designed to suit, in a spirit of simplicity, the varying requirements of the celebration. Bayreuth is now a national shrine to which the army on furlough is sent for spiritual recuperation,[16] which means the celebration of an exclusive and personally Wagnerian nationalism, whereas in Berlioz's Euphonia, the works of all great composers were to be played without thought of nationality, and in a mood quite different from that of military *Te Deums* and Funeral Symphonies for revolutionary heroes.

One explanation of this paradox is that Wagner was wedded to the theater and Berlioz was not. Wagner could not easily conceive or compose without a text, and his faith in the mission of the revolutionary and religious poet made him bend his energies to solve a problem which for Berlioz did not exist: how to unite the arts. This among other things led Wagner to worry incessantly about the "origins" of all forms of art. He pondered the Greeks, changing his mind about the ancient chorus, studying Shakespeare and the librettos of Mozart and Weber, searching his heart about Beethoven's *Adelaide* and Ninth Symphony. Finally, he was led to retrace the steps which opera had taken since the famous quarrel that divided eighteenth-century Paris into partisans of Gluck and defenders of Piccinni.

The result was a significant parallel to the return of Darwin and Marx to late eighteenth-century rationalism. Unknowingly, Wagner found himself propounding to his cen-

[16] *PM*, Aug. 13, 1940.

tury a theory which his German forerunner Gluck and his nearer ancestor the Belgian Grétry had written and fought for in the days of the Enlightenment. The theory is simply that music is the handmaiden of poetry. The insistence on the meaning of words, to which song must be subordinated, is an insistence on making opera "rational," on making it like the theater or like "real life," where people do not repeat words any more than they sing their sorrows. No more arias, therefore, but a new *Sprachvermögen*, a new idiom.

Gluck's reform of the opera did not go quite so far, though it was similarly inspired by disgust for the routine habits that had overtaken the Italian opera. These pieces, as Gluck said, "stank of music." Too many airs, too many repeats, absurd plots and virtuoso tricks. A simpler story, couched in poetic words, would give the musician an opportunity to heighten the true human feelings embodied in the verse. With the aid of a skillful librettist, who reworked the Greek legends and borrowed the verse of Racine, Gluck produced a handful of masterpieces which changed the course of French opera and even influenced Mozart. A generation later, Grétry, whose own works are not without charm or power, simply and lucidly put forth the same arguments for the use of musical art as the underscoring of speech. *La musique est l'imitation de la parole.* As speech accompanies action on the stage, so instrumental music and scenery complete the illusion of a self-contained world felt through the most impressionable of the senses.

To this theory Wagner was a convert from the start. It seemed so self-evident to him that he could use it even as an explanation of poetry. The poet makes a constant effort, he says, to strip words of their conventional meaning, and to use them in their original sensory significance so as to bring before the reader the image of the material object which they denote. Here again is expressed Wagner's twofold tendency: the wish for realism, for material or sensory contact with objects; and the justification of the "true" artistic means by which the impossible can be done;

in other words, the real imitation pearl, or—even more briefly—the theater, for there, by definition, everything is real and everything is illusion. Wagner's gigantic effort to unite the arts was an effort to create a world out of whole *cloth*.

No wonder then that Wagner detected something absurd in the Ninth Symphony and was wearied in trying to follow Berlioz's dramatic compositions. They were exclusively musical experiences. They were experiences localized in time and space by a mere title now and then: Romeo Alone; Ball at the Capulets' House; Love Scene; Queen Mab Scherzo; Funeral March for Juliet. No world of illusion, no storytelling, no gesturing actors—only sounds bearing a mysterious relation to feelings in human beings. No wonder, either, that Wagner did not see why Berlioz, a close student and great admirer of Gluck, should condemn Gluck's "impious theory" and consider it fortunate that the master had not been able to carry it out consistently: he had simplified opera and made it tragic, but he had not subdued music or chopped it up into mere expressive accents underneath a verbal text.

Truly, though Berlioz was too intelligent to say so, this Gluck-Grétry theory might pass for a "characteristically French" bit of rationalist and mechanical thinking. Certainly the desire to stimulate the imagination through abstract ideas and painted objects instead of relying on exclusively musical means had something systematic and falsely logical that the world often associates with "the French mind."[17] But seventy-five years after rationalism, in the middle of a century which first gave him all its resources of invention and achievement, another was to

[17] A German critic ascribes a strictly Parisian origin to the supremacy of word over music in Wagner. He blames not only Grétry but Méhul and Meyerbeer, and says there is nothing German about the idea. At this rate, Wagner is French and Berlioz German—a good example of the futility of making art and ideas into national traits. See Eduard Wechsler, *Esprit und Geist*, 1927, 547-48.

attempt the same project in the name of Germanism, irrationalism, and realism combined. Wagner exploits and re-embodies, without truly resembling, the school of Romanticism.

3. The "Ring" and the Book

Wagner's stubborn perseverance was founded on a reasoned and scientific esthetics. . . .
                                        XAVIER DE RAILLES, 1886

He has virtually discovered the means of expressing the character of man and god in pure form, in the form most congenial to his nature, music. . . .
                                        A. E. F. DICKINSON, 1926

The making of his first music drama, *Tristan*, and the re-furbishing and failure of *Tannhäuser*, interrupted Wagner's Penelope-task of the *Ring of the Nibelungen*. It was ended twenty-five years after it was begun, though work on it was not continuous, so that this trilogy also, though in a different way from the spontaneous *Tristan*, represents the Wagnerian "revolution." It is indeed the core of it, combining fragments of all Wagner's successive philosophies and demonstrating in full the operation of the system.

It is a system of systems. In a useful handbook called *The Musical Design of the Ring*[1] we are introduced first to some seventy "motives" comprising only a part of the musical atoms from which the whole symphonic texture is made up. Only about thirty of these are of major importance, as measured by the frequency of their use. "A theme occurring sparsely in three operas is more important than

[1] By A. E. F. Dickinson, Oxford University Press, 1926.

one which is fully developed in two operas."[2] We are thus
aware from the start of a methodical construction, in which
the importance of musical themes depends as much on
their function in tying threads of plot as on their intrinsic
worth or development. But what are these themes in themselves? They consist for the most part of one- and two-
measure phrases signalizing a person, idea, or object.
Thus we have a theme for Brünnhilde, one for Siegfried's
Thought, another for Freia's Golden Apples. No degree of
abstraction prevents the composer from assigning a set of
notes to it—as in "Wotan's will thwarted" or "a woman's
claims"—because, with a few exceptions, the theme is and
remains a purely arbitrary sign.[3] Aside from the bird's song
or the flicker of fire or the ride of the Valkyrie, the Wagnerian motif does not suggest what it betokens. This is why
it has to be learned. It is also why the Ring could, in the
mind of the author, carry a philosophy. The leitmotif is a
device which knows no theoretical limits to its application:
by assigning themes and using them with rigor, it should
be possible to demonstrate Euclid symphonically.

In this lies Wagner's principal innovation. Previous composers from Bach to Berlioz had used recurring themes,
often with dramatic intent, but they had never used the
device with absolute rigor. Nothing like the new device had
been seen since the musical riddles and jokes of the late
Polyphonic period. And in Wagner it is no joke. Meaning
is uppermost, leading first to musical labeling, then dictat-
ing the nature of the vocal parts. These must resemble
declamation rather than singing, so that the various actors
in the drama can make themselves clearly understood. For
this reason also they sing, as they would speak, alone;[4] and
since their solo voices might find a full orchestral commentary difficult to overcome, the orchestra is divided and one
half of it concealed in a pit beneath the stage. Where this

[2] Ibid., 21.

[3] Emmanuel, Histoire de la Langue Musicale, ii, 608.

[4] Except for the Rhine maidens and the chorus of men in Götterdämmerung.

arrangement is carried out, as at Bayreuth, the proper balance is said to be achieved—at the expense of instrumental sound. Elsewhere the unequal contest goes on between the solitary philosophic voice and the brass-reinforced orchestra —often at the expense of the singer.

Upon the stage the characters appear in heroic garb and stature. They are not only gods and goddesses, but giants, gnomes, dragons, and other animals, who represent principles as much as persons, or who appear not only as themselves but also as varying symbols of human passion: Brünnhilde the lover, Brünnhilde as Wotan's daughter, and Brünnhilde the joy of Siegfried's life are different symbols with different themes. Surrounding these walking propositions are the objects of legend or of nature. The magic fire and the forest murmurs are by now familiar musical conceptions, but they are also visual effects. Much of the *Ring* goes on in an atmosphere of cloud, fire, and water, for which the illuminated steam of the machinist is indispensable. Solid objects are likewise represented realistically, Wagner wishing the scene painter to exert his most refined skill, and apparently believing that the united artwork would so far surpass its separate components that painting and sculpture would disappear as independent arts, overcome in fair competition.[5]

Just as the "scenic and musical magnificence of grand opera" had spurred him on to outdo its usual proportions in *Rienzi,* so in treating the subject of the *Nibelungen* Wagner wished to outdo all conceivable spectacles. The *Ring* is consequently of extraordinary size—a three-day festival with prologue, each day requiring some five to six hours of performance. This scale in turn demands of the performers a stamina almost as heroic as that of the figures they portray. An entirely new style of diction was needed, characterized by great strength and vehemence, and largely unaided by melodic contour in the vocal line. The "continuous melody" was for the listener alone, who put it to-

[5] Autobiographical Sketch.

gether from the instrumental and vocal parts: in other words, the human voice was used as an instrument subserving action and poetry. Frequent climaxes, the uttering of philosophical riddles, and long periods of silence, completely altered the prima donna's conception of an operatic role and put a very communicable strain on her (or his) resources of pantomime and style.

Of action properly speaking there is little. There are deeds, chiefly violent, but the conflict is logical rather than actual. The true music drama being a legend, its most effective moments are tableaux, meaningless perhaps to those who do not fully grasp the implications of the story. Still, Brünnhilde's awakening, Siegfried's forging of the sword, Wotan's farewell, and the (motionless) ride of the Valkyries are relatively simple scenes which were bound to carry the audience with them as soon as the music and the picturesquely costumed characters had become familiar.

Once this association was made, the music itself could be separated from its stage image and played in the concert hall, for it was symphonically coherent and its denotative motifs would make interpretation easy. This is the upshot of the system, rational and simple, and it is no doubt what the excellent annotator of the *Ring* means when he says that Wagner has "virtually discovered the means of expressing the character of man and god in pure form." It was a discovery comparable to that of the "direct method" for teaching foreign languages: "The bird is singing," "she waves her scarf," "I forge the sword."

To say that the utility of the Wagnerian system was temporary is to state an historical fact. We now cut, condense, and disjoin his music dramas. From Wagner's point of view to admit that this can be done is heresy. The arts that he had fused should be indissoluble, and according to the praise of his "scientific esthetics" in the eighties of the last century his position was impregnable. It could not be foreseen that in time the *Ring* would fall apart, leaving behind single operas or large fragments of symphonic music. The unifying poem was also held to be no less great than the music, yet few are the living Wagnerians who could face a performance or a reading of the librettos as plays. Whether in translation or in the original, the lines fail to strike us as remarkable for anything but dullness. The short pseudo-Anglo-Saxon meter with choppy stress and alliteration is as wearisome as *Hiawatha*, while the endless search for synonymous phrases drags out most speeches to unendurable length.

Still, Wagner's reputation as a poet and dramatist, and even as "the first to write the books of his own operas," continues to be taken for granted. The truth is that there are better librettos in the despised literature of opera, and among those some were written by the composers themselves.[6] Moreover, in spite of the co-ordinated systems, it would be hard to name the *Ring* as an example of supremely skillful setting to music. The difficulty of fusing the various "layers" of meaning prevented that accuracy of touch which is so conspicuous in Mozart or Weber, so that we are not surprised to find in Wagner some very delicate musical effects wasted on trivial words, or emphases falling on adverbs. Needless to say, there are many contrary examples. Tovey has pointed out how "when the jealous Fricka did hope (in F major) that the domestic comforts of Valhalla would induce Wotan to settle down, Wotan, gently taking up her theme in E flat, dashes her hopes by this modulation more effectively than by any use of . . . tubas and trombones."[7] But in general the flowing together of words and song as if cast in a single mold is rare, both because Wagner is bound by the use of his tags and because he deliberately neglects rhythm. At the same time, his formulizing of "significance" leads him to overdo the piling up of crises by repeating his fragments on rising steps

6 Thomas Campion, author of masques, and Berlioz—to name only two—wrote their own texts and music as occasion required. Boïto, curiously enough, was a better librettist when he worked for Verdi than when he worked for himself.

7 "Harmony" in *Encyclopedia Britannica*, 14th ed., xi, 210.

of the scale. This sort of realism truly represents the hectic passions voiced by the dramatis personae, but it defeats another kind of realism which relies on melodic impressions of longer range, freed from the necessity of underlining sentences. The paradoxical result is that the poem of the *Ring*, though it is supposed to generate all the rest, disappears in performance as a source of either pleasure or enlightenment.

The matter of the poem is in any case a special taste. When it does not consist of passionate exclamations or queries in alarm, it is likely to be the recital of past history, commentary on what is visible to the eye, or discussions of international politics. There are also references to the earlier plays in the series and harangues on what a character's name is—or is not. Again, metaphors like

> With a whelming worm
> I wrestled for it once;
> Shall I barter it now to buy
> The paws of a paltry bear?

seem fairly dry of musical marrow and would defeat any composer not able like Wagner to tap his supply of melody through literary cross reference.

Standing above the literal matter as the music stands underneath it, is the philosophical meaning. To discuss it is an undertaking before which anyone might quail. Not only, as I have said, was this philosophy patchwork, but later critics have found in it everything from Protestant socialism to bourgeois religiosity. Yet it will not do to discard the philosophy as irrelevant unless one is also willing to dismiss the creator of the *Ring* as a mere scene painter in sounds.

There are at least two social and philosophic schemes in the work, tied to Wagner's political and emotional crisis of the early fifties. In his first, Greek period, when he wished to write a tragedy symbolizing the coming revolution, he wrote *Siegfried's Death* and tried in vain to compose the music for it. The theorizing passion was too strong and he had to set down the confused polemics of *Opera and Drama* to get rid of it. He got rid of grand opera, too, while letting off a few shots in Berlioz's direction for the good of his soul. The Siegfried of this period is the conqueror, the man of a better future, possibly even a life portrait of Bakunin. He is certainly a product of social evolution. He is, says Wagner, "the embodied spirit of the eternally working involuntary power in man, in the fulness of its highest and most immediate strength, combined with unmistakable lovableness."[8] Feeling that this Siegfried tragedy assumed on the reader's part too much knowledge of the preceding story, Wagner changed this written portion into what we now know as *Götterdämmerung* and wrote *The Young Siegfried*, which is at present the third play of the series of four.[9]

Following the rapid composition of this new play (in three weeks) Wagner was nervously exhausted and had recourse to the water cure. He added to it vegetarianism and teetotalism in emulation, perhaps, of his radically pure hero. Thereupon came the downfall of the French Republic, and the *Ring* had to do duty as the explanation of present chaos. Wotan became the central figure, and Siegfried—as Wagner wrote to Röckel—receded so far into the future as to become possible only after (and through) *our* annihilation. It is the difference between a Utopia around the corner and a Utopia in the unimaginable time to be, between an unconscious product of evolution of which we form a part, and the mysterious coming of a savior not yet conceived.

Wotan, meanwhile, is all-important as the bearer of our present ills—world weariness, embroilment in the intrigue for the possession of power (the ring), and in the deviation of love (incest) which has been cursed in order to obtain power. The senseless murder of Siegfried typifies the chaos. Over all this is a veil of Schopenhauerian feeling, as when

[8] Quoted in Hildebrandt, *Wagner und Nietzsche*, 1924, 100.
[9] These four remain a trilogy, with prologue, since the Greek parallel was not given up.

Wotan somewhat mysteriously calls Brünnhilde his Will. Wagner makes the daughter of the gods the only character conscious of the interweavings of a deterministic fate. She it is who utters the poet's hints: to Wotan—"Rest, rest, thou god"; and to Siegfried, "Only thou be our lord, Absolute Father and hero!"

As in every one of Wagner's tragic works, physical love and physical force are the two mainsprings of action. They are expressively joined, one often thinks, in the cry of the feminine warriors called Valkyries. Through the renunciation of love, the Nibelung Alberich—allegorically an industrial magnate—obtains the power hidden in the ring, but it brings destruction in its train until it returns to the vegetative maidens of the Rhine, which typifies the center of the universe. That the world is a meaningless round of lust and death must therefore be the philosophy of the *Ring*, for even the intelligent and loving Brünnhilde cannot rise to self-sacrifice or forgiveness. She sacrifices others and seeks revenge.

Yet both in Wagner's original Siegfried play and in his later remarks about the trilogy, it is apparent that his philosophy was something less repetitious, more gaily progressive than is here shown. The truth is that he very faithfully rendered the Darwinian paradox of evolution and extinction—the mechanist's dilemma that everything endlessly repeats and that progress is none the less possible. Wagner accepted praise for having made the gods and heroes live again, yet he kills them all off. He made, as others said, Schopenhauer's pessimism into music, yet he overlooked the philosopher's Christian ethics. The text, carefully picked over by Shaw, will justify its interpretation as evolutionary socialism, but it will also justify a revolutionary, catastrophic, and fatalist overturn which in its very ambiguity reminds us also of Marx.

What is clear enough is that for the public the tale of the Nibelungen is simply an exciting series of fights and love-making. To fight, deceive, scold, and lie are the means of winning gold or women. Few other objects engage our attention. Wagner's choice of a primitive Norse legend for his philosophical regeneration of mankind was bound to yield him only these "lessons." And thanks to the uncertain handling of the allegory, the message can remain at once ambiguous and excessively simple. On the one hand, the "true" meaning of the *Ring* cannot be found by reading texts, and on the other its real effect is to exalt the "heroic" in its narrow meaning of physically strong and morally weak. Wotan may discuss cosmogony with Erda like an academic lecturer, but to the beholder's eye and the listener's pulse, he remains the god of the raging host.

4. *The Master Thinker of Bayreuth*

Talent—or the faculty of appropriating and applying the knowledge of others.

COLERIDGE

Among artists in general, Wagner's place is with
the actors.

NIETZSCHE

When Wagner was an adolescent, as yet unmusical but
with his head full of plays and stories, he saw Weber conduct *Der Freischütz* and decided at once that he too must
lead an orchestra. "Not to be King or Kaiser but to stand
there and direct." The urge to be the leader of great
masses of performing men and women, and to work his
spell over an even greater mass in the pit, was thus fairly
early his ruling passion. It remained the one unchanging
purpose through all his seemingly disparate and even contradictory theories and actions, and it drove him to master
the one institution where success shines most publicly,
where the rule of the autocrat—the star—is an accepted fact:
the theater.

Music was not "the form most congenial to my nature."
For one of his early plays, Wagner tells us, he required
music. "In order to learn this art I became a musician."
The expression would not arrest us, if it did not recur in
many shapes throughout Wagner's career. His gifts were,
so to speak, undifferentiated. He could turn them to any

advantage, as he turned his friends and acquaintances, mainly to the advantage of his own enthronement as *the* artist of his generation.

And this one thing which he truly sought he won. The form of his dictatorship mattered little. As late as his fiftieth year, when sunk in debt and obliged to leave his lodgings in secret, Wagner writes to Liszt that he would be content to save mankind through his poetic plays alone. When, not long after, King Ludwig of Bavaria gave him the means to carry out his artistic desires to the full, Wagner absurdly meddled in politics, even in military affairs, and had to be turned out. Still, the baton symbolized power so strongly for him that he never wholly renounced the lust for conducting. The parallel with imperial might haunts him. In an unpublished fragment, after telling us that if Beethoven had had to be a Frenchman he would have chosen to be Berlioz, he goes on: "Berlioz is a great general. . . . His symphonies are the battles and victories of Bonaparte in Italy. . . . Just as I cannot imagine these without visualizing the hero at the head of the horrendous melee . . . so I cannot imagine a symphony of Berlioz without seeing him at the head of his orchestra."[1]

Wagner's formal education in music, as is well known, was extremely sketchy—hardly a full year of lessons with a not especially distinguished teacher. But it sufficed him, for he was endowed to an extraordinary degree with the power of absorbing what would serve his ends. That he picked up much rubbish along with the good—as for instance his "historical" ideas about drama—was not a handicap. On the contrary, it was excellent decoration which aided the reception of his works by establishing a point of contact with those who already shared the same commonplaces.[2] Wagner was that rare and infallible combination of talents: the born showman and autodidact.

What is surprising is that this capacity was not accom-

[1] Autograph belonging to A. Bovet, published in the *Revue d'art dramatique*, Jan. 1902.
[2] See below, pp. 288–291.

panied by good nature or an easy-going character. His intimates and acquaintances learned this to their cost. Incapable of friendship, Wagner used other human beings for what they were worth to him, but without any subtlety in the handling. His creed, avowed with the disarming candor of the cynical, was "to be shameless towards one's friends, impudent and hard as stone towards one's enemies." Being shameless meant complaining without remorse and taking what could be had: money, shelter, wife, musical or other ideas. To the end, Wagner's was "the beggarly copiousness of borrowed wealth," of which Liszt said afterwards: "One had to give up everything to him, even one's happiness. . . . Von Bülow and I were his first admirers and his first slaves. . . . Von Bülow did it heroically."[3]

Being impudent and hard as stone meant attempting to seduce acquaintances into becoming satellites, and, on their resisting, turning against them. The prime example is of course Nietzsche, who lay under a ban after he had shown the powers of Bayreuth that though a Wagnerian he had a mind of his own. With notables like Meyerbeer or Berlioz, Wagner's system was temperamentally Marxian: to beg and receive favors and at once to neutralize the claim by doing or writing something harmful to the benefactor. Despite his cordial reception of the unknown Wagner, Meyerbeer was soon attacked anonymously and later linked with Mendelssohn and Hanslick in the famous essay on *The Jews in the World of Music*. They were proved to be a racial menace to the world of German art in terms that likened this evil to an inevitable natural law. It made no difference that Mendelssohn was dead and that Wagner was to rob him for the benefit of his own *Rheingold*; that Meyerbeer was near the end of an honorable career; nor that Hanslick was a far from stupid critic exercising his right to express an opinion on a subject he was master of: Wagner never forgave him and went so far as

[3] Juliette Adam, *op. cit.*, 221. Cf. Cecil Gray's "He does not so much sum up the work of others, as Bach does, but rather robs them." *History of Music*, 206–07.

to contrive a humiliating social occasion where the critic would hear himself ridiculed in the lines of *Meistersinger*. At the time of the written attack, Wagner had presumably put opera behind him, but he obviously could not bear rivals even in a despised genre. He had in fact no more artistic pride than he had a code of ethics in friendship. Trampling on others, regardless of fact or of favor received, was good as strategy and morals both.

Where the attraction was greatest, as in Wagner's relation to Berlioz, the behavior was blackest, for here Wagner's cunning has managed to give others the impression that the aggressor and the ingrate was Berlioz. From the first, when the elder man befriended the younger, Wagner felt he must conquer any possibility of feeling grateful. He began with sour-sweet articles in the German press. Later, in *Opera and Drama*, he abused compositions of Berlioz that he had never heard, since they had not been performed where he happened to be, and never seen in score, since they were still in manuscript. Liszt, who was the intimate of both, tried to soothe the injured party who needed no soothing: Berlioz took no notice and called it the risk of war.

Five years later, when Wagner and Berlioz were both in London, the offender courted Berlioz so persuasively that for a time he believed in Wagner's friendship—and so did Wagner. But on top of this rapprochement came Wagner's token of true love—selected portions from *Opera and Drama* reprinted in English in *The Musical World*. Still Berlioz made no reply. He attended the Wagner concerts in Paris and wrote ungrudging praise of what he heard and liked. His criticisms were precise and technical, and were outweighed by his acknowledgment of Wagner's rank among the first of living composers. When *Tannhäuser* was produced and failed, Berlioz gave over his column to a friend who, he knew, would give a favorable account of the opera. Meantime, the "music of the future" had become a byword to which Berlioz's name was persistently attached, as much out of Parisian folly as ill-will. Whereupon the

French master made clear his views on music and art and his reasons for not joining the crusade in behalf of the future. No one, in fact, had the slightest inkling of what the artwork or the music of the future was, since *Tannhäuser* was an old-fashioned opera and *Tristan* was still five years distant from its first performance. But Wagner's role of Prince Pretender made him feel it as an insult that Berlioz had cleared himself of associations with the unknown and had not personally helped out the success of *Tannhäuser*. This lordly levy of tribute, when Wagner became king indeed, was accepted at its face value by the critical world, where it is still echoed, and by none more brazenly than by Berlioz's ignorant compatriots.[4]

Wagner, throughout these middle decades of the century, also worked to dissolve the Liszt-Berlioz friendship. He protested against Liszt's performance of the Frenchman's works at Weimar, and turned his own relation to his most faithful helper, to his veritable "bulldog," into a dubious partnership of interests. After accepting Liszt's fully extended help, from money to false passports (when the musical revolutionist's life was in danger), Wagner was not ashamed to describe him as "a worldly modern, who has also some distinguished qualities and who loves me in his own way . . . which is to wish for me a huge success."[5] This huge success no one helped to bring about more unremittingly than Liszt, with his "worldly" connections and immense capacity for selfless devotion. Yet Wagner never ceased to fear him. He suppressed his works from the concert platform wherever he could, and he only seemed "to uphold him in a pamphlet and in letters which were too effusive to be sincere."[6]

In ordinary life the Wagnerian maxims of shamelessness and impudence were easily combined. They explain the

[4] E.g., the writings of André Suarès and Pierre Lasserre, during and since the war. But see the authoritative *Berlioz* by T. S. Wotton, Oxford University Press, 1935, 205 ff.

[5] To Uhlig, Sept. 19, 1849.

[6] William Wallace, *Liszt, Wagner, and the Princess*, 1927, 97.

innumerable occasions where purposive rudeness lost him
the good will of performers, conductors, critics, and well-
wishers. In Paris, he first courted the Republican opposition to Napoleon III and received their favors. They sold
tickets for his concerts, gave him entrée to the best circles,
and preached him to whoever would listen. A year later,
the diplomatic situation having changed, Wagner dropped
them and went over to the Emperor's friend, Princess Metternich, who pushed through the acceptance of *Tannhäuser*.[7] It is only fair to add in justification of Wagner's
system that it ultimately built up his reputation as that of
an invincible strong man. If the maestro insults your guests
and complains of their presence (as Wagner once did at
George Eliot's), he must be a genius, and one whom the
world will not trample on, for his own foot will doubtless
be outstretched first. The slave mind in both the offender
and his victim, reminiscent of Marx, reminds us also of
nearer potentates ruling over willing sacrificial herds.

That Wagner's toughness was the deliberate and often
compulsive hiding of weakness appears not merely in his
complaining demands from his friends or in his repeated
threats of suicide; it shows also in his desire to lose himself
in the *Rausch*—the intoxication—of crowds, of art, of violence, or of love. His yearning for the *Allvergessen*, for un-
consciousness, whether sexual or religious, is as evident as
the need for self-assertion. The two are related as the head
and tail of the same animal, driven from within towards
satisfaction in instinctual ignorance of the moral law. There
is no reason why Wagner should have observed any particular conventions of his alleged straitlaced epoch, but that
he could accept none, even of his own making, in any realm,
that he should have sought "happiness,"[8] that his notion of
"active enjoyment" as the goal of art should have run by
imperceptible degrees into the belief that music is a

[7] The ensuing quarrel between the two political factions accounts for some of the noise at the first performance.

[8] Compare the Romantics' repudiation of "happiness" as the
goal of life: in Byron, Goethe, Carlyle, Stendhal, and others.

woman, a sexual narcotic—these are things that throw light on the quality of his desire for power at the same time as they show up his violence as a symptom of sham strength.

When he was in the hopeful phase of his revolving temperament, he ascribed to himself the effect that he vainly sought in the experiences of life and art: again and again he speaks of himself as a savior. At one time he writes to Liszt that he wishes to "save Berlioz" by being the poet that every musician needs "as a man needs a woman." This extraordinary fantasy about an artist who in his creative work needed no help from anybody is matched and perhaps surpassed by Wagner's utterances after the break with King Ludwig of Bavaria. Having meddled in things that did not concern him and clumsily played at pro-Prussian politics, Wagner discovered that his Falstaffian behavior had placed his benefactor in a very difficult position. Whereupon Wagner pretended that he, the artist, must abandon his own high concerns, and "save" his liege. The upshot was Wagner's polite and sorrowful banishment by the King. Still this did not prevent Wagner from boasting of the young man as "his best work"—nor from double-crossing him cynically a short while later, when the King, who was still supporting the artist, begged to have the *Ring* first given in Munich. Whatever Wagner's fundamental weaknesses may have been, gratitude was not one of them.

It is no doubt easy to "write off" Wagner's character as abject and think the needful has been said. The reader adds to these details the dubious Wesendonk affair and the sleight of hand by which Hans von Bülow, relieved of his wife, was made to think it was his duty to art to preach Wagnerism. Other artists than Wagner have acted ruthlessly and contemptibly, especially where money and women were concerned. It is therefore thought possible to divorce the artist from the man. Julian Green, looking at Wagner's portrait, says it shows "the face of a stingy land-lord" but reflects that the same man wrote *Siegfried*.[9] It

[9] *Personal Record*, 102.

seems more and more doubtful, however, whether our high-minded division of life and art is tenable. Art is not something that blows through a man as through a megaphone. The events or the character of the man do not cause or explain his art but they affect it. And in the Wagnerian instance, the man and his art purport to be, and are in fact, one. Wagner's works celebrate Wagner's aspirations and represent his deeds. *Tristan* and the *Ring* are pages from his biography. More than that, Wagner's abjection consists especially in his dealings with art and artists. We do not have to like the music of those he betrayed in order to admit that it was a betrayal of art to act as Wagner did. We do not have to agree with Hanslick in order to see how contemptibly the mature composer could act towards a fellow critic. The truth is that it was not his art that Wagner strove to impose, but himself. It was as the master magician of Bayreuth that he wanted to succeed. Hence he could have no critical or personal ethics. He must damn, praise, cheat, and lie about the very ideals which he presumably revered but really only used. The common faith in struggle and evolution helped to round out the beauty of such a career. With Wagner success meant being "musical master of the world in fifty years." Mozart, Weber, Beethoven, and the living could then be cast on the scrapheap of discarded attempts, for no amount of plausible blurb such as Wagner occasionally loved to write about great names could disguise the notion of a victory to be won, not against his century, but against his fellow artists, past and present.

With the completion of *Lohengrin* in 1848, Wagner felt that his evolutionary step had been taken. He felt like a god: "With that work, the old world of opera comes to an end. The spirit moved over the waters and there was light." Yet it is an error to suppose that Wagner's feelings on this point had the fixity of an intellectual faith. His evolutionism is as uncertain as Darwin's. In the *Lohengrin* days he read Plato and Aeschylus and reminded himself of the father of Greek tragedy. The *Orestes* trilogy was then for him the highest point of art and its norm. In his essays of a few years later, he combined this rather arbitrary decision with the usual cant of Greek "interpretation": Apollo was for him the national god who conquered the "chaotic" Python, an example which Sparta followed in war and Athens in the theater. The absolute artist (namely, R.W.) was Apollo come to life and giving the people "reality." Whether this reality is Platonic, that is, a hidden essence, or material, that is, the charming of the senses in the theater, is difficult to say, particularly since we must raise our altar not only to Apollo the nationalist, but to Jesus the anarchist. The Aeschylean drama goes ill with anarchism, but it does not matter very much what Wagner really means, for he is not thinking: he is talking great thoughts.[10]

Yet no sooner have we accepted the twin rule of these incompatible deities, than in *The Artwork of the Future,* dedicated to Feuerbach, we are asked to consider man as the only standard of thought and art. Music, which was formerly but a means to the end of drama, is now an equal in the union of all the arts. We follow a number of neatly symmetrical theories about the "origins" of the various arts, ending with a consideration of Beethoven and Shakespeare in relation to the Greek past and the Wagnerian future. From this scholarship it appears that Beethoven is both the last of the absolute musicians and the first of the programmatic. A poem underlies all his works, though the orchestra alone is incapable of giving the true idea of these poems, even with a printed explanation. Beethoven and Shakespeare should have joined their powers for a really complete work of art. Anyhow, absolute music is no longer music but an *Unding,* a wretched no-thing.

[10] Uhlig, who was not stupid, could not understand. Wagner explains: "I have grouped, according to their nature, the diverse species of art, in order to be able particularly to show through them as a whole, the evolution of art as a whole, in its relation

At the same time, in spite of Shakespeare, we learn that the true poem springs in lyric shape, not from the individual but from the community. It ripens slowly into the highest form of culture—the drama. Wagner being a dramatist rather than a melodist, we hear no more about the lyric; and in any case he is not pretending to do anything more than forecast the true artwork of the future by denouncing and destroying the false forms of the present.

Here we may interpose the comment that this hodge-podge of ideas is confusing only with respect to the things it describes. No one would go to it for an understanding of Shakespeare or the Greeks. Yet it gives a remarkable foretaste of the Wagnerian product itself. The structure of the *Ring,* for example, is both "regular" in the ordinary manner of the operatic libretto, and "lyrical" in the manner of the rhapsodical poet. Wagner conceals its symmetry under his various devices for building up continuity. The tableaux are there, though there are no set divisions. Speech, action, and music are "realistically" continuous, but the advantages of the "well-made play" are not given up. The result is not lyrical, dramatic, or frankly operatic: it is music drama.

As soon as the "brain cramp" which Wagner says accompanied his theoretic effort had passed, the fit of composing came upon him again. Apollo had to be dethroned and Dionysus, the god of musical intoxication, was hoisted into his place. Greece itself changes while you watch: it is no longer the serene, calm, complete culture that you had been led to admire. That cliché is replaced by the opposite and equally convenient one of the Greek mind as a symbol of movement, becoming, strength, and struggle—in short it is music. The poem is thrown over, its firm structure being no longer needed as the skeleton beneath the flesh of music, song, dance, and scenery. The orchestra alone is now the mysterious "ground of an unending general feeling" out of which "individual feeling may grow to its highest fulness."

to the evolution of human nature up to our modern ideas of what art is." Jan. 12, 1850.

It almost seems as if "absolute music" had regained its rights.

This mystery, however, does not take us (as we might think) into the realm of spirit. The modern theater is with us more than ever. Shakespeare is proved superior to the Greeks because he has got rid of that unrealistic makeshift, the chorus, and the history of all the arts is one of gradual improvement *since* the Greeks. The plastic arts have been perfected for the benefit of the stage manager: "What the landscape painter can only suggest through brushwork and the delicate mixing of pigments, he will here bring to the utmost deceptive power through the artistic employment of all the means put at his disposal by the science of optics and lighting." Progress is both mechanical and Darwinian, intellectual and social. "The march of this evolution is . . . not a cyclical return but a forward progress toward the attainment of the highest human potentialities. . . . Organic becoming is but the growth from lower to higher, the evolution of superior organism from inferior. . . ."[11]

We have had, in short, our choice of analyses, both proving by natural evolution that Wagner's still amorphous conceptions are logical. First the evolution was downwards: culture had degenerated since the Greeks and the time was ripe for regeneration. Next, the upward progress of the arts in modern times has given us Shakespeare and Beethoven, whose hands had missed touching and so left the world lacking the truly realistic work of art, a work of art sprung from the poet and from the people, chiefly poetic and chiefly musical, Apollonian and Dionysiac, with a bouquet of anarchistic Christianity and Feuerbachian materialism.[12]

[11] *Gesammelte Schriften*, iii, 12, 343; iv, 11, 353–54.

[12] A word should perhaps be added here about Wagner's more obvious belief that instrumentation and orchestration also improved by evolving. His second study of Beethoven, proposing corrections in the instrumentation of the Ninth Symphony, aroused protests, but was finally accepted as "logical"—at least by Wagnerians. Wagner was amazed that Beethoven, inheriting the orchestra of Haydn and Mozart, should have been able to

All this is high learning and not something in which "the people" would recognize its handiwork. The further source of Wagnerian theorizing is therefore the national idea—more specifically, Germanism. Like Marx, Wagner left his native land desiring its political unity above all other national goals, and like many of his other compatriots he could not dissociate this desire from personal and cultural judgments. Indeed, he sought out Greek parallels because they were expected to shed light on German affairs through the legendary kinship of the two peoples.

During his first Paris stay, Wagner was already a student of the difference between German *culture* and French *civilization*—a traditional distinction among Germans and one which most often reveals only the inability of the foreigner to distinguish between French culture and French frivolity, between the thinking minds of the nation and the empty ones of the *boulevards*. Wagner's examples betray this incapacity. He discovers, apropos of the *Freischütz*, that the German word W*ald* has no equivalent in French: *bois* is superficial and silly. How very French and very civilized to say *bois* instead of W*ald!* The proof is all the simpler for its neglect of the right word, which is *forêt*.

The conscious desire to be deep acquires more serious significance when Wagner discusses the "origins" of German art and impugns Mozart for composing operas to Italian texts. Before the *Magic Flute*, which has a German text, Mozart's music is cosmopolitan. Weber, of course, marks an epoch in Germanism by his choice of a native legend in *Der Freischütz*, but it is still recognizable as opera. It is not German, much less Greek. Cosmopolitanism in culture, Wagner feels, is fatal, and in view of Bee-

---

express himself with it. Wagner "helped him out" with alterations not required by the obsolescence of instruments. He thereby fostered the deplorable tradition of arrangements and "new readings." Moreover, his changing of the orchestral balance in his own works from the ratio ¾ strings–¼ wind to ⅔ and ⅓ has accustomed our ears to a thicker orchestral texture, which may well be the reverse of an improvement, though it was required by the "progress" from opera to music drama.

thoven's neglect of the stage, the Germans do not as yet possess a national art.

This Germanism ran counter to Wagner's revolutionary, Bakunin-sprung notions of an internationalized Europe, but the former feeling was the earlier and stronger. Long before the adoption of the *Wibelung* legend, Wagner had toyed with the idea of a play to be written around Frederick Barbarossa, conqueror of the southland. He also admired the later Frederick, of Prussia, and numbered him among his chosen heroes: Achilles, Jesus, Sakya Muni, Siegfried. In Dresden, as we saw, Wagner's bent toward Caesarism was clear. Exile only strengthened it. On his return following a special amnesty, he had given up all links with the revolution. He told Count von Beust with a straight face that the earlier episode had been "an unfortunate misunderstanding."[13] To his friends he said that his actions had been *undeutsch* and he proved it by pointing out that there was no native word for "democracy." He made overtures to Bismarck, though in a spirit of condescension, for after the publicity of his adoption by King Ludwig, Wagner acted as the natural representative of German art. He composed, unbidden, a march for the inauguration of William I as Emperor, and found himself commanded to meet him after the first performance at Bayreuth. There Wagner had already told his audience: "You have seen what we can do. It now lies with you that we should have an art."

The new empire and Wagner's rising star were two manifestations of quickened national pride following the humbling of Denmark, Austria, and France. Wagner had every reason to glory in this coincidence, for Paris still haunted him, an object of fascination and hatred. He had starved amid its luxury, half won its fashionable world, and created a scandal when he expected a triumph. He finally conquered it—and very easily—when he was dead. But he would have had to be a magnanimous man instead of a

---

[13] Beust, *Aus Dreivierteljahrhunderten*, i, 78.

conqueror had he not rejoiced to see the German armies encamped around Paris. He wrote an ode for the occasion, and when the city fell, a one-act play which was meant to make merry over the event. His mistake was to publish it.[14]

By this time Wagner's way with the German public had been made, principally by *Die Meistersinger*, which was an instant success. This was due in large part to the simple meaning and obvious fun of the plot, but it also owed something to its nationalist contents, summed up in the closing couplets:

> Let fall to dust
> The Holy Roman Empire,
> And live for ever
> Our holy German art!

This became the theme of Wagner's appeals for funds with which to build Bayreuth, and fittingly also the motto chosen for this foundation in 1882.

In the interim, it had done Wagner only temporary harm to become known as anti-Semitic and to talk learned nonsense about race. As early as 1850 he had taken pains to show that climate had no effect on art—else Germany, so long without art and still with the same climate, was doomed. The real "conditioning factor" was race. Twelve years later, Wagner discovered Gobineau, who returned the compliment, each becoming the other's public admirer. The French Count, who was an amateur sculptor, made busts of Valkyries, and declared the *Ring* to be the artistic embodiment of his own *Essay on the Inequality of Races*. This was true insofar as the *Ring* is a tale of decline and fall, but Wagner's optimistic nationalism overlooked this point, just as he overlooked Gobineau's denial that the Germans were Nordic and his affirmation that music was the gift of

[14] *Eine Kapitulation*, written 1871, published 1873. Its appearance somewhat delayed the spread of the Wagnerian passion among the French and made critics and musicians say things as silly as the piece which called them forth.

the Negro race to the hopelessly mixed Europeans. The vision of Wagner and Gobineau implicitly agreeing in the Villa Wahnfried that Wagner must be more Negro than Nordic gives the story of their friendship a much-needed touch of high comedy.

But this was no more isolated a "misunderstanding" on Wagner's part than his repudiation under that name of his whole revolutionary past. Wagner was attracted by the ambiguous. His learning, his kaleidoscopic faiths, his uncertain "depth," belong to the same murkiness of mind and character. He had no simplicity anywhere about him. He tried once to explain viva voce to Berlioz how the perfect work of art grew from an inner capacity which received objective impressions from without and transformed these according to the laws of general metaphysics and individual psychology into a product which, etc., etc. "I understand," replied Berlioz, "we call it digesting." Wagner's prose is a fair warning. It has been compared by the most eminent authority on the subject to the long, slow, and sure development of Wagner's musical thought.[15] It may be so, but it is likewise a badly overladen and tortuous medium for polemic or theory. Abounding in superlatives, prolix in vague analogies, and skillful in effusive praise which is immediately withdrawn, Wagner's writings stand as the incorruptible witness of his obliquity. Yet, throughout, the art of showmanship saves him from bathos. The casual reader feels confident in the man who can write that "Antiquity had only one poet—Homer," who deduces from this that Homer was a seer because he was blind, and who concludes that it was the desire to show men the reality seen by a seer which made Homer a poet.[16] This is reasoning indeed, though the meaning escapes.

In life—a more difficult medium than prose—the ambiguity would have been more excusable had it seemed less impudent. Before the success of Die Meistersinger, honest Mathilde Wesendonk could not understand why Wagner

[15] Ernest Newman, Preface to Schubert's Letters and Diaries.
[16] "On Poetic and Musical Invention."

should scorn money and public favor in letters which also unfolded his plans for attaining both. He apologized for the comic opera and prayed she might forgive it as he would forget it. Wagner had spoken as if Liszt's worldliness were abhorrent to him, but when Wagner's friends, who were paying the piper, remonstrated with him on his careless extravagance, he exclaimed: "I am built otherwise, I have sensitive nerves—beauty, glamor and light I *must* have. The world owes me what I require! I cannot live on a miserable post of organist like your master Bach! Is it such an unheard of demand when I ask that the little bit of luxury that I enjoy be given to me? I, I who hold a thousand enjoyments in store for the world!"[17] The Buddhist beggar whom Wagner envied in his low moments obviously had the tastes of the average sensual man. His vegetarianism itself was purely Pickwickian. Drawn from the messianic pages of a retired French colonel,[18] Wagner's renunciation of animal food was but another idea in the air. He grew angry when the children—his own and Cosima's—took it seriously. But the last word on the Wagnerian ambiguity must go to the significance of *Parsifal* and the Regeneration doctrine that filled his mind and his Bayreuth writings after the establishment there in 1876.

Cosima Liszt von Bülow, with whom Wagner had been living after her separation from her husband, was a devout Catholic, but not so devout that she had not become a Protestant convert in order to obtain a divorce. After her remarriage she exerted a strong religious influence upon a mind still open to new forms of salvation. This time it was Christianity, orthodox, yet passionate, tearful, and with the old demon of sensuality to be conquered. One of its results was the reworking of the legend of *Parsifal* into a sort of tract, ritual, and music drama all at once. Again, Wagner made a lucky hit. The devoutness of the play was transferred to its maker, putting the seal of holiness on the pub-

[17] Quoted in Hildebrandt, op. cit., 145.
[18] J. A. Gleizès, *Thalysie ou la Nouvelle Existence*, Paris, 1840, 3 vols.

lic's adoration of the master. People went to the new drama to celebrate Good Friday while enjoying, à la Wagner, the easy conquest over the ballerina seductions of the second act. Everyone remembered not to applaud and sat through the long allegory with the most in-churchy expression. So popular did the drama become within ten years of its composition that Cosima Wagner thought of reserving the right of performance exclusively for Bayreuth.

What Parsifal himself represents in his author's philosophy is not clear. The "pure fool" that he is supposed to be does not belong to the German original of the myth, where Parsifal is a gay and faithful lover who ultimately becomes the father of—Lohengrin. Nor do the real saints of history much resemble him. He suggests rather the common man's idea of a saint, combined with the villager's respect for a "natural." In Wagner he was also the symbol of the new humanity emerging with innocence from the temptations of the world—as did Tannhäuser. Only Tannhäuser was at least a poet. Parsifal has no utility, no power or idea but one: purity. Wagner was weary of the struggle and at last personified himself up to date. His work was now done, the work of the future had become the Bayreuthian present; artistic evolution had reached its end. It was for the rest of mankind to become regenerate in its turn by taking to heart the Wagnerian word in all its contradictory fulness.

5. Perfect Wagnerites

The noble Doctor Wagner all must know,
The first in all the learned arts is he;
. . .
Wisdom increasing, daily making clearer
How thirst for knowledge listener and hearer:
. . .
No name or fame beside him lives,
'Tis he alone invents and gives.

GOETHE, *Faust*, Part II

The first of the Perfect Wagnerites was the youth who mounted the throne of Bavaria as Ludwig II in 1864. Six years before, as a boy of twelve, he had read Wagner's dramas and had become a devotee. This was typical of the generation that raised Wagner to the pinnacle: first the written word, then the music. At fifteen the prince saw *Lohengrin,* and Wagner, unknowing, became his "educator and leader." The artist having broadcast appeals to crowned heads to endow Germany with an art of its own by giving him the means, it became Ludwig's object to fulfill the request, in spite of Wagner's revolutionary writings which the King's entourage put in his way to scare him off.

In the spring of 1864, when Wagner, still fleeing creditors, was writing his own epitaph in despair,[1] a royal em-

[1] "Here lies Wagner, who never amounted to much, was not even knighted, never achieved anything, not even a degree from

bassy was despatched inviting him to come to Munich, virtually on his own terms. The miracle had happened, Wagner was dumbfounded, then jubilant. The first moments between the pair, said he, were loverlike. They spoke out of the fulness of their hearts, each the longed-for fulfillment of the other's dream. When the performance of the *Ring* had been decided on, Wagner wanted to fall down and worship, and the King was in a transport of reciprocal adoration.

Wagner was the first to cool down. He immersed himself in plans to build a Richard Wagner Theater, in his new love affair with Cosima, and in conflicts with a naturally jealous officialdom that he did nothing to charm or placate—quite the contrary. He gave his pride an airing and neglected the King, though he wrote for him a tract on *The State and Religion* which shows, once again, how quick the poet was to seize contemporary moods and raise them to the dignity of theories. A Christian influence is visible in the new revelation, but without any worldly mission, rather a giving up of the world, with art as a sedative. Between Cosima's faith and the King's dreaminess, Wagner was reverting—purely on paper—to his make-believe renunciation. The business of establishing a theater was going on, but art had become a "noble illusion, a turning away from reality, a cure for life which is indeed not real, which leads one wholly outside life, but thereby raises one above it."

The King was not, as has been too often said, crazy. He was merely a timid and wounded spirit appalled by *Realpolitik* and the intrigues of a court. Wagner's union of art and religion in a realm beyond the state would hardly discourage the prince from wishing to act Lohengrin in a blue silk costume, and it would certainly encourage others to bemuse their discontent in an era of frightening prosperity and misery. Wagnerism offered every conceivable satisfaction. To a blasé public in search of new sensations

a university." Quoted in F. Panzer, *Wagner und das Deutschtum*, 1933, 1.

it gave the skillful mixture of sexuality and bigotry of *Tannhäuser;* to the spirit of national *Gemeinschaft* it gave the jolly complacency of *Die Meistersinger;* to the aggressive, the *Ring,* and to the devout, *Parsifal.* The literary could feed on doctrines and allegories and the musical enjoyed the "accurate thridding of labyrinthine things." For the first time poets, painters, sculptors, and scribblers of all sorts found a musician who saw the world through their eyes and made his own easy to grasp through theirs. They could wholeheartedly praise and expound to the less articulate some mysteries which could be understood, and music which, by its tireless repetition of simple themes, many really came to enjoy. Persuaded moreover by all they saw and heard and felt that here was true profundity, these artists and their followers hailed the new art and entered the new church with a reverence that in their day no other new establishment could command.

Both in England and in France it was the rising Symbolist Movement in the arts which first adopted Wagnerism as a cult. Though most great artists have had to be imposed at first by a small band of admirers, it would be silly to speak of Beethovenism or Blakism. But the circumstances of Wagner's coming into public notice helped form the ism and gave it special cachet. A King had chosen an Artist as his master, a people had adopted a man's work as the expression of their spirit—both in the lifetime of the creator himself. A city had been dedicated to his uses, and his rare and difficult music made money. An artistic generation starved of recognition, success, and religious balm, would find in Wagner its indirect vindication and would prostrate itself at the feet of the man who was the heir of Bach, Beethoven, Shakespeare, and the Greeks, and "better" than them all.

Symbolism in England began with the Pre-Raphaelites and it was a German, Franz Hueffer, who imported Wagnerism into their circle about 1869—the year of Berlioz's death. Hueffer was a Ph.D. in Philology as well as a disciple of Schopenhauer, and his reception at the house of Ford

Madox Brown, the painter, gave him a wide circle of hearers for his fluent advocacy of the new German art.[2] He preached so vigorously that even his amiability could not redeem the subject. But his persistence was soon rewarded by news from Germany and Belgium telling of the success of *Meistersinger*—an opera that appealed to every artist by its vindication of art. The group of English Wagnerites grew fast. Swinburne, the younger Rossettis, Forman (the Shelley scholar) and his brother, Arthur Symons, George Moore, were exposed and converted. Hueffer married Ford Madox Brown's younger daughter,[3] settled permanently in England, and as music editor of *The Times* became the Wagnerian authority until his death in 1889. By that time, a Wagnerian Society had been founded in affiliation with the Universal Wagner Society, and a periodical, *The Meister*, established under the direction of W. Ashton Ellis, who undertook to translate and publish in English all of Wagner's prose writings. In less than a decade after the composer's death, "Wagner night at Covent Garden" had become a regular feature of operatic life and "being a Wagnerian" conferred superior status.

Nor did the "advanced," freethinking, and socialist elements lag far behind. The naturalist novelists, Hardy, Gissing, Bennett, Galsworthy, were Wagnerians. Hardy thought Wagner a great painter of nature, and though Galsworthy ended by breaking away, the theorist of the contemporary esthetic movement, Walter Hamilton, did not hesitate to count Wagner as a force in naturalism. Wagner had replaced the original untruth of opera by the natural truth of continuous melody, leitmotifs, and so on. The

[2] His friend William Bell Scott wrote:

> There's a solid fat German called Hueffer
> Who at anything funny's a duffer
>   To proclaim Schopenhauer
>   From the top of a tower
> Will be the last effort of Hueffer.

[3] From this marriage was born in 1873 the late Ford Madox (Hueffer) Ford.

mythical apparatus was explained away as permitting the communication of crude truths about life and death to an unprepared public.[4] This did not prevent the decadents and anti-naturalists from finding Wagner's art to their taste. Aubrey Beardsley, who approached it in a spirit of mockery, was finally engulfed in its sensuality, and produced for each of the stories one or more characteristic designs. The sex question was being discussed and Wagner's plays contributed as much light to it as these drawings, Swinburne's ballads, and Baudelaire's *Fleurs du Mal.*

Perhaps this is why still others put Wagner forward as a pioneer of Humanitarianism, much to Samuel Butler's amusement.[5] George Bernard Shaw became a Wagnerian at a moment when his position as the most readable music critic could powerfully aid the movement and it was he who urged the new Fabian Society of socialists to reprint Wagner's *Art and Revolution* as one of its tracts. The motion was defeated, but it showed how far Wagnerism could reach. Bohemians, decadents, bourgeois, socialists, and other-worldly enthusiasts merged their differences "in a frenzy of love and devotion."

The pitch was raised so high that Shaw himself saw— exactly as he had seen with Marx—that someone must cry halt. He undertook the difficult task of pushing Wagner as a musician while combating the deification of the man. He made Wagnerites but ridiculed the Wagneritual. Thoroughly familiar with the music of the nineteenth century before Wagner, Shaw knew how much the new idol had taken from his predecessors. The truly faithful, like W. A. Ellis, were as innocent of musical knowledge as Parsifal was of sin, and they resisted it with the same fortitude. They denied that anyone before Wagner had put any dramatic qualities into music and they described the scoring of Donizetti or Meyerbeer, which they had not heard, as "a few arpeggios."[6] Shaw finally saw that the tide was too

---

[4] *The Esthetic Movement,* 1882, passim.

[5] *Butler: A Memoir,* by H. F. Jones, ii, 373.

[6] Shaw, *London Music in 1888–89,* 1937, 30.

strong to stem; he chose rather to harness it to socialism. He reinterpreted the *Ring* in the light of Wagner's early hopes of revolution and stressed with the aid of biography the distinctions between early, middle, and late Wagner. The result was *The Perfect Wagnerite*, "a book of devotion" as he called it in a gay note to his publisher, "an Imitation of Christ affair" for the use of Covent Garden audiences, which should have "gilt edges, leather binding, clasps, and a bookmarker of perforated card with a text worked on it in wool."[7]

In France, though the socialist tinge was absent, Wagnerism left an even deeper mark on the mind of the generation that closed the century. The uses of Wagnerism in England were social and philosophical; in France, there added to these the artistic and esthetic. With defenders among older men like Baudelaire, Gasperini, Challemel-Lacour (a politician and pessimist), and among influential women like Judith Gautier and the Comtesse d'Agoult (Liszt's first love and Cosima's mother), the tradition was carried on from the *Tannhäuser* days to those of the symbolist poets and the writers of the incredible *Revue Wagnérienne*. Neither resentment at the defeat of 1870 nor political feeling against Wagner's turncoat behavior in France and Germany, nor the knowledge of his many acts of ingratitude to his former hosts, prevented his sway from becoming complete. A second Franco-German war in 1914 hardly affected it. It would be a splendid spectacle of admiration for art rising above ordinary human passions if one did not plainly see that the gratification of stronger and often irrelevant instincts was the force behind the initial choice and its maintenance. Certainly musical taste had little to do with the growth of the movement: rather, taste followed it. The thoroughly Wagnerized poets from Villiers de l'Isle Adam, Verlaine, and Baudelaire, to Mallarmé, Stuart Merrill, René Ghil, Henri de

[7] Grant Richards, *Author-Hunting*, 1934, 138.

Régnier, Catulle Mendès, Paul Valéry, and Paul Claudel[8] betrayed in their verse and prose how much literary theorizing had to do with their bending the knee. They were for the most part as unmusical as poets generally are, and they remained, also for the most part, Wagnerians and nothing else.

Edouard Dujardin, the founder of the *Revue Wagnérienne,* had had, it is true, some musical education and was a composer of sorts. But his main achievement after the *Revue* is to have influenced Joyce's work through his novelistic device of the "internal monologue."[9] As Dujardin admitted much later, he founded the *Revue* not to propagate the works of Wagner the musician but of Wagner the great poet, the great thinker, and especially the creator of a new form of art.[10] At the same time he became, in his own words, a Cook's Tour clerk for Bayreuth, a press agent for the performances taking place the world over, and an interpreter of the Wagnerian revolution to the French. His formula—"the new Wagnerian art re-creates the complete feeling of reality by appealing to all the senses at once"— suggests a patent medicine, but it worked. The *Revue* lasted only three years in its perfervid stage but it left Paris almost more Wagnerian than the home of the master.

The absurdities said and done during this crusade form an amusing chapter not only in the history of criticism, but in the mythical tradition of "French logic." For one thing, a number of its heroes, like Houston Stewart Chamberlain and the *Revue's* co-editor, T. de Wyzewa, were foreigners who wrote French with noticeable awkwardness. Yet their style harmonized perfectly with that of the native contributors, particularly Dujardin's, for the symbolists were achieving by art what the foreigners had by nature. The *Revue* was advertised by its own strangeness. It openly declared the French language inadequate to its new subject matter

[8] Claudel's retraction came very late, though with great violence; see *Figaro,* March 26, 1938.

[9] In *Les Lauriers sont Coupés,* 1888.

[10] *Revue Musicale,* 1923.

and only regretfully announced to its amazed subscribers that after a given date it would be written in intelligible language.

Behind the verbal affectations lay philosophical mysteries: Dujardin's promise of reality was combined with de Wyzewa's egocentric mysticism.[11] Wagnerism was explained as both "the real thing" and the projection of the self into the apparent forms of the outer world—a bit of pseudo-Fichtean Orientalism which sank particularly deep into the soul of Barrès, then in his Hegelian and Marxist phase, but which he dropped very soon, only to become a rabid blood-and-soil nationalist. He never admitted how much Wagner had had to do with this transformation but his early articles show how easy the transition was. Whether truly Wagnerian or not, the mysticism of the ego did not prevent the "scientific" naturalists like Zola, Huysmans, Hennequin, and Léon Daudet from joining the ranks. "It was dumb if you like," said Daudet some years ago, "but what we admired most was the librettos."

The poets moreover paid homage to Wagner in verses which were often easier to understand than their prose. Twice during the life of the review there appeared sonnet sequences by various hands, exalting Wagner's works and sounding the evolutionary theme of perfection just attained. Wagner includes and surpasses his predecessors: Mozart is a limpid stream, Beethoven a mighty river, and Wagner is the all-englobing sea.[12] Better yet, "Wagner is the synthetic revelation to which Racine and Bach, Hugo and Berlioz, and that great precursor, Beethoven, have contributed their special efforts, their visions, and their voices. . . ."[13] This artistic tutti-frutti was not even necessary: we have the co-editor's assurance that "for works of art to transform a race there is no need of their being

[11] The gifted but half-crazed *illuminatus*, Péladan, worked Wagnerism into his cycle of twelve realistic novels on "Latin Decadence."

[12] *Revue*, Jan. 15, 1887, passim.

[13] *Ibid.*, 1885, 130–31.

known; so that despite our ignorance [of music] we have all been powerfully influenced by this new art of Wagner's."[14]

The avowed ignorance of music was occasionally repaired by having a music critic write an article, but this was not necessary either: once the handbooks of leitmotives had been published, almost anyone could learn to discourse on the scientific construction of the music dramas. One of these technicians could find in *Die Meistersinger* a single motif from which all the other eighty-three were "organically generated" and could point to the realism of having 96 per cent of the music a mere notation of normal speech inflections.[15] These Wagnerians were of course purists who insisted on the scenic display: "To perform the Forest Murmurs without scenery or pantomime shows a complete lack of understanding. . . . Wagner is not a musician, he is a dramatist seeking to reproduce the whole of life. . . ."[16]

This kind of criticism was bound to have nationalist implications, and the sources of the Wagnerian legends were argued about at length: were they German or Celtic? Hans von Wolzogen, head of German Wagnerism, preached Aryan art with the help of the "renegade Englishman" Chamberlain, and showed that Wagner was far more than a German artist. He was "a necessity of the modern spirit." The barbarian invasions of the Roman Empire came up quite apropos to prove the blood bond between Germany and a part of France, and this in turn brought up the political issues that were then uppermost in the recently defeated country. The party of revenge against Germany, led by would-be fascists like General Boulanger, Paul Déroulède, and the anti-Semitic publicists, were nevertheless for Wagner. The republicans, feeling there was something progressive and high-minded about Wagnerism, swore allegiance also. Politicians like Roche and Monod, novelists like Mirbeau and Mendès, campaigned in the press for the

14 *Ibid.*, 168.
15 *Ibid.*, 315.
16 *Ibid.*, 1887, 44, and 1885, 76.

performance of *Lohengrin* at the state-subsidized Opéra-
Comique. The patriot Rochefort suggested it be de-Ger-
manized for public use: "*Lohengrinno,* by Ricardo Wag-
nero." Wagnerism was excellent publicity for all parties to
the dispute. At long last Wagner had conquered Paris and
was the leader of *all* its contending factions: only the annual pilgrimage to Bayreuth united them in silence.

Even scholars like Romain Rolland and Henri Lichten-
berger hardly kept their heads. The latter declared that
Wagner had translated the abstract ideas of the philosophers into forms of beauty and emotion. Another critic said
that Mozart had "failed" because music was incapable of
psychological delineation and could only express propositions. Weber, said a third, was a child compared to Wagner, and mature young persons of twenty announced that
the taste for the *Freischütz* overture was something one
outgrew at fifteen.[17] Nothing like Wagner had been seen
since the Renaissance; he was a whole Renaissance in himself.[18] Romain Rolland summed up the intellectual background of these convictions: "I remember having been
dominated by the Wagnerian idea when the Wagnerian art
was still half obscure to me. When it befell me not to be
able to understand a musical work of his, my confidence
was not shaken. I was sure that a genius whose mighty
thought had convinced me could not err, and that if his
music escaped my grasp, the fault was mine."[19]

Among the composers, Saint-Saëns, Vincent d'Indy,
César Franck, and many lesser ones succumbed—with better reason—to the spell. When the first-named reasserted
his independence, at least in matters of theory, he could
say with the knowledge of experience: "Artistic faith has
become dogmatic and authoritarian; it hurls anathemas,
condemns former beliefs as erroneous, or allows them as a

[17] *Lettres de l'Ouvreuse* by Henri Gauthier-Villars, 1890, 126.
[18] Camille Benoit, *Richard Wagner* (Extracts), 1887, Preface.
[19] *Musiciens d'Aujourd'hui,* 7.

preparation to the reign of the new law. . . . Intolerance, fanaticism, and mysticism have followed in its train."[20]

The Wagnerian vogue in Germany can be imagined as being on the same scale. It was, if anything, more learned. The *Bayreuther Blätter* saw to it that all the Wagnerian outposts were well defended. A friend like Gobineau was celebrated and buried with full honors. Musical masters and rivals were kept in their proper place, "indispensable works" like those of Chamberlain or the *Wagner Encyclopedia* of Glasenapp were recommended, and the *Regenerationslehre* implied in *Parsifal* was taught as a preventive against European decadence.

The nation at large naturally enjoyed a proprietary interest in the artist's nationalism. His rise to fame coincided with that of the nation to the rank of great power and his victory was that of German culture over its old enemy, the French. Nietzsche might say that the victory had been purely military and had left the cultures untouched, the readers of Darwin and Spencer knew better. A racialist like Ludwig Schemann, founder of the Gobineau Society, told his audiences that he could hardly exaggerate the significance of Wagner in cementing the national union or strengthening German hegemony.[21] The critical opposition, rallying around Brahms and his *German Requiem*, had but a poor chance of diverting the torrent.

In the year of Wagner's death—a month after Marx's—a solid work entitled *Bismarck, Wagner, Rodbertus*,[22] and bearing the motto "Monarchisch, national, social," argued with a great show of reason that German destinies must follow the paths broken by the three great German ideas of the century: Bismarck's Caesarism, Rodbertus's national socialism, and Wagner's artistic nationalism. Wagner, in

[20] *Portraits et Souvenirs*, 187.

[21] *Wagner in . . . Nationale[r] Kultur*, Goslar, 1877.

[22] Moritz Wirth, *Bismarck, Wagner, Rodbertus: Drei deutsche Meister, Betrachtungen über ihr Wirken und die Zukunft ihrer Werke*. Leipzig, 1883.

fact, receives the fullest treatment, technical and biographical, for without him the work of the other two cannot be co-ordinated and made popular. Many men in one, Wagner created a spiritual center for the nation. His example must not be allowed to die, Bayreuths must spring up in every province, and younger composers without imitating him must nevertheless not stray from the line. Fortunately, according to the author, *Don Giovanni* was no longer the German people's favorite opera as it had been in the old cosmopolitan period: it was now replaced by *Tannhäuser* and *Lohengrin*.[23]

Ten years later Wagnerism was a bond of union wherever German speech and thought had currency. More popular than ever at the court of the new German Emperor after the pilot Bismarck had been dropped, the new art was felt to exemplify the virtues of the Prussian army. The chancellor Hohenlohe had always been a Wagnerian, even in the difficult Ludwig days, just as Wagner had been from the start an absolutist, ready to hitch his star to the Prussian bandwagon. Now the accumulated creeds of four decades were fused in the Pan-Germanic agitation and the "Aryan" mysticism that ushered in the new century.

Certainly, the title "Universal Wagner Society" was no exaggeration. For perhaps the first time in its cultural history, the United States received the new tidings from abroad without delay. There were musicians here ready to play the new works "until the public liked them," writers like Whitman willing to say that Wagner's was "the music of *The Leaves*," and commentators proud to illustrate their subject or display their insight by allusion to the new art. One such use of it deserves to be quoted in full, for it combines all the features of the Wagnerian fever: poetic, musical, social, nonsensical, and at the last, the hint of a philosophic disappointment at not having been given the promised "reality." The writer, it is worth noticing, was a

[23] *Op. cit.,* 151.

Harvard professor giving the last of his Lowell Lectures on English Composition:

There is no single example of this more notable than the phase of fine art which I am disposed to think most characteristic of this last half of the nineteenth century: I mean the music drama of Wagner. Anyone can appreciate how great a poet Wagner was. In *Siegfried,* for example, when the Dragon lies sleeping on his hoard, Wotan comes to warn him of the approach of the hero who is to slay him; and from the depths of his cave comes the growling answer,

> Ich lieg' und besitze.
> Lass mich schlafen . . .

I lie here possessing. Let me sleep. In seven words, Wagner has phrased the spirit that made the French Revolution what it was; that among ourselves today seems to many so terribly threatening to the prosperity of our own country. But Wagner is not only a poet; most of you, I think, who have let yourselves listen, must have felt the indefinable power of the endlessly interwoven melody by which he seeks to express in music, too, the thought and emotion for which poetry alone is an inadequate vehicle. Perhaps you must go to Bayreuth to know the rest. But certainly at Bayreuth, where every engine of modern art was at his disposal, Wagner has brought all the other fine arts to his aid: architecture in the simple lines of the darkened theatre itself, where the music of the instruments fills the air one knows not whence; painting, in scenery, in costumes, in groupings of heroic figures, where for once the pageantry of the stage is treated as any great painting; even sculpture, as when, through the whole celebration of the mystic sacrament, Parsifal stands motionless as any figure cut from marble. No one art of expression was enough for Wagner; and it was at last his fortune to control them all. Yet when all was done by this man, who seems to me the greatest of modern artists . . . the final reality, the real thought and emotion which all this marvellous thing would express, is as far away as ever.[24]

The fine irrelevancies of such a passage, the zestful absurdities penned by European and American critics, the many meanings of these many passions clinging to half a dozen operas, the reason of the worship of a "mere artist" by a generation that had let so many die in neglect, could, at the time, be perceived by very few. Only one man of the first rank, Nietzsche, took in the tragicomedy at a glance and saw in it the portrait of an age. His remarks were taken lightly, though the warnings they contained should have been heeded all the more seriously that among Wagnerians he had held an early and a uniquely favored place.

[24] Barrett Wendell, *English Composition*, N. Y., 1891, 278.

6. Nietzsche Contra Wagner

But the systematic philistine education which has come to power, just because it is systematic, is not culture; and it is not merely bad culture; it is the opposite of culture.

NIETZSCHE, 1873

Nietzsche was before anything else a great culture hero; as a critic of art he has been surpassed by no man.

A. R. ORAGE, 1922

No greater mistake can be made than to consider Nietzsche's break with Wagner a personal quarrel resulting from a difference of opinion about music. It is much more. It is the first critical repudiation of the second half of the nineteenth century by a herald of the twentieth. It is consequently the key to the twisted cypher of the Romantic-Realist conflict, and the symptom of the chaos created by Darwinism, socialism, nationalism, and popular culture between 1875 and 1900. Caught at the junction of these rushing streams, Nietzsche's thought was heaved up like a confused crest and scattered in all directions. That is why his work, although it is made up in part of fragments and aphorisms, must be taken as a whole and not piecemeal. His "friends" the apologists of violence and his opponents the defenders of democracy err equally in taking sentences out of their context and metaphors away from their intention. No less misleading is it to sample his anti-Wagnerian polemics.

It was in 1869, only ten years after *Tristan,* that Nietzsche, under the spell of its music, came as an unknown of twenty-five to Wagner in Tribschen. A philologist by profession, Nietzsche had been attracted to the figure of the struggling artist. First taken up, then deposed, by a king, Wagner was continuing the fight, as it seemed, "against the century." That alone endeared him to Nietzsche, who like most beginners in the career of art was looking for a master, a judge, a hero whose deeds he could sing. The affection with which Wagner responded begot also in the orphaned Nietzsche a feeling akin to the discovery of a second father. But whereas the younger man's devotion was without *arrière pensée,* Wagner's contained the usual dose of self-seeking: he saw a champion sent by fate to convert the men of the rising generation. Nietzsche's ideas on the musical origins of Greek Tragedy fitted in confusedly but satisfactorily with Wagner's old notions on the subject, and lively talks together smoothed out any glaring contradictions. Wagner became a Nietzschean as quickly as Nietzsche a Wagnerian.

Any cross purposes were so far submerged in a league of artists against Philistines. Nietzsche was thoroughly conversant with music, he played the piano like a gifted amateur and had even composed a few "tone poems." He was also a poet and a trained scholar. Wagner was therefore talking to his peer in culture and, for all he knew, in creative power. He was in fact talking to his superior in critical insight; for not long after the friendship had been made fast, we find Nietzsche beginning to jot down his private doubts about Wagner.

It had been planned between them that as soon as *The Birth of Tragedy* was published, Nietzsche should strike out with an essay—perhaps a book—on Wagner. But the critic delayed. He wrote instead the first of his *Thoughts out of Season*—the famous assault on David Strauss, the representative of false culture, false science, and false spirituality. Of these unpopular "thoughts" Nietzsche wrote another, and a third. Only in his fourth and last, seven years after their first meeting, and after Wagner had established himself at Bayreuth, did Nietzsche devote a hundred short pages to his chosen master.

The pages are not only short, they are constrained and diffident. There can be little doubt, as a modern critic has shown, that Nietzsche was already aware of his main objections to Wagnerism.[1] These are in truth implicit in the first of the four *Thoughts* and are summed up in the term *Bildungsphilister*—educated Philistine—a nickname of Nietzsche's invention to stigmatize not merely Strauss but the generation to which he spoke, the Wagnerian generation. The *Bildungsphilister* is the cultural enthusiast, the canting faddist, the torchbearer of civilized mediocrity, some of whose thoughts embellished our last chapter.

Between the first and fourth of the "Unseasonables," Nietzsche had gone to Bayreuth and it had been for him a revelation in the wrong sense. He had seen the stage effects, beheld the symbolic menagerie in action, heard the shouting heroes and heroines, felt the musical thrills ebbing and flowing over the united sensorium of the audience—and he had seen the master magician beam with delight at the public response. Nietzsche could still feel that it was not the time to speak out. Wagner's professed aims were as good as ever: a national art akin to Greek tragedy, combining music and acting, and not seeking to make money out of the boredom of the upper classes. But all the aims might be lost through a vulgar compromise with a vulgar audience. Crude and high-priced, Bayreuth combined snobbery with sightseeing, and was steeped in sensuality and beer. Nietzsche took a sorrowful farewell of the place where the new art might have come to birth. Tears stood in his eyes as he sighed, "And that was Bayreuth!"

The break with the Wagners—for Cosima had much befriended him and was the first to discern his "treachery"—

[1] Hildebrandt, *Wagner und Nietzsche, Ihr Kampf Gegen das Neunzehnte Jahrhundert*, Breslau, 1924.

was brought on by Nietzsche's next work, *Human, All Too Human*. It is the record of his passage through darkness, his plunge into positivism and science, which he uses against his society without remorse. Here are found the first hints of anti-Wagnerism, mixed with suspicion of all forms of faith. Antinomies in the manner of Proudhon combine with satire drawn from Darwin and the socialists and are turned against them as well. Cosima's devout soul was shocked, but she comforted herself (and Nietzsche's sister) with the idea that their friend and brother was mentally sick. He would recover and return to them. He never did, though intermittent letters were exchanged among the two Nietzsches and the two Wagners, ambiguous in tone, seeking some impossible ground of reunion. These notes might accompany a new book or a score: from Wagner came the last music drama *Parsifal*. This was the end of the end. Nietzsche was revolted by its thick sanctimonious atmosphere. The notes *Contra Wagner* were accumulating, and Nietzsche was about to seek abroad a spiritual calm which neither his native land nor his professorial conscience could afford him. Yet with a delicacy which the subject of the notes would have found superhuman, Nietzsche did not publish until five years had passed over Wagner's death.

Nietzsche had not been mentally sick. He had only taken Wagnerism seriously and tested it. Not conceding that what was new art to the half-educated public of Europe was necessarily made so by their decision, he judged Wagnerism by its effect upon him. His intimate acquaintance with the quality of genius from Plato and Pascal to Stendhal and Schopenhauer made him feel that in Bayreuth art took a step downwards in order to reach, not the people, but the middle classes of a decadent era. Everything in Wagner was designed for them: the size and crudity of the show, the aura of technicality and religion, the figure of the author as a wonder-worker, the association of nationalism with the turgid dramas, and finally the music. The music was not separable from the rest; it was crude, pretentious, and turgid too. It lacked the two things that define and give intellectual form to inarticulate sounds: rhythm and melody. It was the opiate of the people.

The tricks of the master did not escape the one-time disciple. Nietzsche saw that music drama is only theater writ large and pompous. The wooden structure of the plays is concealed by a false continuity of verse and sound. Like any Meyerbeer, perhaps even less skillfully, Wagner pulls his subject about to satisfy some conventional stage demand: two whole acts without a female voice are unbearable; the heroines, however, are busy elsewhere: never mind! Wotan will wake up Erda and discuss philosophy for want of small talk. The effect is achieved and no one will inquire too closely—except an artist.

Wagner the theorist, Nietzsche sums up by ascribing to him three rules of procedure: "Whatever Wagner cannot do is wrong. Wagner can nevertheless do many things, but he will not, from rigor of principle. Whatever Wagner can do, no one can do after him, no one has done before him, no one shall ever do again. Wagner is a god."[2] Before Wagner, music had had no need of literature to help it. Is it possible that Wagner feared his music would be too slight, too easily understood without the paraphernalia of theory and symbol? Or is it rather an answer to the demand of the musically illiterate for something to give importance to their nervous thrills? In any case, Wagner's music is decadent and for decadents. It lacks gaiety, strength, intelligence, freedom from gross material aids; above all it lacks artistic integrity: it comes out of a bag of tricks.

This is the "Wagner Case." Six months later, the debate grows wider. Wagnerism has become the symptom of the European malady which it is Nietzsche's mission to combat and, if possible, to cure. Music has become an opiate because the world of the late nineteenth century is too dreadful to be faced, and those who have made it are too stupid

[2] Nietzsche's *Werke*, Klassiker Ausgabe, Leipzig, viii, 32.

and cowardly to remake it. Materialism and loss of faith have generated their seeming opposite, a makeshift mysticism of the senses. In it sensation itself disappears; as in *Tristan*, sensation is for the sake of forgetting self, love is for the sake of death. All ideals meanwhile have become falsehoods. Morality is an indecent sham; brutality masquerades as strength; positivism is the name for a disgusted skepticism; science and education are professional make-believes sheltering the mass mind. Nowhere is anyone found saying "yea" to life, loving his fate, knowing his mind or shaping his world. It is "the Bayreuthian era of civilization." The theories of Darwin and Marx preach fatalism, chaos, and a Utopia coming thereafter through nobody's fault.

These are the reasons for Nietzsche's knowing that he is at the antipodes from Wagner, who condones all this and gives the patient a soothing drink. Nietzsche scorns most the two things Wagner stands for most—Germanism and anti-Semitism. To be a good European, an anti-German, a lover of "Mediterranean" music, an anti-pessimist, and a witness of the rebirth after decadence, one must be first an anti-Wagnerian, a wholehearted detester of the "Music Without Any Future."[3]

When Nietzsche gathered some of these ideas upon the Wagnerian issue and published them, he himself was near the end of his career. In another year his mind was gone. In addition to disease he had borne the strain of grasping and reproducing the contradictions of his age. This is what makes him of perennial interest to the historian of ideas and of immediate importance to the present. For Nietzsche was among the first to see that the *thoughts* of his epoch

[3] Title of section four in *Nietzsche Contra Wagner*. As an example of Mediterranean music, Nietzsche instanced *Carmen*, which has puzzled certain commentators, for the work is too slight to oppose the Wagnerian machine. It is nevertheless a pointer in the direction of Romanticism, both musically (Bizet is a genuine pupil of Berlioz, says Nietzsche) and dramatically (Mérimée's tale as the basis of the libretto).

were heading men towards catastrophe. Unlike other prophets of decadence, he saw that it was not this or that group
which was the obstacle to peace and self-culture, but the
corrupted minds of men in all groups. He used the Germans as examples of a peculiarly sodden complacency just
as he used Wagner as a symbol of anti-culture, but their
removal would not uproot the common tradition of science,
positivism, pessimism, and shabby morality which blighted
Europe. Occasionally he used the French or the Italians as
models of true culture. This was doing them too much
honor, or rather it was using certain superior minds in foreign countries to emphasize the mass vulgarity of his own
land. Those superior foreign minds could have pointed to
the same vulgarity at home, as did Gobineau in his best
writings. The problem was on a continental scale and
Nietzsche alone, it seemed, was raising his solitary voice in
an overpopulated desert.

This may be one reason why his words are violent and
his metaphors military. He must make his contemporaries
understand by using the language of competition and struggle which they already knew. They misunderstood nonetheless, for all were partisans and accustomed to overlooking
a good half of what is said. They took Nietzsche's flattery
and forgot his warnings. And still today, Germans and anti-
Germans tug over the body of Nietzschean doctrine, mis-
taking strength and force, anti-morality and immorality,
superman and brute. Devised to stress the unity of mind
and life, Nietzsche's use of biological similes encourages
racialists and nationalists, but his Superman bears only a
verbal resemblance to that fancied by Eugenics Societies.
The Nietzschean ideal is not the improved *homo sapiens*
that Darwin hints of, nor the shadowy hero that Wagner
buries in the *Ring*. He is rather the Shavian revolutionist,
Jack Tanner. Yet Nietzsche is no socialist. He is against
all manifestations of mob and snob, against militarism,
against the principle of nationality, against brutish conquest
on any field by the uncultured force of numbers. His superman is strong in that he can stand alone, that he thinks by

cerebration and not imitation, that he acts by refined instinct and not by rote or rule. Hence Nietzsche's detestation of Caesarism, from Bismarck down to Caesar himself —their strength being not their own but a mass of coagulated weaknesses.

Nietzsche's overthrow of Christianity has the same roots. It is never Jesus, whom Nietzsche always treats with respect, but the popular Christ of the churches whom he attacks as the cultivator of weakness and the abettor of complacency. Nietzsche's psychological discovery is that there can be no fertile graces, no gentleness, without strength. For this reason he rejects Darwin in favor of Lamarck. The former's unholy promise of an evolution taking place haphazard, without thought, merely as the result of a crowd's trampling itself to near extinction, revolts him. How can the survivors come out any closer to the superman than they went in? It is not in individual fights or in mass actions that the qualities of the new race can be bred. He cannot in truth tell us how it shall be done, for although he uses the word "race" which belongs to his "period vocabulary," he denies anything like inborn qualities, particularly in himself. No one acknowledged more freely the debts he owed to his many masters, his helpers of all lands and creeds.

Among them one notes many romanticists of every age, from Hölderlin and Schiller to Stendhal and Pascal. Yet in his early and middle periods, Nietzsche continually attacks *Die Romantik* and *die romantiker*. This is another clue to the false perspective common to the second half century, for what Nietzsche despises is the thin imitation of romanticism by the second generation of its practitioners; it is the romanticism of the realists, the romanticism of Wagner . . . or of Emma Bovary. Occasionally Nietzsche is harsh in his judgments of the earlier men, of Byron or Schiller or Carlyle, but in the end, having relived in himself the successive moods of the century, he was brought back to a new romanticism. He had described a full though not a closed circle. He now rejoiced in the "delightful diversity of types and prodigality of forms" which nature and true culture jointly permit. Like Gobineau, he gave up all mechanical ideas of producing the new elite. It can only spring spontaneously by self-culture. Finally, he rediscovered and restated the romanticist relativity of all knowledge, the futility of applying scientific cause and effect to life, and the primacy of faith. Independently of Samuel Butler, Bergson, Poincaré, or William James, he became a Pragmatist and a proto-Freudian. His fragments on the Will to Power show that he has broken with all the riddles and false antitheses of the positivist era. Art is not opposed to reality but to morality and philosophy, that is to say, art is the opposite of convention and routine. Art is creation of the real, not, as in Wagner, a sedative. The Will to Power has nothing to do with the Darwinian instinct of self-preservation; it is the need of self-knowledge and self-assertion without which nothing great can be done. Only in fine natures does it bear fruit. The common yearning for overlordship, for satisfying the ego anyhow, is a sign of weakness that spells slavery either way. The Nietzschean ideal is simply the quenchless desire of man to be conscious, cultured, and free.

7. After Wagner: What Is Art?

> I wish to see Wagner uprooted, however clever he
> may be, and I don't doubt he is: but he is an anti-
> artistic, and don't doubt it.
>
> WILLIAM MORRIS

The Nietzschean view of art was doubtless too difficult for
the public to extract from his contradictory and allusive
sentences. It was much simpler for the "well-informed" to
echo here and there an isolated outburst against morality or
a hymn to reckless strength, and to unite Nietzsche with
Wagner and Ibsen as the prophets of the new life. On the
other side, the defenders of a purely imaginary "established
order" condemned all three, with Tolstoy, Dostoevski, and
"those Russians," likewise as symbols of degeneration.[1]
The century that ended to the tune of Natural Selection,
Socialism, and Anglo-Saxon Supremacy did not distinguish
disharmony within the parts, it merely sensed it somewhere in the orchestral mass.

And although this chaos of tendencies was felt as mark-

[1] Two books published at the turn of the century give the temper of the moment: Max Nordau's *Degeneration* and H. S.
Chamberlain's *Foundations of the Nineteenth Century.* Though
the thesis of each is incoherent, these two works are not the
"obviously crazy" productions they have been called. Their
success at the time shows how little obvious their folly actually
was to readers familiar with Galton, Lombroso, Karl Pearson,
and other scientific "authorities."

ing the end of a period, the impression that remained with the majority was one of cultural accomplishment. It was typified equally well by the carrying of the White Man's Burden and by Wagner. Conquering all difficulties, an artist had triumphed and had been declared a great man: the age could not be so materialistic in the bad sense as some had charged. The public, rather, was flattered by the thought that it had known enough to choose him and to learn about art at his capable hands.

With Wagner the "life of art" became a recognized substitute for life itself. Not only was Nietzsche not understood, but thoroughly lucid writers like George Bernard Shaw and Romain Rolland[2] were unable to depict the relation of art to society and religion, or to vindicate art from the charges of a Nordau, without being interpreted as saying that culture was exclusively the reading and making of books, the talking about pictures and concerts. Similarly, the social function of art was simply the depicting of industrial horrors in documented novels. The essentially Wagnerian confusion of art with both reality and unreality could not be disentangled, for the question of what was real and what was not could not be solved intelligently in an era which saw only Matter and non-Matter as the criteria of real and unreal. In any case, art had won the place that Wagner hoped it would win: that of absolute dominance, at least in the speech of the educated. Art for art's sake, which was a mild and redundant ideal, gave way to life for art's sake.

But this unlikely esthetic awakening of all Europe was so self-conscious that it was hard to distinguish it from the general faith in moral mechanisms which filled the spas and hydropathic establishments, the "new thought" studios and theosophic chapels. The few who kept their heads vainly raised their voices in behalf of simplicity and a direct use of the good things in life, which happen to include art.

[2] His long novel, *Jean Christophe*, which educated a whole generation to music and social thought, remained popular on the Continent until the World War.

In the year of Wagner's death, for example, the English critic Edmund Gurney advanced the idea that the public had the right to look at pictures and listen to music that interested it, and no duty to endure any other. It already seemed a paradox to say: "Most students of the *Oper und Drama* must have admired, as in a dream, the earnest minuteness with which every sort of conscious reference, theoretic and practical, is read into the past history of opera and its public; the only point of view omitted being that which recognizes in the genus opera-goer . . . a wholesale indifference to theory, and a quite unpractical habit of enjoying what it may and enduring what it must."[3]

Gurney went on to analyze with an accuracy we can appreciate today the advantage which Wagner's artistic practices gave him as the weaver of spells over musical and unmusical alike. "Wagner professes to 'cast off Beethoven's shackles' and to 'cast himself fearlessly in the sea of music' where . . . sinking, he finds himself naturally in the variegated home of invertebrate strains. . . ." To us as listeners this means "*our* enforced flurry, *our* active impotence. But their creator is wise in his generation. Give the public from a couple to a score of firm bars they can seize and feel reliance in, and keep their eyes employed; and on these terms their ears will be quite content to stray about . . . for the next quarter or half hour. . . ." The critic rightly deplores Wagner's success in "making the expressiveness itself mechanical and independent of any impressiveness whatever." Finally, Gurney puts his finger on the secret of the great nonmusical appeal of the new art. It is the "prosaic fallacy that the essence of music is vague namable expressiveness, instead of definite unnamable impressiveness."[4]

The word "prosaic" tells the story. Wagnerism made art a demagogic approximation to a dimly sensed truth, a form of free public education, an adjunct of the newspaper press.

[3] "Wagner and Wagnerism" in *The Nineteenth Century*, March 1883. Reprinted the same year in *Topics of the Times*, ed. T. M. Coan, 158, 169.
[4] *Ibid.*, 190.

It confused giving art to the people with making the people think they could learn its meaning in a few easy lessons, and promised outsiders that they could *hereinstudieren* themselves into the elite. It was the confusion of vulgarity with popularity; and in so saying it is necessary to redefine vulgarity, for in this same period the word acquired a new meaning. Originally it meant what belongs to the crowd and is liked by it; the crowd being the common people, rough and untutored. It is this sort of vulgarity that salts Shakespeare's plays or Hogarth's scenes, and is seldom absent from great art. But with the advent of industrial city dwelling, popular crudity was lost. What had been rough became falsely polished, pretentious, apish, and cheap. The common people of former ages had made folk songs and folk tales and had sung them themselves; the new plebs had cheap songs and cheap tales made for them by hacks in imitation of the high-class product. A new vulgarity, known by its falseness and pride, henceforth permeated culture.

As regards Wagner's share in purveying a superior brand of it, it is significant that in his later musical output, which was designed particularly for the lay public, there is not a folk tune or the reminiscence of one, not a vulgar passage in the primary sense of the word. He speaks to a theater-bred audience, even when he poetizes nature, and he is at his worst when he tries to give sailors or apprentices a catch to sing. The theater sophisticates everything into the vulgar decency of the genteel.

It was the smelling out of this vulgarity that made William Morris turn against Wagner so early. As a socialist and a man who was trying to reintroduce art into a mechanical society, Morris might have been expected to sympathize with the innovator whom Francis Hueffer depicted in such attractive terms. But the reading of the *Ring* was conclusive. Morris knew the original legend just as he knew the Venusberg story, and he felt that Wagner's handling was not only an alteration but a perversion of these ancient poems. The poet may always take liberties, since recapturing in modern speech the simple realism of the early versions is impossible, but to transform the human drama into a farrago of wandering discussions, the characters into wooden symbols of doubtful integrity—that was to be an anti-artist.

Nor was Morris altogether alone in his feeling. The materialist poet John Davidson, who had begun as a Wagnerian, soon decided he must write new ballads on the themes of the legends that Wagner had spoiled. He must as it were disinfect them. More violently still, the American critic John Jay Chapman, who felt so much at home in Germany and was so well disposed towards a new dramatic art, could find no simple explanation of his intense disgust at Wagner. But of the sharpness of the sensation he did not doubt: "The essential lack in Wagner is after all a want of sanitary plumbing. No amount of sentiment or passion can wholly make up for this. One feels all the time that the connection with the main is fraudulent. I should be grateful to you or anyone else who will tell me . . . why I am against him body and soul, sleeping and waking, and think him a bad man and a bad influence."[5] Henry Adams's objection, like Ruskin's, was on grounds of literary form. Neither could feel any sympathy—much less enthusiasm—for a system that merged all distinctions of dramatic structure, even that of moods. Like the Bernard Shaw of later years, they grew tired of losing themselves in the bottomless sea of harmony, and for his part Adams was only willing to drink it "in short gulps."[6]

The fiercest attack, though the most easily discounted, came from Tolstoy. He also had gone through a transvaluation of all values and had emerged as a primitive Christian and an apostle of peasant simplicity. He did not merely wish to destroy modern art, he replaced it under his own hand with a truly popular folk literature; he did not merely

[5] To Owen Wister, Jan. 7, 1895. See also in M. A. de Wolfe Howe's valuable life and letters of Chapman a later comment, p. 271.
[6] Letters, ed. Ford, ii, 335.

announce his renunciation of the world, he lived its precepts as a cobbler with only one shirt. Meantime he defied Europe and scorned its new treasures in a pamphlet, *What Is Art?* containing a chapter on Wagner which at once became famous. The description of *Siegfried* was only too true: "When I arrived, an actor in jersey and tights was seated in front of an object intended to represent an anvil; his hair and beard were false; his hands, white and manicured, had nothing of the workman's; the carefree air, the bulging stomach, and the absence of muscle betrayed the actor. With an incredible hammer he struck, as no one ever struck, a sword that was no less fanciful. It was easy to see he was a dwarf because he bent the knee as he walked. He shouted for a long time, his mouth strangely open. . . ."[7]

The rest of Tolstoy's analysis of the *Ring* derides the monotony and pettiness of the human motives it presents and the inartistic pretense it makes at an illusion which it does not produce. Its further pretension to being a moral and a popular art Tolstoy exposes without mercy, showing it to be instead a boring and insidious product of overcivilized, artificial exclusivism. These objections would of course apply to most operas, certainly to all operas produced with an eye to stage realism. How great art could be achieved in unaffected simplicity in the midst of a contrary-minded civilization Tolstoy showed in his later tales and his *Four Reading Books* for children, but he did not touch again upon opera or dramatic music.

It was nevertheless from Russia that the purely musical emancipation from Wagnerism was preparing. The European recognition of Moussorgsky, Balakireff, Borodin, and Rimsky-Korsakov marked the return to simplicity and folk inspiration, to the use of musical rather than scenic devices in dramatic music. It was from these men, whose works had accumulated during the Wagnerian sweep, that the French Impressionist school of Debussy and Ravel gained the strength and knowledge to pierce through the wall of in-

[7] *What Is Art?* ch. xiii.

terwoven leitmotifs. The Russians had found keeping their independence a hard fight; what had saved them artistically was their devotion to native music and legends and the example of their two masters, Glinka and Berlioz.

As early as 1868, the Imperial Music Director Vladimir Stassoff was writing to the dying Berlioz in Paris how his immediate circle felt: "We do not think that Wagner is a prophet of the future. We think rather that he has made music regress from its status in Weber; though the prestige of a German name, the word 'future' attached to his music, the show of scenery and costume, will no doubt produce an effect on a public little developed musically."[8] From Glinka's orchestration and use of folk tunes, from the lessons contained in the scores which Berlioz left with the Russians when he visited them twice during his career, the Russian "five" and their pupils fashioned their own ideal of lightness and clarity and discovered a preference for melody and nuance over harmonic and orchestral massiveness. Opera regained its rights and dramatic effects returned to Mozart's and Weber's practice over Wagner's head.

The French School, working in the midst of a flourishing Wagnerism, found its own emancipation much more difficult. Its style became a sort of negative offprint of the Wagnerian—discontinuous, all nuance and slight construction, with harmonies as sensuous as the Wagnerian but more sparse. It was also wedded to literature, not only for its inspiration but for its interpretation: the scores are marked with precise or poetic tags. In the opera, it hardly dared compete with the man who had captured the place of Meyerbeer. Yet the one attempt by Debussy suffered from the same affliction of making the music subserve the words, whence "the maddening repetitions in Wagner's operas, [akin to] the maddening repetitions in *Pelleas*."[9]

Music was thus left "weak and exhausted by the fierce Wagnerian domination and hag-ridden by the alien and equally pernicious influences of literature and the plastic

[8] October 5/17, 1868. Reprinted in *Revue Musicale*, May 1930.
[9] Constant Lambert, *Music Ho!*, London, 1933, 29.

arts."[10] Artistic questions, wrongly put and confusingly answered, were left in a chaotic state; legitimate efforts to expand musical or other means of expression were misjudged, great personalities of earlier periods were misrepresented, and critical perspective on all past art was foreshortened until a reaction in the form of surrealist parody was inevitable. Erik Satie's telling Debussy after a performance of a piece marked "Dawn—Noon—Afternoon" that he liked especially the little bit around half-past eleven is the fitting dissolution in laughter of the mechanical conception of meaning in art.

Forward-looking critics and their readers may agree that Wagner is an end, a monument that shortly turned into an attractive ruin, and provided fine fragments for the museum. They may say that he is farther away from us than Mozart or Berlioz,[11] and they may begin to do justice to Weber, Verdi, Meyerbeer, and Rossini. They may even rehabilitate the critic Hanslick.[12] But the world does not move like an army behind its vanguard; it straggles behind rather like the black guard. In the same way as we find parts of the world not yet ready for Darwin and not quite sure whether Marx is a living agitator, so the bulk of the listening public still finds Wagner at the threshold of the temple of culture. Commercial and educational needs still give Wagner the preponderance over every other composer. New interpretations of the *Ring* continue to appear, Wagner Dictionaries, with their usual hero-centering of history, find a sale, and opera houses the world over live handsomely off Wagner. Among musicians, he is still presented as the only many-sided composer, among teachers and students it is still most convenient to utilize his well-indexed musical

[10] Cecil Gray, *History of Music*, 209.

[11] Paul Rosenfeld, *Musical Portraits*, 10, 87.

[12] On Verdi and Rossini, see the works of Francis Toye; on Weber, the Stebbins biography already cited; and *In Defence of Hanslick* by Stewart Deas, recently published in London. N. Slonimsky's *Music Since 1900* also contains valuable indications of old and new attitudes, in chronological order.

form for teaching and learning dramatic music. Conductors, finally, know that they can be sure of a certain kind of response by playing or recording anew the Ride, the Murmurs, the Good Friday, or the Love-Death.

On a more exalted plane the contributions of Wagnerism hold their own. Art is still entangled in precious theorizing and historical justification. It is held to be a product of evolution just as the artist is held to be a product of his times, and the world makes demands in consequence. The artist must defend himself in print and show how others are wrong, for all artists are presumably seeking "solutions" to contemporary problems. At any one time only one solution is valid, hence only one artist has "the answer." The artist is made into a kind of research scientist and sociologist combined. He must have opinions, not only for his private use, but for his public work, and through it he must exert an influence upon all matters of social concern. To avoid frivolity, art must teach, alter the course of history, and regenerate mankind. It deals, in short, with the conduct of the will, the improvement of the State, and the purification of the soul. This naïve error of the French Revolution, carried on by Wagner, has become an implicit assumption in the world of art, and a positive command in that part of it which is Marxist.

Again, critics who find in myths the explanation of the power and meaning of art find in Wagner the chief of their band. For him and them, all myths are related, are one myth; and that one is a symbol of human life which successive works of art play variations on. The genetic fallacy glories here in its fullest reduction of the complex to the oversimple. But the newer names of Freud and Thomas Mann give it the color of authority, supported by the traditional scholarship of the evolutionary century.[13] In music proper, evolutionism has flourished particularly in Wagnerian studies, whence it has spread to the past and present

[13] In a telling essay, Dorothy Sayers assails this fallacy, using, as it happens, the *Tristan* legend and its reduction by scholarship to a marriage-by-capture story. *Begin Here*, London, 1940, 105–06.

of the art. As W. D. Allen has shown, there have been two main schools, a Darwin-Wagner school, largely French, and a Spencerian, largely Anglo-American, whose musicology has strengthened our belief that art grows and improves, not logically but biologically.[14] The language of much of our criticism betrays this faith and our judgments take on the deceptive coloring: "Weber," says Dennis Arundell, "never produced a prize bloom, nor perfected a single species . . ." implying, it would seem, that the artist's task is set, competitive, horticultural.[15]

A kindred form of evolutionary analogy affirms that melodies "grow" from root tones, chords, or simple musical figures. This in turn leads to the notion that composers express observations of fact and laws of nature by their choice of musical ideas. Thus the heaviness of gold at the bottom of the Rhine has been found "expressed" in the repeated chord that underlies the long opening of *Das Rheingold*. The most elaborate treatment of music (chiefly Wagnerian) on these principles is to be read in F. W. Robinson's *Aural Harmony* (New York, 1936), where we are told that "the major triad, being found in Nature, is natural; the minor triad, being man-made, is less natural. . . ." From this it is said to follow that certain chords are fitted to express static and others dynamic feelings, and this in turn enables us to find "God-like and human love" simultaneously expressed in the first chord of *Tristan* or stability insured in the Valhalla motif. The great masters are supposed to have recognized these "natural laws," and we in turn need no longer find Wagner's harmony "enigmatic" so soon as we learn this type of analysis.[16]

Again, Wagner's personal preoccupation with revolution remains a criterion with which we judge his contemporaries

---

[14] *Philosophies of Music History*, N. Y., 1939, 269 ff.

[15] *Heritage of Music*, ii, 134.

[16] On this theory the very "dynamic" opening of Beethoven's Third Symphony ought to be as restful as Valhalla. In Mr. Robinson's book see especially Part I, pp. 23–4, 26–7; Part II, 6, 11, 100, 105, 175.

or prod our own. It does not seem to matter that his was a pitiful example of incoherence and self-seeking, nor that after having been touted as a revolutionist, he should now appear as a dangerous forerunner of fascism.[17] Like the Russian censors of Shostakovich, modern critics are ready to believe that art grows directly out of political ideas and that bars of music carry political meanings. And for the same reason, again in the spirit of Wagner, nationalists and would-be nationalists try to impart a quality of the soil to their music or their painting.

The belief in a direct linkage between art and its source makes also for the fallacy of art-as-illustration. This is perhaps the most dangerous legacy of Wagnerism, the hardest to combat in a world supersaturated with mechanistic ideas. Whether in Salvador Dali's setting for the *Tannhäuser* Bacchanale—indeed in all ballets made from music not designed for the purpose—or in more ambitious attempts to "educate the masses" by combining skillful film sequences with music from the masters, the Wagnerian error of pictorial duplication goes on unabated. It is a danger not to music alone, though that is bad enough; it imperils the very idea of art, which by its nature can never enter into a one-to-one relation with anything else but its beholder.

For art, though precise, is never systematic, consequently its "interpretation" can never come from formal "notes" or explanations in another medium. Art has to do with the real world, of which it is a concrete extension; it has to do with morality and social life, of which it is, in Matthew Arnold's phrase, a criticism; hence its language cannot be learned bookishly, apart from the experiences which both art and life afford. It certainly cannot be learned by juxtaposing the symbols of a less familiar art with those of another, more familiar. Neither music and pictures nor music and words, nor pictures and words nor words and words,

---

[17] See Henri Malherbe on Wagner as revolutionist, Peter Viereck's articles in *Common Sense* (1940) showing Wagner as a fascist, and the correspondence in the *Nation* (fall of 1940) on the same subject.

will together teach the meaning of the arts. Interpretation may from time to time be necessary, but it can never supply continuous "equivalents" of whatever kind—poetic, technical, or visual.[18]

To suppose that it can is to repeat the error of mechanistic materialism, the effort to understand one definite sensory experience through another. This may, within limits, be legitimate in science; but its error even there is that the medium of translation distorts. It lets through only so much as is common to both experiences, the unique part of each being lost when looked at through the lens of the other. There is, in short, no pinning down of any subject, object, or idea so that it can be fixed, carried about, and combined with kindred expressions from other arts, as in the system with which Wagner captured and ruled the willing imaginations of his age.

[18] In Schweitzer's classic work on Bach, composers are divided into "poetic" (Beethoven and Wagner) and "pictorial" (Bach, Berlioz, and Schubert). This seems an unfortunate terminology to describe the difference between the use of "atmosphere" and the use of melodic line to achieve what is in both cases nonpictorial. No one has ever seen music, though things can be shown while music is playing so as to link the two through habit.

IV

The Triumph of the Absolute

Dogmatism . . . is nothing else but the view
that truth consists in a proposition.

HEGEL

1. The Triumph of the Absolute

THE GENEROUS IMPOSTURE

> An enthusiast sways humanity by . . . dinning it
> into our ears that this or that question has only one
> possible solution; but when once he is gone, an
> army of quiet and uninfluential people set to work
> to remind us of the other side and demolish the
> generous imposture.
>
> STEVENSON

I have now reviewed some of the episodes in our intellectual history which led me to say earlier that this book had but a single subject: the inherited form of thought which still constricts our minds. It now remains for me to sum up and say a brief word in behalf of the living opposition which has already put its stamp upon the twentieth century.

To brand the still dominant heritage with a single word, one could say simply "Evolution." But it is a special kind of evolution. The idea of development which made its way into every thinking mind in the first half of the nineteenth century was philosophical; it was a way of understanding things and it implied purpose. The Evolution which triumphed with Darwin, Marx, and Wagner, in the second half of the century, was something that existed by itself. It was an absolute. Behind all changes and all actual things it operated as a cause. Darwinism yielded its basic law, and viewed historically, its name was Progress. All events had physical origins; physical origins were discoverable by science; and the method of science alone could, by revealing the nature of things, make the mechanical sequences of the universe beneficent to man. Fatalism and progress were as closely linked as the Heavenly Twins and like them invincible.

Their victory, however, implied the banishment of all anthropomorphic ideas, and since mind was the most anthropomorphic thing in man, it must be driven from the field, first in the form of God or Teleology, then in the form of consciousness or purpose. These were explained away as illusions; those were condemned as superstition or metaphysics. The blind play of forces known as struggle replaced purpose. The vast arena of nature was pictured as a scene of "desperate" conflict. Through geology, timeless room opened backward behind us and made possible the lucky survivals insuring progress. History was a sieve that worked. Man was the residue.

Marx took up the theme in the next higher register. History—man's history—was the record of dialectically competing classes, whose motives were as simply biological as those found in Darwin. Earning a living and fighting those who make it hard were the two forces that explained the past and propelled history. Environment, as in Darwin, was made up of things. In both these worlds man responded like a machine, and out of the same physical necessity— compared to which everything else was ideological rubbish —a perfected society was produced. History was a sieve that worked. The proletarian Utopia was the residue.

With Wagner we take another half-step upwards and reach an uncertain twilight region—part biological, part social, and (this is the half-step) part esthetic. But the pattern is the same. Art has its evolution, which follows the development of races and nations, the progress of culture ultimately requiring the union of the arts in a popular synthesis of sociological import. The *Ring* accordingly cele-

brates in turn the superman-to-be, the fall of the old gods
through the curse of gold, and the triumph of Germanism,
in one long tale of blood, lust, and deceit. The spectator
of this saga finds surcease from a harsh world in the music
drama which was the goal of the Greeks, and, dimly, of a
few moderns now surpassed. History is a sieve that works,
and the residue is the artwork of the future.

So much for doctrine. Its strength cannot be gauged
apart from the special virtues of its form and the personalities of its makers. Its form was System, a clear claim to the
title of *ism*. From each of these isms the public learned
that the riddle of the Sphinx had been solved, but that the
solution was somewhat technical and intricate; a new language was to be mastered, whose universal use would revo-
lutionize the world. Yet at bottom lay a simple principle.
The survival of the fittest, the theory of value and surplus
value, the leitmotif and its function, were the patent props
of the three constructions. The public could thus enjoy the
double pleasure of simpleness and profundity. The chaotic
universe of change was made rational by the ordinary fact
of struggle; the anarchy of social existence was organized
around class hatred; the tumultuous sea of harmony in the
music drama could be charted with a guide to the motifs.
The beholder began with a matter of fact and could reach
symbolism and true knowledge with only an effort of application and memory. Physical struggle led to survival,
physical labor to value, physical object to musical theme,
and at the end each system yielded the most exalted objects of contemplation; the adaptation of living forms; a
perfect state; a religion of art and the regeneration of
mankind.

In knowing how to lead the most enlightened men of
their time through these experiences, our three men gave
proof of great gifts as teachers. Little of what they taught
was original or novel, but: as Samuel Butler said, "When
people, to the end of time ask, who taught us about evolution, we must reply, Charles Darwin"; as Shaw said of the
exploitation of labor, "It is easy to show that Mill and

Cairnes and Sidgwick knew it and said it, but the fact is that the average pupil of Marx never forgets it, while the average pupil of Mill and the rest never learns it"; as Paul Rosenfeld said of Wagner, "He is the great initiator, the compeller of the modern period."

Part of their success in reaching and teaching a great miscellaneous audience lay, surely, in their being somewhat less than great thinkers. When their systems are examined they appear unusually, almost incredibly, incoherent, both in thought and in form. Of the many books which Darwin, Marx, and Wagner have left us not one is a masterpiece. With their work as a whole our practices show that we are not satisfied. We cut them, abstract them, reorder their parts to make them palatable: they failed in artistry at least. Imperfectly aware of their intellectual antecedents and impatient of exact expression, they jumbled together a bewildering collection of truths and errors and platitudes. They borrowed and pilfered without stint or shame, whence the body of each man's work stands as a sort of Scripture, quotable for almost all purposes on an infinity of subjects. Their systematic tendency thus lies half within, half outside the work they have left. For just as each of them found a "bulldog" to defend the hoarded treasure, so each found hosts of eager systematizers who made the master's message more orderly than it was. The age that found itself in their pages could certainly collaborate in improving them.

This implies no disrespect of their powers. Their genius was par excellence the genius of taking pains; they were colossal workers in an age when patient industry was regarded as the highest intellectual virtue. Science had made it so. As would-be scientists,[1] they most naturally presented themselves as recorders of what was—secretaries of the universe taking down its dictation. And though in

[1] Lest this be taken as disrespect to Darwin, I quote Sir Clifford Allbutt: " 'Scientist' seems to me as proper as 'artist' or 'naturalist' . . . but it should signify the professional worker; hardly the great amateur such as Boyle or Darwin." *Notes on the Composition of Scientific Papers*, 3rd ed., 1922, 42.

Darwin this image of himself led to a stubborn modesty, in Marx and Wagner it produced an equally impressive arrogance. As he commanded willing friends, they commanded willing slaves. They were teachers, not finders, and all the more revered for their belief that they were only teaching what they found in nature or history. The world, as Marx said, must come to his views, not as to a dogma, but because it must learn through his mouth what the world itself, big with evolutionary future, contained. The three evolutions gave birth to three religions.

It makes little difference whether today we have lost some of the first enthusiasm for the artwork of the future, whether we think the Survival of the Fittest an encumbrance to science, whether Marx's theory of value has been discarded. We still feel that Darwin vindicated science against orthodoxy, that Marx set us on the track of a science of society, and that Wagner made art a serious social concern.

More than that, we are imbued with the spirit in which their work came to birth. We are all evolutionists, not merely in the legitimate sense of accepting what science tells us about genetics and genesis; we are evolutionists in the sense that on our own account we explain things by their origins, take conditions for causes, and cannot resist the lure of profundity. The *surface* of things, their *present* state, their interpretation by consequences instead of antecedents—all leave us intellectually at sea. As Montaigne said, *ils laissent les choses et courent aux causes*. So we fly to the answers by which Darwin, Marx, and Wagner made their philosophies persuasive—Natural Selection, economic interpretation, national, racial, or pictorial meanings in art. Seeking clues and not wisdom, we distrust the philosophy that might show us that even these principles can be suggestive without being adequate explanations of what they profess to explain.

We use even more aggressively certain other beliefs from the same source: that struggle, for example, must mean war and hatred, that the individual counts for nothing and the race for everything, and—by a natural extension of this last idea—that sexual activity is an end in itself, so native to the universe as to constitute a sort of personal salvation. We no longer even think of these as ideas belonging to the second half of the past century; we think of them as matters of fact.

Oddly enough, we find as many widespread popular notions, presumably derived from our three masters, but which run counter to their distinctive theories. Darwin thought he had slain Lamarckism, but ask people at large why giraffes have long necks and they will tell you that in times of scarcity some of them stretched up to the higher foliage. Ask others how socialism triumphs, and they will say: "Active propaganda and loyal obedience to heroic leaders"—the immanent dialectic of history is an afterthought. Go to another group and inquire whether they prefer Wagner's music in the opera or in the concert hall and they will probably choose the latter; yet were the master alive he would forbid the playing of his preludes on symphonic programs. These contradictions follow those in the minds of the makers. Darwin ended by disowning Darwinism, thinking he had poorly set forth his ideas. Marx said that for his part he was no Marxist; and Wagner at the height of his power felt that the Bayreuthian effort was *Unsinn.*

This may be the normal lot of world-historical characters in times of mass participation in culture. No idea can seep down very far without taking on the color of the minds that receive it. Yet one would have thought that with Darwin, Wagner, and Marx the distance traversed and the distortion inflicted would not be very great. For one thing, it was not the masses that hailed them, but rather the middle mass: the educated, newspaper-reading, opinion-making public. For another, the three masters did not tower above their followers. Neither by origin nor by temperament were Darwin, Marx, and Wagner aristocrats. Darwin was a conventional, broad church, "anti-poetic" soul; Marx a self-centered, headlong reformer, suspicious of elegance, manners, and superiority; Wagner an average sensual man, attached to his "little bit of luxury" and spellbound by the theater. What raised them above the crowd without rendering them unpopular was their massive powers of work and self-assertion, their colorful careers and employments, combined with their responsiveness to the intellectual moods around them. They undoubtedly thought they were fighting their century; but in reality they were leading a part of it—the heavier battalions—against the other part. It made their strength, insured their place in history, and also gave their work that encyclopedic quality, that false appearance of unity and revolutionary newness, which has raised a barrier between us and their predecessors, and which—all questions of preference apart—deserves the title of imposture.

REVOLUTIONS COME BEFORE THEIR TIME

> Few things are more benighting than the condescension of one age for another.
>   WOODROW WILSON

But, it may be objected, this "encyclopedic quality" only proves their greatness. All great men sum up their age, and we go to them rather than to their predecessors because we prefer the full impact of one comprehensive mind to the fragmentary revelations of lesser ones. This view is plausible but it begs the question; indeed it begs several questions. One is at liberty to admire Darwin, Marx, and Wagner, but for that admiration to be solid, it must rest on the qualities they displayed, not on supposititious ones. Now it is arguable that we cannot do without Marx, Darwin, and Wagner as a triune summary of their past, but if this be so then we cannot also rank their work as revolutionary departures. Yet this is the usual, and seemingly the greater praise which they receive.

If, again, it be asked why it makes the slightest difference who first enunciated some principle or other, the reply must be that if credit in these matters is so slight a thing, then no difficulty should be made about giving it to the man who came first by a quarter century or more, and who received jeers instead of compliments for his pains. Lamarck is a case in point. It may be tedious to be reminded that there were strong men before Agamemnon and denouncers of social misery before Marx; but it is even more tedious to be told that Western Europe lived in an industrial fool's paradise until Marx shook it out of its dream world; particularly when we find the awakening by Marx beginning in the eighties, and then only through the popularizing of works which in their original form would have been better calculated to increase slumber than to abolish it.

Or yet it may be urged that no one is original. Complete originality is a myth, certainly. But that it is easily possible to be more original than Darwin, Marx, or Wagner should be clear from a reading of these pages.

There is, besides, a reason of immediate moment why the question of originality must be gone into. We have seen that our three men represent a double cultural movement taking place in their day: the gathering up of many ideas and tendencies established in the early nineteenth century and a return to the mechanistic assumptions of a previous era. We know further that in diverting Romanticist thought from vitalism to materialism, the three "realists" knotted together so many incongruous strands of thought that confusion is apparent in their work and chaos in the acts of their disciples. Consequently, their "summing up," far from saving us the trouble of going back to their sources, compels us to do so. Since 1900 a steadily increasing interest has driven inquiring minds to re-examine the earlier period. Historians of science have gone back to Lamarck and Erasmus Darwin; economists and sociologists have renewed acquaintance with Proudhon and the Utopians; artists and critics have begun to rediscover Weber and Berlioz and other Romantics.[2] Not that any of these were

[2] One may note the growing stature of Coleridge as a thinker and critic, the rescue of Shelley from the fiction of the ineffectual

ever totally forgotten: there was no lapse of memory; merely a half century of neglect, abuse, and misconstruction which for all practical purposes was worse than oblivion: a man had better be unknown than half-known or known disparagingly for what he did not do and never said.

At the present moment, however, the Romantic period is once again threatened with disfavor owing to its supposed paternity of fascism.[3] By an understandable error, the Romantics, with Wagner and Nietzsche added, are made responsible for the outburst of "irrationalism" in totalitarian countries, where indeed many theorists proclaim the kinship. This accusation is stricken with the same historical confusion as affects our three men, and here is not the place to undertake the unraveling of it;[4] yet it should be clear that if Wagner, for instance, is called a "romantic," although living and working in the post-romantic age like Nietzsche, then he cannot be given the credit of having made a fresh start and put form and vigor into mere romanticist gropings. Moreover, Nietzsche, heralding the twentieth century, combated everything that Wagner stood for, particularly his commonplace cultural Germanism. How, then, can they both be seen fighting side by side for the new German order, except through a double misconception of their beliefs?

The chief obstacle to thinking straight in this situation is the word "Romantic." It means so many things that some have concluded it means nothing. Unfortunately, partisan use likes double meanings, and calling a man romantic can be made to suggest that his ideas are either foolish or dangerous. Romantic is thus a fitting parallel to Utopian, few critics being willing to admit that just as romanticism is a constant tendency in human beings which a certain epoch

---

poet (see Carl Grabo's writings), the new lives of De Quincey. (Edward Sackville-West), Mazzini (Stringfellow Barr), the work of Edmund Blunden on the Hunt circle, the truer appreciation of Delacroix (Walter Pach) and Vigny (Louise Bogan), and many similar rediscoveries.

[3] Written in 1940. [Note to the Second Edition.]

[4] The task was attempted in *Romanticism and the Modern Ego* (1943). [Note to the Second Edition.]

happened to value, so Utopia is simply the country at which mankind is perpetually landing when it carries out some premeditated plan. A world with airplanes is Leonardo's Utopia. Hence the character of a proposed Utopia is to be judged by its likely consequences, and it is at this point that the reassessing of the Romantic-Utopian period is imperative.

Romanticism contained all the leading ideas that we ascribe to Darwin, Marx, and Wagner: evolution, natural selection, the contradictions of capitalism, class struggle, scientific sociology, dramatic music, and "popular" art—I need not list them all again. Nor was it devoid of realism, though this was an inclusive realism that embraced the world of feeling and fancy as well as the world of matter. It preferred the concrete to the abstract, but recognized ideas, dreams, romance, as having reality too; in this it stands apart from the age that followed it. Now if these convictions represent a revolutionary departure from the orthodoxies of the enlightenment, then the revolution in thought belongs in the period 1800–1850 and was completed before Darwin, Marx, and Wagner. Nor was this a purely theoretical revolution; the practical work was well begun and its scope can be measured by the success of the later comers. This is an historical generality: it is the obscure and accursèd precursor who creates. When Marx tells Engels he wants to finish off "these donkeys of Proudhonians . . . who have done such harm," he does not see that they have made his advent possible. When he says that *Capital* will be a scientific weapon that may bring the revolution nearer, and compared to which the efforts of Mazzini for thirty years amount to nothing,[5] he forgets that without thirty years' armed revolt and ceaseless agitation by somebody else, preaching "the" revolution would be unintelligible and without effect. An evolutionist ought to have known that the workers who first break ground are indispensable to those that—in the double sense—succeed.

[5] Letter of Sept. 11, 1867.

Of course, the main reason why our three evolutionists neglected their own forebears while urging the development theory was that they thought they were bringing realism and science into what had been error and folly. Their realism, as we know, consisted in adopting the insights while denying the aims of the Romantic philosophy as a whole—the aims by which all Utopias and ideas and works of art are to be judged.

What the Romantic philosophy had achieved was to bring back into favor certain social purposes and human attributes that the materialism of the eighteenth century and the violence of the French Revolution had obscured. Rousseau, alone in his century and ahead of the Revolution, forecasts the achievement: he made clear the function of feeling in life and in the work of reason; he stressed the twin realities of the individual and the group; and he stimulated science, together with the love of nature and the direct worship of God. After him poets and artists innumerable, naturalists like Oken and Goethe, theologians like Schleiermacher and Newman, philosophers like Schelling, Fichte, Emerson, and Thoreau, historians and reformers like those I have previously named, joined in a diversified world movement which we may disdain in our ignorance, but which wrestled with our present problems and offered solutions on which we have not yet improved.

Still the movement failed. It was caught between the French Revolution, whose hopes for man had yet to be given social embodiment, and the violent consequences of that revolution, which meant the hopeless quartering of Europe: two groups at odds in each nation, and every nation at odds with every other. The "realism" of the French Revolution, and particularly of its offspring Napoleon, had begun the unification of Italy and Germany and inoculated them with nationalism. And this at the very time when machine industry was everywhere increasing the gap between rich and poor. So the Romanticist doctrines of cooperation and association, of democratic inclusiveness, of social experiment, and of cultural individuality, struggled in vain against these two agents of disorder, and succumbed at last before the new political strategy, which was nothing but "nationalism" applied to class, race, or country. The Romanticists having noticed that struggle was a universal fact of experience, their word was redefined as struggle-for-life, with death implied as the punishment of incapacity. Morality became a hindrance to success, again at the very time when science was questioning religious revelation in matters of geology. In the resulting mêlée, ethics and religion went under, while government, confusing production with prosperity, spurred on an industrialism which it believed to represent scientific progress. The philosopher could plausibly say:

> Law for man and law for thing,
> The last builds town and fleet,
> But it runs wild,
> And doth the man unking.

Whence by an easy transition came the new materialism. Things are in control, things are absolute, and mankind must learn their ways instead of trying to build Utopias with purpose and by design.

This in brief is the story of the similarity and difference between so-called Romantic and self-designated Realist. The Realist seemed to offer a simple way out. He proposed a hopeful but fated "order," though one based on the perceptions, critiques, and teachings of his Romantic predecessors. But the simplification meant that in any given realist Utopia—and there were many—only the best, the few, the high, the low, the many, the elect, or the pure would find a place. Fated evolution was single-tracked and exclusive. The argument behind it was that it was scientific, natural, whereas the Romantic order of diversity in unity had been merely wished for and had not come to pass. This last statement was true: possibly the Romantic order was defeated by the presence of believers in the other.[6] Waiving this

[6] At a critical time during the middle watch of the century, Lassalle recorded his sense of a changed atmosphere: "To think of this general descent on the part of the middle class in the land

point, did that second order get established? The answer is all about us, painfully compelling us to take stock of our ideas, even if it means going back into our culture the astronomic distance of 150 years and getting used to names that have not the familiar and comfortable ring of our more immediate masters.

And the upshot of the survey is that unfortunately ideas and not things ride mankind. The belief that things will co-ordinate themselves for our greater good if only we learn their ways is itself an idea. It might be a true one if men were as obliging as things. But to test it would require that men be first left out of account; then, armed with the laws of "things as they are," science would return to a world where there are both things *and* men, men whose wills, habits, ignorance, and passions are harder than the rocks and more fluid than the sea.

Historically, this contradiction was betrayed in the actions of the would-be realists, than whom no reformers were ever more busy in propaganda, cajolery, denunciation, and abuse, more inclined to ascribe to ideas and ideologies the errors of their opponents. Not only did they seek mastery over things, but over men's beliefs, making it fatal to display faith, admit doubts, or pursue an interest in design. Their success was such that today we read without surprise, but rather with reverence, that among our experts on the mind, the psychologists, "there is no word which sounds as bad . . . as purpose."[7] And in our consequent naïveté, when we find the political leaders of aggressive nations speaking of their will, purpose, or designs, we cry "Roman-

---

of Lessing and Kant, Schiller and Goethe, Fichte, Schelling and Hegel! Did these intellectual heroes merely sweep above our heads like a flight of cranes? . . . What is the curse that has disinherited the middle classes, so that from the great work of civilization which has been completed among them, and from all this great atmosphere of culture, no single drop of refreshing dew has ever fallen upon their steadily decaying brains? They celebrate the festivals of our great thinkers because they have never read their works. If they had read them they would burn them." *Capital and Labour*, 1864.

[7] Koehler, *The Place of Value in a World of Facts*, 1938, 55.

ticism again!" not seeing that either it is a purpose in the psychologists to deny purpose, or if purpose is an illusion, that neither Romanticism nor fascism can be accused of having one—let alone having the same.

History, it is said, loves conquerors and never undoes her injustice to the vanquished. It is certainly easier to let prejudices rest when nothing depends upon their being uprooted. But the search for the historical sources of our present calamities is chiefly carried on by those who would leap over the backs of the Realists to find in the Romantics more unresisting scapegoats. This proves at any rate that history is not a solid block—as the realists taught—and that we can choose our models by an act of purposeful reason. Progress, then, is not fated any more than decadence, and the Romantics were right to make room for the human will and the possibility of design. The accusation now brought against them testifies to their achievement. Since Darwin, Marx, Wagner, disclose how Romanticism indirectly furnished the modern era with its leading ideas, Romanticism, we must conclude, was a useful failure; and we conclude also that the later assault of these same ideas in mechanized form was a success that we may well have reason to regret. We must not, and in truth cannot, repeat the many errors of Romanticism, but we can and must slough off the illusion of Realism and find again our true beginning among the *data*, though not the solutions, of the Romantic revolution in thought.

THE METHOD OF ZADIG

> TOYS: Should always be scientific.
>> FLAUBERT, *Dictionary of Accepted Ideas*

> Man thinking must not be subdued by his instruments.
>> EMERSON

It is of course the connection of this vast political, religious, and philosophic issue with science that binds us to our conflicting ideas. We dare not escape even if we could, for fear of running counter to scientific method. Darwin and Marx fastened the fetters upon us, and Wagner conceded their right to do so by aping their methods and offering dubious anodynes for relief. The threefold result is that today the name and ways of Science have put on the garb of authority and become "scientism"; that the public has remained unenlightened by the superb achievements of science (it merely gapes at its wonders, incapable of critical judgment); and that the danger of an attack against science for its alleged sins against humanity is as possible in democratic countries as it has proved real in fascist. Science needs therefore to be criticized, taught, and defended anew on its own impregnable grounds.

Scientism is the old Huxleyan belief that nothing is outside the scope of science and that it can furnish answers to all human problems. It goes hand in hand with the Marxian denial of the efficacy of ideas, and it makes science a substitute for philosophy, art, and religion. Our dependence upon the manipulation of things is thus enforced as an absolute dogma which conceals itself. Protest against it is branded as "the new impudence"[8] and a return to the "robust materialism of Huxley" is called for as a safeguard against the wickedness of all other thought. Scientific humanisms of various kinds are offered as panaceas, and the English school of biologists vie among themselves in preaching materialism, Darwinism, and Marxism as science— therefore as authoritative.[9]

Our nineteenth-century training makes the questioner of any given scientist's dictum seem an obscurantist, an enemy of science as such, when in fact the fundamental question modern man should put and try to answer is: What is science?

Thanks to evolution, we have come to think of it as a great impersonal army marching forward without cease,

[8] Lancelot Hogben's characterization of C. E. M. Joad, who wrote that specialization in science could lead to material and moral dangers. L. Hogben, Dangerous Thoughts, 117.

[9] See the writings of Bernal, Needham, and J. B. S. Haldane.

ever sure of its present position and with its rear train secure from attack. We like to have it so, for what we admire in science is not so much its adequacy—of which as laymen we probably know little—but its apparent fixity: "Now we know." It is this weakness in ourselves which has enabled so many scientists to exploit their zest for lecturing and our wish to believe, while holding over us the claim of being masters of reality. Thus beginners being introduced to the study of science are told: "Finally, it is to be hoped that the students will see that science must face realities and that talking and argument which may be useful in some situations will not reveal the secrets of nature."[10] This is worthy of those earlier scientists who could not tire of explaining how patient they were at their "quiet, painstaking work," how "thoroughly" and "critically" they examined their evidence, as if they held a monopoly of these virtues,[11] and as if their published work did not reveal as much haste, inconsistency, and reversal of opinion without notice, as the works of ordinary men.

Science as a Delphic oracle exists only in the popular imagination and the silent assumptions of certain scientists. At any given time there are only searchers who agree or disagree. The March of Science is not an orderly army on parade, but rather a land rush for the free spaces ahead. This means a degree of anarchy. Besides, fogeyism, faddism, love of stability, self-seeking, personal likes and dislikes, and all other infirmities of mind, play as decisive a part in science as in any other cultural enterprise. This inevitable condition should neither be deplored nor hushed

[10] From the syllabus of an Introduction to Science given in a large university in 1937. Curiously enough, considering this fantastic disclaimer of the place of discussion in scientific work, the course was given in a building on which is engraved: "Speak to the earth and it shall teach thee."

[11] The pedant's self-regard is nothing new. Compare the preface to Peter Buchan's *Ancient Ballads of Scotland* (Edinburgh, 1828): "No one has yet conceived . . . what patience, perseverance, and general knowledge are necessary for an editor of a collection of ancient Ballads."

up. It is in fact what makes us admire the power of the methods which by creating conventions and testing them enable men to measure, plot and control events.

Overlooking the creativeness of hypothesis, we tend rather to imagine a science of pure discovery, of organized observation and common sense, which Darwin called his "true Baconian principles" and which Huxley called "the method of Zadig." He was referring to Voltaire's story in which the hero Zadig acts precisely like Sherlock Holmes: he notices traces of the passage of the King and Queen's favorite animals, tells in which direction they have gone, and so is suspected of magic. The modern scientist is supposed to be doing the same thing on a higher plane, his magic being to enunciate "laws" after having gathered "facts." To these laws, following Marx, we ascribe coercive power over things, so that when a well-known biologist wants to impress his views, he warns us that "the wages of biological sin is death."[12] In these analogies, the meaning of scientific law, which is simply the most convenient statement of the way things behave, is lost in pseudo-moral metaphor. With theory and fact likewise. We believed Darwin when he said that for five years he collected facts and "did not allow himself to speculate"; we believe Lancelot Hogben when he says: "Since Marx was a genuine scientist insofar as he made a close factual study of capitalism . . . he was able to advance hypotheses which have been brilliantly confirmed by subsequent events."[13] The "factual study," says an economist, represents the "scientific approach," as against the "theoretical."[14] The truth is that hypothesis, imagination, creation, must precede the collecting of facts; after which what we may expect is not scientific law, but descriptive generalities or measured relations, that may find a place in completed Theory.

Facts themselves are not the "hard" or "cold" items to

[12] A. E. Hooton in the *Atlantic Monthly* for Oct. 1939.
[13] *Op. cit.,* 150.
[14] Colin Clark, *The Conditions of Economic Progress*, 1940, *passim.*

which we constantly appeal in order to silence our opponents. They are in a sense products of our ingenuity and often inseparable from our hypothetical interpretation of them. Most statistical fallacies come from neglect of this usual obstacle, just as our imputations of ignorance or bad motives come from supposing that our "undeniable facts" are direct messages from experience which can mean only one thing. The physical scientist has, of course, long passed this stage and has had to devise imaginary entities which will represent what he cannot easily fix in the stream of sensations. When he comes from his laboratory to tell us that a piece of wood is a whirl of electrons, he is speaking of scientific things with scientific warrant, but his facts have left the realm of "common sense"; our physical objects have become his scientific objects; and his tests of truth and error have left the range of the "simple experiment" open to ordinary inspection. The progress of physical science has therefore been not so much the storing up of standardized facts as, in the words of Cassirer, "the discovery of ever-fresh special methods of thought."[15] But what physicists have learned from the history of their science has not yet been learned by the biologists, which accounts for the curious fact that while some physicists are becoming a new sort of "vitalists," most biologists are still for the most part mechanists—like the ordinary man.[16]

Two things have betrayed us: the loose incorporation into our culture of the precise speech of science and the failure to teach science historically; so that many scientists themselves know their confined techniques without knowing what their operations mean or imply.[17] Historians and social scientists have been still worse offenders. They have

[15] Quoted in R. B. Haldane, The Philosophy of Humanism, 1922, 188.

[16] An instance of a businessman who is a convinced mechanist opposing a man of science who is a vitalist can be found in the entertaining exchange of letters between Professor Herbert V. Neal of Tufts College and James F. Porter. Vitalism and Mechanism, Science Press, Lancaster, Pa., 1934.

[17] For examples, see Sir Clifford Allbutt, op. cit.

made a show of aping science and have pilfered its vocabulary without excuse. From Lester Ward, comparing the contact of cultures to the union of ovum and spermatozoon, to Veblen's saying "dicotyledonous" when he meant "twofold," the abuses of analogy and the parading of profundity have achieved the corruption of sociology. Little wonder that "scientific" and "unscientific" have lost all definite meaning and become mere terms of emphasis: "The kind of juggling that has gone on [in the budget] . . . is unscientific and wasteful."[18] Read: "juggling is wasteful."

Such habits of speech and thought have plunged us in a state of scientific piety where we dare not call our soul our own. After causing the moral distress and disorder of the period 1860–1900, the dogmas of Evolution permitted the growth of a swarm of false ideas about the necessary opposition between science and religion, science and philosophy, science and art, throughout which science—or rather scientism—acted in an aggressive fashion of which it has not yet purged itself. The popular mind still infers real and unreal from "objective" and "subjective," and opposes the "fancies" of art to the "truths" of science. Yet slowly the opposition has made itself heard and achieved certain gains. Purpose was rescued from the debris of late nineteenth-century materialism and recognized where it had never ceased to be—in the world of living beings. At the edges of the organic world it may be hard to define what is living and what is not, but there need not be much difficulty about recognizing that society is composed of the living and that man is not a machine. After willfully, heroically, forgetting it, the rediscovery could not come all at once, nor even make much headway in the years between 1859 and 1900. It was left to our century to undo the simple uniformity and false neatness of a bandbox universe.

18 Editorial in the *New York Times*, Apr. 3, 1940.

V

The Reign of Relativity

Damn the Absolute! WILLIAM JAMES

1. *The Reign of Relativity*

The more a thing knows its own mind, the more living it becomes.

SAMUEL BUTLER

The opposition to dogmatic science began, as we know, in the seventies, but it made little headway against the current until thirty years later, when protest from all sides and new theories in many fields proved the objections unanswerable. At the same time appeared many expressions of doubt by some of the stoutest proponents of the earlier materialism. Like Mill in an earlier day, the great Darwinists—Huxley, Spencer, Romanes, Tennyson, Morley—closed with statements of scientific uncertainty and sometimes of religious belief. Others, such as Alfred Russel Wallace, Conan Doyle, and Oliver Lodge, joined the ranks of the spiritists.[1] It was not all science-weariness: the head-

[1] Leuba's inquiry into the religious faith of American men of science before the first world war showed that belief in God prevailed among 43.9 per cent of the physical scientists who gave replies, 30.5 per cent of the biologists, 48.3 per cent of the historians, 46.3 per cent of the sociologists, and 24.2 per cent of the psychologists. The philosophers' answers precluded any statistical computation. *The Belief in God and Immortality*, Boston, 1916, 221–81.

long plunge into materialism, as we saw with Wagner, easily
leads to mysticism, and it is not too much to say that there
is no fanatical and fantastic mysticism like that of the dis-
illusioned, or awakened, or simply heedless materialist; for
his belief in matter is itself a faith in the unseeable—in
the famous "pincushion hidden by innumerable pins"
which Coleridge uses as the perfect analogue of Matter
hiding behind sensible phenomena.

The traditional opposite of Matter is of course Mind, and
unfortunately the division is ordinarily made in such a way
that a "believer in mind" is put down as one who scorns
material things. He presumably lives on very thin air and
does not bother to dodge missiles. This choice of views
was supplemented at the turn of the century by a third
which sought to destroy equally the mysticism of Matter
and the mysticism of Mind. It would distribute mysticism,
as it were, throughout experience, common and uncom-
mon: the fact of growth is as much a miracle as it is a
commonplace. The new outlook accepted on the one hand
all the demonstrations of mechanism in life, but said, This
is not all; and on the other it declined to reaccept Vitalism
with its supposed partnership of spiritual and material substance that led to even greater difficulties.

The late J. S. Haldane, uncle of the contemporary materialist J. B. S. Haldane, undertook his lifelong biological
research on the principle that each science must make the
kind of assumptions appropriate to its subject matter.
Nothing, in his view, warranted the decision that the basic
ideas of physics must obtain throughout the universe. By
very exact measurements on respiration and other bodily
functions, he found that the usual laws of physics concerning gases and liquids did not apply within the living animal.[2] He found that the organism, far from being acted
on wholly from outside, had the power to maintain its environment constant. Life, he concluded, is an element; we
cannot without distorting experience reduce it to constitu-

[2] He was, by the way, the inventor of the British gas mask used
in the first world war.

ent factors, for it is not a mechanical product: it acts. Far from repudiating the services of physics and chemistry, Haldane insisted on their use as the only means of arriving at exact conclusions in biology. What he combated was the gratuitous faith that the mechanical laws of these two sciences would ultimately "account" for life.

Haldane's position was the very one that Lewes had begun to expound in his *Physical Basis of Mind* some decades before, and it is apparently a difficult notion to assimilate, since we find critics disregarding its simple statement and insisting on putting Lewes among the materialists and Haldane among the Vitalists. What they are, actually, is scientific relativists. That is, they relate their results to a defined set of circumstances. The assumptions which permit the slicing off and temporary forgetting of a part of experience for experimental purposes do not permit the permanent exclusion of that part in the ultimate *scientific* account. Adhering to this intellectual discipline has the effect of restoring the organism to the realm of life. A living being is not a machine nor does it merely "respond," it *behaves*.

Whether this purposive behavior is conscious or not is another question which hinges partly on words and partly on the philosophic work of the period under discussion. It is, as we know, the period of Charcot, and the French school of psychiatrists, of Freud, F. W. H. Myers, and William James.[3] The study of hypnotism, hysteria, double personality, and telepathy made great strides, yielding the therapeutic techniques and the vocabulary which in the intervening forty years have enlarged our means of understanding human behavior. But it is still beset not only with uncertainties but with confusions. Freud, for example, insisted that his work was based on the assumptions of materialistic science and that it ought to be accepted as such by physicians and biologists. This exposed him to contemp-

[3] The pioneer work of Dr. John Kearney Mitchell (father of S. Weir Mitchell) on therapeutic hypnotism, though published in 1859, was relatively unknown in 1890.

tuous criticism for many years, because it was obvious that his work did not include the kind of "proof" which mechanism requires. Where was the unconscious? And how could the paths taken by repressed emotions be traced from unconscious to conscious? Freud had no answers, for the reason that his conceptions no longer implied telephone wires carrying messages back and forth in the fashion of the mechanist. The need for contradictory concepts like "unconscious mind" was a sign that observed effects demanded a new view of the human person.

William James's classic *Psychology*, published in 1890, drew attention to the same difficulties with even greater clarity. Summing up as it did all the valuable results of mechanical psychology, the book also showed James's awareness that measurable outside experience was not the whole of experience and mechanism not the whole explanation of given reality. The book disposed of Spencer, the "simple-minded evolutionist," whose ideas were those of the majority among James's scientific and lay readers. At the end, in the chapter "Necessary Truths," James works clear of the doubts which he has raised and suggests the view of science and of mind which he later formulated as Pragmatism.

Independently, Bergson had also emancipated himself from Spencerism, while Le Dantec, Samuel Butler, and Nietzsche were thinking on converging lines about mind, truth, science, and reality: a quiet revolution was taking place. Even the sociologists participated. Giddings, the propounder of a new sociology in America, announced to the New Orleans Congress of the Economic Association that two causative factors were at work in society: the original stimuli from the immediate environment and the traditional products of past social life kept alive in the present —how? As ideas. Causation was still at work, but at least the notion of automatic response to physical environment was losing ground. Cooley was blandly demolishing the work of Galton about genius, race, and human faculty. Veblen, though a social Darwinist by self-designation, dealt with man as the teleological creature par excellence, and made the instinct of workmanship central to his critique of contemporary institutions. Lastly, Boas was founding the new anthropology with his Lowell lectures on the Mind of Primitive Man, in which the simple evolutionary dogmas, the egotistical European judgments of primitives, and the mechanical notions of culture by diffusion and imitation were discarded in favor of renewed empirical observation.

In physics, the quantum theory of Max Planck and the Relativity theory of Einstein were having a decisive effect on scientific mechanism. The quantum, computed by Planck, suggested that the idea of infinitesimal, continuous changes in material things was false. There were perceptible "droplets" of matter, not endless streams—or rather, effects could be measured only in discrete quantities, and therefore we must cease assuming the stream and assume the droplet instead. The favorite nineteenth-century means of conjuring away difficulties by the "slow small cause," whether in philosophy or in physics, was going into the discard about the same time as Einstein—following the Michelson-Morley experiment in search of the "ether"— demonstrated the need for discarding the notions of absolute space and absolute time as distinct dimensions. Absolutes were going down one by one before statements of relations. The observer as a mind, a fact, a reality, was reentering the universe from which he had excluded himself lest the cosmos appear anthropomorphic. Knowledge itself was relative. Lenin might call the work of these scientists and critics "bourgeois reaction," and combine his renewed materialism with an admission that the existence of matter was not necessary to it, but with or without reason, a new reign of consciousness, purpose, teleology, relativity, and pluralism was being quietly ushered in with the new century.

THE THOUGHT OF THE TWENTIETH CENTURY

> Pragmatical: originally 'one engaged in affairs . . .
> and accomplishing the business which properly con-
> cerned him.'
>
> TRENCH: *English Past and Present*

In the light of these facts it is unfortunate that the idea of relativity should have first become popular twenty years later and in single association with the name of Einstein. Not that he and his work are not significant in the movement of ideas, but that the special nature of his researches casts an air of mathematical mystery over a simple idea. Besides, in the ever-confused state of the public mind, the kindred word "relativism" has independently acquired a flavor of contempt, as if it denoted a kind of looseness—the lazy man's way. That it should be deemed so is a paradox, for the word "relative" bears on its face the idea of a fixed connection. Whatever is relative is related, that is to say, tied to something else. Mathematical functions relate quantities in a fixed or variable manner, and it is the possibility of plotting these relations that has enabled modern science to cope with innumerable problems of motion, currents, strength of materials, blood reactions, leading to the most practical and immediate of the benefits we enjoy.

Indeed, it is not in science that relativism is objected to. It is the relativity of all knowledge that frightens those who want their faith guaranteed. Yet all relativism means is that every truth has limits and that taken out of its limits any truth can become error; it means that absolute rules delude, and that the transforming of relative rules into absolutes is a source of violence—it does violence to facts or to persons. "The first thing a principle does nowadays, if it really is a principle, is to kill somebody." The old problems of the casuists all arose from the rigidity with which rules are commonly stated and enforced. For example, is a man

honest who does not always tell the truth? Certainly not!
Well then, is he to tell the homicidal maniac where his
victim has just gone? Certainly not again. The casuist la-
boriously works out a rationale: he relates the rule to
circumstance. But if we admit this exception to truthtell-
ing, are not people going to hide dishonesty under the name
of conditional judgment? No doubt. There has been no
way yet discovered of preventing either absolute or relative
rules from being disobeyed or from cloaking hypocrisies.
The only safeguard is in the conscience of the free agents
we call men. There is no guarantee in greater dogmatism
about rule.

This is not to deny that one accustomed to absolute com-
mands and dogmatic propositions may greet the discovery
of relativism as a license to irresponsibility. The commonplace that morality is not universal, but is relative to time
and place, strikes the untutored mind as an assertion that
there is no morality at all. The teaching that artistic beauty
is not fixed or universal is taken to mean that there is no
"real" beauty, that anything can mean anything, and that
chaos is the only truth. These colossal *non sequiturs* imply
the false propositions, "unless morality is absolute, there is
no morality; unless beauty is fixed once for all and for all
men, there is no beauty," which is equivalent to saying that
what foreigners eat is not food. In all the circumstances of
life the standards regulating conduct and judgment are
fixed enough, and the problem is not to make them stiffer
and less amenable to change, but on the contrary, more
flexible in order to be more precise. Hence the right understanding of relativism must lead not to greater laxity
everywhere, but to greater firmness in moral intention,
greater precision in intellectual, greater subtlety in esthetic.
This is probably what Hamlet meant when he spoke of a
rule being more honored in the breach than the observ-
ance: he did not mean that it was more often broken than
not, he meant it was truly followed when it was apparently
broken.

The problem is left of how we shall judge when we may

or may not go counter to the rough and ready rules by which we are wont to guide our preferences, and it is here that the Jamesian doctrine of Pragmatism illuminates the problem. James says that we shall know a truth by relating its consequences to its avowed purpose. Something is true, not because it has been repeated often, not because someone in authority has said it, not because it copies the world outside, not because it has been deduced from an infallible generality; but because it leads as accurately as possible to the kind of result that we have in mind. Pragmatism, in other words, takes a stand in opposition to the genetic fallacy which bade us look at the antecedents of a thing, an institution, or an idea in order to discover its meaning. Apply the pragmatic test to the music drama, and all the rubbish about what the Greeks had in mind becomes irrelevant. Pragmatism does not discard the historical method, far from it, but it recognizes that before economic history, or evolution, or any other interpretation, can light the path ahead of us, some kind of purpose, standard, or basis of selection must be implied. And it asserts that moral and intellectual honesty require the implied basis to become explicit: the scheme must be tested by concordance between our goal and our achievement.

It is easy of course to debase this method by saying that it leads to the cynical acceptance of whatever "works." But here again this debasement is possible only by those who have the narrowest notions of what they mean by "work." If the critic assumes a person of dull sense and vicious habits, it is true that *that person's* pragmatic test will validate almost any infamy; but with that supposed person, a set of absolutes will lead to identical results and offer less chance of redress, since the infamies will be committed in the name of truly moral, religious, or esthetic canons. The sanctity of the rule shields the offender.

The superior value of the pragmatic test is that it forces the user to reveal to himself and to others what his aims are, and so furnishes his critics with his own yardstick for measuring him. Those to whom the pragmatic analysis of thought is uncongenial accuse it of the very things which display its virtues. One says, "The objection to . . . all varieties of pragmatism is that the ultimate interest . . . to which thought is instrumental remains very arbitrary." And another, "A thing is not truth till it is so strongly believed in that the believer is convinced that its existence does not depend upon him. This cuts off the pragmatist from knowing what truth is."[4] Both these objections are in reality testimonials. The first shows that starting points are arbitrary and should be stated before results can be judged true or false. But this arbitrariness, which is inevitable, is not capricious. Purposes are always based on some sort of previous experience, not picked out at random; and the merits of our purposes must themselves be tested by experience at large, personal or historical. "Before we can say certainly that a thing is true . . . it must not only think true, but feel true, sense true, do true."[5] In other words, pragmatic judgment is a mode of escaping from that blind trust in a rule of progress which has dogged scientific and philosophic thought for three generations.

As for the pragmatist's being unable to know truth because he cannot forget that it depends on him, that is the clear-sighted word of a gifted American who was part philosopher, part fanatic, and altogether a great critic. His fanaticism unfortunately made him reluctant, like many other people, to accept a self-aware method of judging his own purposes. It seems as if it were indeed too much to ask persons of a certain temperament that they view their opinions, their tastes, their conclusions, as valid but not universal. For them, absolutes are an emotional need; but whereas a variety of absolutes can coexist in a pragmatic system like democracy, no absolute system can include plural choices. Such temperaments must consequently work for their own supremacy even more than for their stated ends, or else be doomed to frustration.

There is more than this political convenience to the

4 H. B. Parkes and John Jay Chapman, respectively.
5 A. R. Orage, Readers and Writers, 1922, 187.

pragmatic rejection of absolutes. Pragmatism enlarges our total comprehension by showing how separate truths are relative to the act of knowledge and the reality of experience. Against the view that the mind simply copies the outer world, the pragmatist differentiates sharply between the "concepts" or ideas which he forms as a result of living in a given time and place and the "percepts" that are his experience.[6] The percepts are flowing, continuous, vivid, yet not transmissible save through the concepts—incomplete, lifeless, cold—which he shares with his fellow creatures.

It follows that when we use for our living purposes a concept, be it as simple as "democracy" or as complex as "the law of evolution," we must beware of confusing concept with experience and believing that the one is the exact copy of the other. The one is an instrument by which we arrange our relations to things; though it is not an instrument fashioned wholly by our fancy: the objects of the world are given us, and so are the relations, but we take from them what interests us, what we need, what we hope we can use to create new realities. All thinking is, in this sense, wishful: it is not the offprint of what is; it is relative to our desire and capacity for knowing what is. And that is why Haldane is justified in saying that the concepts of physics seem to him inadequate for dealing with what he experiences in his biological laboratory. He is trying to be, in the strictest sense of the term, a "realist," for he does not stubbornly attach to the ideas of matter and motion the quality of "sole reality"; he observes in a frame of mind compounded of knowledge and self-knowledge, and is ready to follow his experience in the shaping of his concepts. Having shaped them, he is not likely to think that they were given him ready-made by the stuff he handled or by a

[6] For example, the modern logic of relations has established that "a class is not a fixed collection." It is a construction of logic. "A member of a class, being a concrete individual, cannot be a part of it in any literal sense. Membership is a peculiar and subtle relation." Langer, *Introduction to Symbolic Logic*, 117.

fixed scheme of transcendental powers. Acknowledged or not, the pragmatic test is a characteristic form of twentieth-century thought, springing as it does from a critique of science,by men who had all the scientific qualifications for making it.

It is also the form of thought of which our century stands in need. For everything in our mechanical, remote-control civilization tends to alienate us from the concrete and to make us operate with concepts. We recognize verbalism as a menace but fail to see that when we first detect it in ourselves or another, we have probably been spending many moments out of touch with reality, keeping ourselves going by conceptual substitutes, arguing, hoping, spinning plans in a perceptual void.

The quality of our concepts bears on our ills, just as the quality of our purposes and means bears on our ends, which is not only why I have thought it worth examining the history of our inherited materialism, but also why the problem of our century seems to me to be principally a problem in communication. Forty years and more have elapsed since the characteristic forms of thought of the twentieth century were first created in opposition or modification of the past. Yet how limited are the circles in which these new forms have made a difference! How often have our inertia and inattentiveness twisted them back into a likeness of what we already know! The new anthropology, which views culture as a whole made up of values rather than parts; the new physics, with its relinquishing of cause, continuity, and mechanism; the new psychologies, with their stress on the irrational, the purposive, the *Gestalt* in perception; the new biology, equidistant from materialism and vitalism; the new logic and its philosophical implications—these symptoms of a new era in thought seem hardly to have left their native haunts among the professions; or else have left this shelter only to be distorted and debased. Freud's thought is a good example of the way in which work devoted to freeing man from thralldom through the use of intelligence has been blindly misinterpreted as proving the necessary slavery of man to "unconscious urges," and the advisability of giving loose rein to them because they were scientifically there. As if anyone had ever doubted the existence, the importance, or the irremovability of sex! To be sure, Freud combined with his tested therapeutic technique many social and moral speculations which still want verification; but his intent, the emancipation from the disorders of the emotion, has been turned by ignorant popularization into its contrary absolute, and led a whole generation to believe that Sex was the new devil or divinity, cause of all its ills and salvation as well, explanation of all of life, art, biography, and human character. The path to freedom was once again barred by the materialistic faith in causation from beneath and the worship of concepts as things.

OF HUMAN FREEDOM

The beginning and end of all philosophy is—Freedom.

SCHELLING, 1795

In the long run men hit only what they aim at.

THOREAU

Once upon a time there was a philosopher learned in mathematics and the sciences, who taught his contemporaries with the greatest success that all they knew and needed to know was the exact relations between the physical objects to be found in the visible world. Assume that everything is touchable, he said, use your ingenuity to make every natural effect impress itself upon your sense of sight close to a measuring scale, and in course of time you will infallibly become masters of your own destiny.

No sooner had he said this than this unhappy man (whose wife, like that of Socrates, was not the best of companions) met a charming and affectionate lady who was, alas, married to a convict. The philosopher and the lady

fell in love; but the love had to remain a passionate friendship and a short one, for within a year the lady died. Then
the philosopher, transfigured by his glimpse of a new world
of feeling, was led to review his work and saw it was inadequate. Making no secret of the reason for his change of
mind, he began again to teach his disciples a new, an expanded gospel, in which the scientific intelligence played
but a minor role. In fact it was openly depreciated. Happiness, for him, now lay solely in the exercise of the affections. He coined the word "altruism" and proposed a new
religion of self-sacrifice in behalf of humanity. Love was its
principle, order was its foundation, and progress was its
goal.

But the habits of half a lifetime were not so easily transformed, as could be seen in the further details of the new
religion. Everything was co-ordinated and systematized as
in a textbook. He who had said that there was no freedom
of thought in science, and therefore science should guide
mankind, now said that anyone who took any care at all for
his personal interests should be regarded as vicious. All
activity should point to a single communal end; to insure
which, a benevolent state socialism, a hierarchy, and a ritual were instituted. A supreme Pontiff ruled the world, a
dictatorship of three bankers ruled each nation. The single
High Priest of Humanity ensured the total suppression of
independent thought, for as the prophet kept repeating, it
is the intellect that needs to be reined in and subordinated
to the affections. He proposed a holocaust of books and a
crusade against men of thought. Yet at the same time the
ritual provided that certain passages from the poets should
be read at stated intervals and that temples be built in
sacred groves, for the founder came to think that positive
science was truly akin to fetishism and should be organized
as such. The earth became the Great Fetish, and the master became convinced that truth was independent of any
proofs: rather, truth was the flower of his own thought,
partly because he was following in the great line of thinkers
that began with Descartes and Leibniz, and partly because

as a measure of "mental hygiene" he now took care not to read any books. The followers grew fewer but they obeyed.

What I have written is not a parable of my own invention. It is the story of Auguste Comte's positivism and its transformation under his own hand, a few years before the appearance of the *Origin of Species*. It would be comforting to say that the French theorist of evolutionary science went mad as a result of his unhappy passion; but the books which expound the Religion of Humanity contain so much that proves his mathematical and analytic mind unimpaired, that we are not allowed that consolation. And when we compare these dogmas of 1850 with the doings and sayings of some of our contemporaries, we may be entitled to think that the explanation of both aberrations is to be sought elsewhere than in insanity. We may, that is, call them insane only in a philosophical, and not in a pathological sense. Is it not, after all, easy to understand how Comte's sudden and violent awakening to the life of feeling, combined with an intelligent dissatisfaction with pure positivism, made him throw overboard his whole baggage of evolution, scientific overlordship, and the use of reason? And if this is understandable, is it not possible that the sudden conversion which he went through in his short life-span may bear some faint analogy to what the world is living through at the present time? The mysticism of matter and reason breeds the mysticism of passion and recklessness, not in all men but in enough of them to make Comte —or Wagner—represent mankind.

The points of similarity between Comte's second Utopia —which Mill called "the regime of a blockaded town"— and totalitarianism need no enumeration, but it should be noted that the country where theory and practice have gone farthest in the direction of Comte's later proposal is also that where the organization of positive science reached a degree of perfection that was but recently the admiration of the world. We can therefore sympathize with those who would forestall the spread of this self-devouring passion by a ban upon all feeling, by glorifying reason as almighty, and by taking their oath that science is our only savior and master. They only forget that it was a course of these self-denying ordinances that preceded Comte's overturn and the dictatorship he advocated: anti-individual, anti-intellectual, and using science with deadly destructiveness to establish the High Pontiff of Humanity on his Fetishistic throne.

Rationalism is no bulwark. If we view reason and feeling as enemies, instead of as a team without whose equal pull nothing can be done, if we discard James, Bergson, and Freud as "anti-intellectualists" and pray for the return of Huxleyan robustness, we are indeed lost. To play at being tough is a bad sign. We can, on pure nerve, do violence for a time to one half of our nature, but the unreasoning reason of man takes revenge against the claims of reasoning reason by exaggerating the primacy of the will. Men do not live by bread alone: if nothing better offers they will take circuses, even circuses in which one directly participates as wild beast and victim both. Mankind has of late felt the need of periodic bloodlettings to clear its brain. It is a crude method, and there is no reason why it should not be improved upon; but since the crudity has been allied with a swing from rationalism to voluntarism, it must be that both these things are legitimate and demand co-ordination. The fact that they can be co-ordinated is proved by individual experience, to which Freud's work precisely adds its confirmation. Reason and feeling are not at war from their natures, they are fused elements which we separate only in reflection. But man has freedom to change the channels between his feelings and his ideas. In this freedom lies the germ of all other freedoms: he can choose purposes. He has no need to have *complete* freedom in order to have *some* freedom, and it so happens that he has the one which can generate all the others.

But he can even more easily bind himself—or be bound by others—through his beliefs. It is a commonplace that ignorance is a form of slavery; it is less easily recognized that knowledge also binds. The intellectual puritanism with which scientific evolutionists and economists fought social legislation, or with which mechanists treated their own religious or moral insights as "illusions," shows how far the possession of truths can paralyze men. Our own modern habit of immediately calling everything unfamiliar, everything we dislike, an "illusion" is a sign of our bondage to the belief in matter. There are enough illusions of inadvertence without making the creeds, the wants, and the perceptions of others into illusions which we must first uproot before we can live together in peace. Even an optical illusion represents a genuine experience, misclassed or misinterpreted. As for the two great illusions—of pure Rationalism and pure Voluntarism—they, alas, refute themselves with terrific certainty.

What then can be done to make our knowledge, and particularly the sciences, be our servants instead of our masters? First the recognition that facts, as facts, are neutral; second the recognition that the knowledge of causes is no magic defense against evil. "To understand why one is jealous, ill-tempered, or sadistic does not prevent one from being jealous, ill-tempered, or sadistic."[7] When we know why we are such, we may decide that the reason is trivial and that we will change our habits. But the will is indispensable.

This means that in our personal and social work, in our criticism of men and ideas, we can never trust to a single, magic formula of change. We cannot work through "matter" and by "changing living conditions" make everyone healthy, wealthy, and wise. Nor can we rely on empty moral preachments where physical conditions bind the will. The stupid child cannot be scolded or bribed into scholarship: straighten his eyes and give him glasses and *perhaps* he may improve. But don't think that free eye clinics will make a nation of Lincolns and Shakespeares. The task

[7] C. E. M. Joad, *New Statesman and Nation*, Oct. 2, 1937.

is endless, the need for imagination and new appropriate action can never cease.

Our only guides are our interests, viewed in the largest possible sense; our interests made as self-aware as possible, since it is unlikely we can attain what we do not want, and impossible to want what is not conceived as attainable. Purpose is distributed, a morsel in each of us, not overarching our fate with guarantees. Whatever may be true of the animal past of man, his evolution in society has been the story of purposes achieved against odds, of striving, with luck occasionally aiding, but more often of brain directing brawn to a dim or clear imagining ahead.

But are there common goals, consented to as the residue of civilized experience? The study of history and origins is here in point, though its results are no more binding than those of science. In this view, the cherished ideas of Western Europe need not be jettisoned every generation—a verbal trick at best—but used pragmatically after being stripped of their claims to represent unchanging facts. Progress, for example, is a valid notion if divorced from automatism and viewed as one aspect of historical reality. We plainly see that in transportation, for example, progress has been made. We fly where we rode. The error is to suppose that this progress has been a pure addition of comfort or wisdom or peace. We have paid for this progress in innumerable ways, as we have for all other "advances," no matter how beneficent.

That is why there has been, since the end of the last century, a far from negligible protest against the machine age. We have increased discomforts along with comforts, misery along with ease, speed of communication with bewilderment and folly, power of construction with power of destruction, means of cure with means of moral and physical suffering, until the most thoughtful swallow their pride for the rest and wonder whether we are not the most wretched humans that ever existed. When we are not on the brink of self-pity we are ready to immolate someone else for what we know to be our collective sins of omission, our fatalism and forgetfulness that we are all members one of another.

Having got rid of Design with loud huzzahs, we are suddenly sorry to find our handiwork faithfully reproducing the image of our superior theories. With Huxley and others we denied the principle of human equality,[8] asserting the inborn supremacy of certain races instead—only to wake up in a world taking this science literally. We did not see that Equality was a concept for dealing out justice among incommensurable human beings. Supposing that equality was either a fact or not a fact, we mistook it for identity or uniformity, which the simplest observation disproves.

We made the observation and felt we were geniuses a cut above Rousseau and Thomas Jefferson, whom in our pride we had neglected to read accurately. The limits and the means of achieving political equality we therefore discarded in favor of automatic competition. For with Darwin and Spencer and Marx we had discovered the virtues of the free-for-all and accordingly made fun of human brotherhood. But eighty years later we solemnly aver that competition is destructive, that nobody really likes war, and that its existence must be due to the conspiracies of the mad or the wicked.

Lastly, we denied Liberty, from a myopic acquaintance with animal reflex and molecular movements, but now that we have been in truth reduced to reflexive rather than reflective creatures under the bombardment of something fiercer than molecules, we begin to suspect that there are some good things to be said in behalf of freedom—even if only that it seems a fairly widespread human desire and a universal assumption in our everyday dealings.

In the midst of all this imaginary "toughness" and "realism," we tried certain antidotes. Dimly sensing that individual wills and minds must have something to do with personal and collective misery, we tried art and the sacrifice of self to society. We became Wagnerians and Positiv-

8 *Essays*, i, 305 ff. (1890).

ists—or what is much the same, Marxists.[9] We even mixed
the two and made art for Marx' sake, while criticizing all
past art and artists for not having created in fact the world
of our dreams. We sought the scientist, but found him—
whether physical or social scientist—shut up in his discipline, not as an escape, for he was confident of soon finding
the clue that would free mankind from its bondage, but as
an expression of his faith. He would gain and give salvation.

All these faiths have been at bottom monistic and materialist: they have disregarded the pluralism of the world
of experience, or called it chaos so that some order—imposed, not fitted—could make all things fixed and convenient forever after. Man-made ideas have been transmogri-
fied into eternal substances to be worshiped. Looking on
the universe, man first denied that he was there and then
complained that there were other men obstructing his work
of tidying up: the scientist denounced the artist and the
theologian; the educated denounced the uneducated; the
leaders their followers; nation fought nation and so on
down to race and class, not because of any permanent pleasure they took in it, nor even always from pressing need,
but from a fantastic sense of duty, until clear-eyed men
hopelessly exclaimed, "To change fundamental opinions
and redirect desires is not apparently to 'do' anything at
all."[10]

To reverse such ingrained habits of thought and work
cannot be done in an instant. It will take as much work
and a very different kind of thought in a fresh direction.
But the difficulty of the task should only spur our efforts
in the one realm which we have under some sort of immediate control: our minds. Failing this, the possibilities
which Henry Adams foresaw seem likely to come true all
at once: cynical pessimism among the leaders of mankind;

[9] "A positivist held in his hand, without possibility of argument, the past, the present, and the Future." Juliette Lamber
Adam, whose first husband was a Positivist leader in the forties,
in *Mes Premières Armes*, 4.
[10] Norman Angell, *The Fruits of Victory*, 1921, xvii.

a vast revival of semi-religious superstition; a brutish dictatorship by capital or labor.

Even if this should come, the present advice would not be needless. Nothing lasts forever, nothing "wins out in the end." There is always a rebeginning, and even if we ourselves do not learn in time the knack of living together in large numbers, and solving the problems that our best gifts create, at least the future archeologist will find it written that our century, coming after a time of systematic mechanism, proclaimed in a hundred ways that men have minds, and that purposeless work is not for the sane.

INDEX OF NAMES AND TITLES